AMERICAN CRISIS BIOGRAPHIES

Edited by

Ellis Paxson Oberholtzer, Ph. D.

The American Crisis Biographies

Edited by Ellis Paxson Oberholtzer, Ph.D. With the counsel and advice of Professor John B. McMaster, of the University of Pennsylvania.

Each 12mo, cloth, with frontispiece portrait. Price $1.25 net; by mail, $1.37.

These biographies will constitute a complete and comprehensive history of the great American sectional struggle in the form of readable and authoritative biography. The editor has enlisted the co-operation of many competent writers, as will be noted from the list given below. An interesting feature of the undertaking is that the series is to be impartial, Southern writers having been assigned to Southern subjects and Northern writers to Northern subjects, but all will belong to the younger generation of writers, thus assuring freedom from any suspicion of wartime prejudice. The Civil War will not be treated as a rebellion, but as the great event in the history of our nation, which, after forty years, it is now clearly recognized to have been.

Now ready:

Abraham Lincoln. By ELLIS PAXSON OBERHOLTZER.
Thomas H. Benton. By JOSEPH M. ROGERS.
David G. Farragut. By JOHN R. SPEARS.
William T. Sherman. By EDWARD ROBINS.

In preparation:

John C. Calhoun. By GAILLARD HUNT.
Daniel Webster. By PROF. C. H. VAN TYNE.
Alexander H. Stephens. BY LOUIS PENDLETON.
John Quincy Adams. By BROOKS ADAMS.
John Brown. By W. E. BURGHARDT DUBOIS.
William Lloyd Garrison. By LINDSAY SWIFT.
Charles Sumner. By PROF. FRANKLIN S. EDMONDS.
William H. Seward. By EDWARD EVERETT HALE, Jr.
Frederick Douglass. By BOOKER T. WASHINGTON.
Jefferson Davis. By PROF. W. E. DODD.
Robert E. Lee. By PHILIP ALEXANDER BRUCE.
Stephen A. Douglas. By PROF. ALLEN JOHNSON.
Judah P. Benjamin. By PIERCE BUTLER.
Thaddeus Stevens. By PROF. J. A. WOODBURN.
Andrew Johnson. BY WADDY THOMPSON.

To be followed by:

Henry Clay	Edwin M. Stanton
Ulysses S. Grant	"Stonewall" Jackson
Wade Hampton	Jay Cooke

D. G. Farragut

AMERICAN CRISIS BIOGRAPHIES

DAVID G. FARRAGUT

by

JOHN RANDOLPH SPEARS

Author of "History of Our Navy,"
"Our Navy in the War with Spain," etc.

PHILADELPHIA
GEORGE W. JACOBS & COMPANY
PUBLISHERS

359.0092
Sp 3d

Copyright, 1905, by
GEORGE W. JACOBS & COMPANY
Published September, 1905

34453
January 1957

To the Men of the American Navy,
Good and True, Every One,
Who believe with Admiral Farragut that

" The Best Protection Against the Enemy's Fire
is a Well-Directed Fire from Our Own Guns."

ACKNOWLEDGMENTS

In preparing this biography of Admiral David Glasgow Farragut, I have been assisted in the most liberal and cheerful spirit by Captain Loyall Farragut, the son of the admiral, and author of "The Life and Letters of Admiral D. G. Farragut." It is with hearty thanks that I acknowledge my indebtedness to him and his work.

I am also under great obligations to Mr. Charles W. Stewart, Superintendent of the Library and Naval War Records, Navy Department, Washington. Through his courtesy, I have had the use of hundreds of documents, gathered from Union and Confederate sources, which have not yet been published, but are to appear in the "Official Records of the Union and Confederate Navies." From these documents I was able to gather much valuable fresh material. And it may not be out of place to add here that by consulting other original sources of information I have been able to correct a few errors that appear in other works relating to the admiral, and to throw new light on events with which he was connected. The story of the war with the West India pirates, for instance, was written after a careful search of the Naval Affairs volumes of the American State Papers. "War Papers" printed by the "Loyal Legion" have proved of great value, while such private memoirs as those of James K. Hosmer have been gathered and searched with care.

Finally, I have to thank Captain A. T. Mahan, United States Navy (retired), for services kindly rendered.

JOHN RANDOLPH SPEARS.

CONTENTS

ILLUSTRATIONS

CHRONOLOGY

1801—David G. Farragut born July 5th at a ferry across the Holston River, near Knoxville, Tenn.

1807—March 2d, his father, George Farragut, is appointed a master in the United States navy. In the fall of the year the family removes to New Orleans.

1808—June 21st, death of his mother. His adoption by Commander (afterward Commodore) David Porter.

1809—Leaves New Orleans with adopted father and goes to Washington.

1810—December 17th appointed midshipman in the United States navy.

1811—August 9th, joins frigate Essex, under the command of Captain David Porter, and sails on a cruise along the coast to protect American commerce.

1812—June 18th, Congress declares war against Great Britain. July 3d, Midshipman Farragut sails on Essex, Captain David Porter, for cruise against British commerce. August 3d, British sloop of war Alert captured. September 7th, arrival in port. October 28th, sails to join Commodore Bainbridge's squadron for cruise in East Indies. December 12th, on way to Brazilian coast, the British packet Nocton captured.

1813—January 26th, Essex sails from St. Catherine's Island for cruise in the Pacific. March 3d, ports stove in on one side—narrow escape from foundering. March 26th, captures Peruvian man-of-war Nereyda for attacking American whalers. April 17th, arrives at Galapagos Islands. July 9th, Farragut appointed captain of whaler Barclay that had been recaptured from the enemy. A mutinous whaler captain subdued. During September news received that a British squadron is in pursuit of Essex. October 23d, arrives at Nukahiva to refit Essex.

1814—February 3d, arrives at Valparaiso in search of British squadron. February 8th, British frigate Phœbe and sloop Cherub arrive. March 28th, Essex drags anchor in squall, puts to sea, loses topmast, anchors near beach and is attacked by the two ships of the enemy at 3:54 P. M., being captured at 6:20 P. M. On July 5th, Essex Junior arrives in New York harbor with Farragut a prisoner in cartel. In November, he is exchanged.

1815—Ordered to the Independence for first cruise in the Mediterranean.

1816—Ordered to the President for cruise in the Mediterranean.

1817—October 14th, obtains permission to go to Tunis with Rev. Charles Folsom for study. During a visit to ruins south of Tunis, his eyes are seriously injured by a sunstroke.

1818—Returns to fleet and joins the Franklin.

1819—While cruising in the Mediterranean, he is made executive officer of the schooner Shark, frequently having full command of her.

1820—Ordered home for examination for promotion. Arrives at Washington, November 20th, but fails to pass the examination.

1822—Cruise on coast of Mexico as deck officer of the sloop of war John Adams.

1823—In February sails on schooner Greyhound in fleet under Commodore Porter for cruise against the West India pirates. Made executive officer of the Sea Gull, the first steamer to see active service in the American navy.

1824—In command of schooner Ferret in war against West India pirates. Returns to Washington with yellow fever. September 2d, marries Susan Caroline, daughter of Jordan and Fanny Marchant, of Norfolk, Va.

1825—January 13th, promoted to lieutenancy. Watch officer on Brandywine for cruise on European station.

1826—Returns to Norfolk for shore duty and leave of absence.

1828—December 28th, sails for the South Atlantic station on sloop of war, Vandalia.

1829—In November is sent home because of defective eyesight.

1832—December 4th, ordered to Natchez as executive officer.

1833—Sails in Natchez to Charleston to aid in quelling the nullification troubles. May 8th, sails to the South Atlantic station.

1834—March 6th, ordered to command of the schooner Boxer, and sails for home.

1838—August 7th, ordered to command of sloop of war Erie, and to cruise on coast of Mexico to protect American interests while French naval ships are blockading and capturing Vera Cruz. Makes careful studies of the coast and of French ships.

1840—December 27th, Mrs. Farragut dies.

1841—February 22d ordered as executive officer to line-of-battleship Delaware, for cruise on South Atlantic station. September 8th, promoted to commander.

1842—June 1st, in command of sloop of war Decatur.

1843—In February returns home in ill health. On December 26th, marries Virginia, eldest daughter of Mr. William Loyall, of Norfolk, Va.

1844—Executive officer of the line-of-battleship Pennsylvania at Norfolk Navy Yard.

1845—Second in command of Norfolk Navy Yard.

1846—On April 24th occurred the first fight in the war with Mexico.

1847—February, ordered to command of sloop of war Saratoga for service against the Mexicans and sails, determined to take the fort at Vera Cruz called San Juan de Ulloa "by boarding," but arrives after the surrender (March 26th) to General Scott. Serves on coast of Mexico.

1848—February 19th. arrives at New York, and is ordered to Norfolk Navy Yard.

1850–1851—Draws up ordnance regulations for the navy and lectures on gunnery at Norfolk Navy Yard.

1852—Conducts important tests of naval guns at Old Point Comfort.

1854—Ordered to San Francisco, where he establishes the Mare Island Navy Yard.

1855—September 14th, promoted to captain.

1858—Ordered to command the steam sloop of war Brooklyn in cruise on Mexican coast.

1861—Beginning of the Civil War. April 17th, Virginia state convention votes to secede from the Union. April 18th, having long since determined to remain loyal to the Union, Farragut goes North with his family and settles at Hastings-on-the-Hudson. In December, ordered to Washington to take command of an expedition against New Orleans.

1862—January 9th, formally invested with the command. February 2d, sails in the steam sloop Hartford from Hampton Roads for the mouth of the Mississippi River. February 20th, arrives at Ship Island. April 18th, the mortar flotilla opens fire at Fort Jackson. April 20th, fleet ordered to prepare to pass the forts guarding the river. On April 24th, passes the forts. On April 25th anchors at New Orleans. On April 28th, Forts Jackson and St. Phillip surrender. April 29th, hands the city over to General B. F. Butler. In May cruises up the river to Vicksburg and back. June 6th, leaves New Orleans for another cruise to Vicksburg. On June 28th, passes Vicksburg batteries. July 16th, promoted rear-admiral, the first of that rank in the American navy. July 20th, reports his return to New Orleans.

1863—March 14th, dashes past Port Hudson batteries with Hartford and Albatros. In June, aids in attacks on Port Hudson. July 3d, Vicksburg surrenders, placing the Mississippi under control of Federal forces. On August 1st, sails for New York to repair the Hartford and other ships of his fleet. August 13th, enthusiastically received by citizens of New York.

1864—In January, returns to Gulf Station with view of capturing Mobile. On June 18th, receives a sword presented by the Union League Club of New York. August 5th, battle of Mobile Bay. August 6th, Fort Powell evacuated and destroyed by Confederates. August 8th, Fort

Gaines surrenders.   August 23d, Fort Morgan surrenders.
In September, on account of ill-health, is unable to accept
command of expedition against Fort Fisher at Wilmington, N. C.   November 30th, sails for New York.   December 31st, promoted vice-admiral, the first to hold
that rank in the American navy.

1865—In January, employed for a brief period on James River,
Virginia, to repel an expected Confederate raid.   April
4th, visits Richmond, the Confederate capital, after it had
been captured by the National forces.   End of Civil
War.

1866—July 26th, promoted admiral, the first to hold that rank
in the American navy.

1867—June 17th, hoists flag on steam frigate Franklin and on
June 28th, sails for cruise on coast of Europe where he is
most cordially received.

1869—Visit to the Pacific coast.   Taken seriously ill while at
Chicago on his way East.

1870—Goes to Portland, Maine, to take charge of the reception
given to H. B. M. ship Monarch that brought home the
remains of the eminent philanthropist, George Peabody.
During the summer, cruises to the Portsmouth, N. H.,
Navy Yard, and on August 14th, dies there at the home
of Rear-Admiral A. M. Pennock.   On September 30th,
public funeral is held in New York City.

INTRODUCTION

IF I were asked why I supposed the history of the first American admiral was worthy of preservation, I should reply first of all, "Because he was a typical American citizen." For though David Glasgow Farragut was born in a log cabin on the American frontier, during a period when the frontiersmen depended upon game for their meat, and cultivated their land with their long rifles within easy reach because the Indians were liable to attack them at any time, yet he attained by good work a world-wide reputation. His father was a leader among the hardy neighbors of the region, not because of inherited rank or wealth, but by right of good heroic qualities; while his mother was a woman who could, and did, protect her children from deadly peril by force of arms. For his inheritance Farragut had ability and ambition. But as for book-learning, he had fewer days in schoolhouses than the poorest child in the land may have at the beginning of the twentieth century. It was for an unschooled boy from the backwoods of Tennessee that the American people were glad to create in their navy the ranks of rear-admiral, vice-admiral and admiral.

Farragut was a model sailor. After a midshipman's warrant was procured for him, he had no one to push him up in rank. To the end of his life the

memory of the many boys who entered the navy
after him, and became lieutenants before him,
rankled in his mind.   But in the end he got what
was better than any promotion—a thorough training, and the story of this training alone makes the
history of Farragut's life worth telling.   For after
making full allowance for what he learned under
his first instructor in the arts of war, he was a self-
made admiral.   Though turned into steerage after
steerage where his shipmates thought and talked
of nothing so much as a frolic on shore, Farragut
never lost an opportunity for acquiring knowledge.
When his ship was ordered to lay up for the winter
at Port Mahon, where life for the boys was one prolonged "lark," Farragut sought and obtained permission to go away with the fleet chaplain and
spend the time in study.   And long years before
the Bureau of Information was established in the
Navy Department, Farragut spent his leisure
moments in sounding out reefs in foreign ports and
in making notes on the rigging, guns, fittings and
practices found aboard foreign ships.

Yet he was no "goody-goody."   When a prisoner
on the Phœbe he thrashed one of the British midshipmen in a fair fist fight.   Though he never
fought a duel he would not have hesitated to do so
if challenged, and he was one of the best swordsmen in the navy.   The fact is, his thorough training saved him from the challenges that were thrown
around so readily in his early days, and that is
something for the consideration of those good but
mistaken people who think that any preparation for

war disposes a nation to quarrel-making. While Farragut was never a roysterer he not only held the respect of his shipmates, but he was affectionately called "the little luff," by all who knew him.

In his constant self-training he sought and obtained opportunity. While yet a boy in his teens he had experience as executive officer of a schooner and had learned to handle her in a gale. He served on the first American naval steamer that was engaged in actual war. He obtained command of one of the great steam sloops that were built just before the Civil War and armed with the huge smooth-bores that had been only recently developed.

In short, the Civil War found Farragut the best equipped man in the navy, although his ambition for active service was thwarted for a time. His loyalty to the Constitution he had sworn to defend was unswerving, but because his family and friends lived in the South, he was doubted. In some way, however, it comes to pass that the man who is always ready finds his opportunity. For his first tutor in the arts of war, Farragut had one of the most capable captains in his day—Commodore David Porter—and it happened that a son of the old commodore was able to open the way for Farragut early in the war. Thereafter his course lay plain before him and the work of a lifetime had its fruition.

How he carried his fleet past the forts on the Mississippi has been often told, and the story of the battle of Mobile Bay is found in many books, but certain features of the admiral's character as they appeared during those days can never be described too often. Thus, the plan for the capture of New Orleans was laid down in his orders from Washington, but when after a fair trial he found that it was worthless he had the courage to brush it aside in order to force the fighting—in order to accomplish the work. Likewise when Craven disobeyed orders and lost his life in an effort to get into closer quarters with the enemy, Farragut had only words of praise for him.

That the man who had labored all his life to train himself would make full preparations for a great battle was a matter of course, but one feature of his character stands out most prominently whenever he had such preparations in mind. He never called a council of war to determine whether he ought to fight. His officers were invited to council only that they might consider how best to fight. No man ever had stronger faith in aggressive action than Farragut, and yet he could wait when it was necessary. He had fortitude as well as courage. And with all else he had the inspiration of genius as is abundantly proved by his words quoted in the dedication of this book.

The admiral is memorable, too, because during all his long and laborious career he preserved his sweetness of temper and sense of humor. We will not forget that he was half Spanish. He could be merry when the occasion served, and men who knew him well, when asked what they remember about him best, first of all almost invariably speak of his smile.

Finally we may mention his religious temperament. Of sour-visaged religion he had not a trace. He did not join a church until after the Civil War. But throughout his life he believed in the power and presence of Deity. He would not ask his captains for advice but he would appeal to his God. And his appeals were characteristic. With the torpedoes under the bows of his ship his prayer was, "Shall I go on?" And for every success he gave most hearty thanks.

The greatest of our naval officers was also the most sincere and upright of men. In the history of the leaders of the American people he stands with the highest. Not one word or act of his needs apology or explanation. In his private life he was without blemish, and as an officer of the navy he was a model for those coming after him.

J. R. S.

Northwood, N. Y.

DAVID G. FARRAGUT

CHAPTER I

A BACKWOODS BOY

DAVID GLASGOW FARRAGUT, the first admiral
of the American navy, was born on July 5, 1801,
at a place then called Stony Point, but afterward
Low's Ferry, near Knoxville, Tennessee. The
house stood on the north side of the Holston River.[1]
The main highway from the North Carolina settle-
ments to Nashville, ran past it. Major George
Farragut, the admiral's father, had a license
(granted in April, 1797) to operate a ferry at this
point, and the family estate amounted to 640 acres
of land.

But it should be remembered that this main highway west of the Alleghanies was but a blazed trail
in an almost unbroken forest. Through the energy
of such men as James Robertson and John Sevier,
people from the east side of the range had been led
across the Alleghanies down the Holston, overland
to the Cumberland, and as far west as Nashville.
The settled region west of the mountains was in
form an irregular triangle whereof the Ohio and
Muskingum Rivers were the north line, the Holston

[1] Haywood's " Major George Farragut."

the south line, and Nashville the apex. The Cherokees still owned wide breadths of land in the eastern part of Tennessee, and west of Nashville the
Chickasaws held undisputed sway. It was not until October 24, 1801, that the whites obtained the
right to blaze a trail from Nashville through the
Chickasaw country to Natchez.

The great red war path of the forest-covered valley of the Tennessee lay but a few miles south of
the place where Farragut was born, and beyond
that path was the land of the Creek warriors as
well as that of the Cherokees—a fighting host that
numbered thousands—and these warriors were
steadily urged by the jealous Spaniards at New
Orleans, to exterminate the Yankee pioneers.

The house in which Farragut was born was built
of logs. "Originally it was 40x20, but additional
rooms built later greatly added to its size." [1] The
wolves howled in the near-by forest during the long
winter nights, while the red deer ate the grain in
the narrow fields during the summer-time.

It was the day of log rolling, when the neighbors
for miles around gathered at the new-made clearing
of a settler, and made sport of the work of throwing the fallen trees into huge piles for burning;
and then after a satisfying supper of meats and
"journey cake," they wrestled and ran races by
the light of the moon, jumping on a log and crowing like roosters when they won, and finally danced
half the night away to the music of a well-scraped
fiddle.

[1] Haywood.

But what is of still greater interest in the biography of this man-o'-warsman is the fact that his father and neighbors cultivated their fields with long flint-lock rifles ever at hand to repel the red men that came from the south in search of scalps and plunder. The walls of the Farragut home were pierced with loopholes, like a frontier fort. "I remember," says Farragut in his journal,[1] "that on one occasion during my father's absence, a party of Indians came to our house, which was somewhat isolated, when my mother, who was a brave and energetic woman, barred the door in the most effectual manner, and sent all of us trembling little ones up into the loft, while she guarded the entrance with an axe. The savages attempted to parley with her, but she kept them at bay, until finally they departed, for some reason which is unknown, their intentions having been evidently hostile."

In a letter written to Dr. Lyman C. Draper, on September 20, 1853,[2] Farragut adds that he was five years old at the time. It was therefore some time in the year 1806 that this raid occurred. During the parley the Indians offered to go away if the mother would give them some whiskey. She thereupon opened the door, part way, to comply with the offer, when one of the Indians struck at her with a knife. "But she closed the door by the bar and the knife stuck in the door. They soon after went away."

[1] Quoted in Loyall Farragut's life of the admiral.
[2] Am. Hist. Rev.

George Anthony Magin Farragut, father of the admiral, was a full-blooded Spaniard. He was born in Cuidadela, on the Island of Minorca, in the Mediterranean, on September 29, 1755, and the ancient records of that place show that there was fighting blood in the family as far back as the year 1229. In 1776 George came to America, joined the patriot forces and served with credit during the Revolutionary War. It is noted particularly that at the battle of the Cowpens he saved the life of Colonel William Washington. After the war he went with two comrades to Tennessee where he was employed as a surveyor. But while he was yet living in North Carolina he had become enamored of a maiden named Elizabeth, the daughter of Captain John Shine, of Dobbs County, and at a forgotten date he returned to the Old North State, married her and carried her to Tennessee.

There George Farragut, because of his personal characteristics and military training, became a man of much local importance. He was a typical frontiersman in his ability to turn his hand to any kind of work. Knoxville, for instance, boasts of a house still standing that was built by him. He was a famous hunter—"a glorious Indian hunter, and a great provider in great straits for food," as an old comrade said of him.

On November 3, 1790, William Blount, Governor of the territory south of the Ohio, appointed him muster master of the district of Washington, and a major of cavalry. He was also something of a land speculator, as the old records show, and it was on

December 9, 1796, that he bought the tract where the future admiral was born.

Any one who could gain credit for ability among the patriots of North Carolina during the War of the Revolution, and thereafter obtain rank among the frontiersmen of Tennessee, was, beyond question, an able fighting man. It is natural to suppose that the son of such a man would have similar abilities. But when we consider the inherited fighting qualities of Admiral David Glasgow Farragut we will also remember the picture of his mother, standing by the barred door of her log cabin, axe in hand, awaiting the attack of hostile savages.

Among the leading citizens of Tennessee with whom George Farragut was associated for a number of years was William Charles Cole Claiborne. When Louisiana was transferred to the United States (December 20, 1803), he was appointed governor of the territory and, according to a tradition in the Farragut family, George Farragut removed from Tennessee to Louisiana through his influence. The governor, having "executive, legislative and judicial powers over a vast territory, peopled by heterogeneous races," was burdened with a task more difficult, perhaps, than any ever set before such an officer in America. His position was dangerous as well as difficult, for assassination was a common occurrence among the floating population of New Orleans, while dueling was a pastime with the gentry. It was therefore natural for Claiborne to bring to his support such of his friends as were

skilled in the arts of war. Thomas Jefferson was
President of the Nation and Claiborne stood very
close to him. It is not improbable that when Jefferson developed his policy of building gunboats
for harbor defense, instead of a navy, Claiborne
saw in it an opportunity for obtaining congenial
employment in government service for the venturesome Major Farragut. At any rate, Major George
Anthony Magin Farragut was appointed, on March
2, 1807, a sailing master in the American navy, and
was ordered to New Orleans to take command of
Gunboat 11, a schooner-rigged craft of shoal draft,
carrying four cannon.

From the admiral's letter previously quoted, it
appears that Sailing Master Farragut departed for
his new post immediately after receiving the appointment, leaving his wife to follow him with the
children and such household effects as she could
bring, in a flatboat. This flatboat journey was
made in the fall of 1807.

It is a memorable fact that at the time of the Farragut migration the territory around New Orleans
was a troubled and perilous part of the country because the American government claimed the land
between Lake Pontchartrain and Pensacola as a part
of the Louisiana territory, while Spain, with better
reason, claimed it as a part of Florida. Having
faith in the claim of the United States, George Farragut, on arrival at New Orleans, bought 900 acres
of land "in what is now Jackson County, Mississippi. It was situated at a slight promontory,
called Point Plaquet," since called Farragut's

Point, and lay on the west side of the Pascagoula River, but well within West Florida.

Some of the few incidents of George Farragut's life in New Orleans and the regions roundabout, are of particular interest. For one thing, he made a voyage from New Orleans to Havana in a pirogue —a kind of dug-out canoe built of two tree trunks hollowed out and fastened together. Then, being on duty at the naval station in New Orleans while managing his Pascagoula estate, he was obliged to make numerous journeys across Lake Pontchartrain. For this purpose he used a yawl and he frequently carried his children (he had three sons) with him. Young David wrote afterward that his first experience on salt water was a trip across the lake in this yawl while the wind was "blowing almost a gale." As they passed a gunboat stationed there, its captain invited the senior Farragut to "come on board until the blow is over." But Farragut replied: "I can ride it out better than you can." And that was his candid opinion, for he had entire confidence in his own boat, and a sailor's natural contempt for such craft as the gunboats of that day.

While making these trips the father and his boys often slept on the sandy beach wrapped in the boat's sail. When his friends suggested that he was subjecting his children to great risks he replied:

"Now is the time to conquer their fears!"

Thus not only did David Glasgow Farragut spring from good fighting stock, but he was taught as a child to face peril with unruffled composure.

CHAPTER II

A MIDSHIPMAN IN THE AMERICAN NAVY

IT is a fact of much importance in the life of Admiral Farragut that he was associated in his earliest years with men who made their names memorable in American history. The influence of Governor Claiborne has been mentioned. Still more influential were the Porters of the old navy.

While Sailing Master George Farragut was on duty at the New Orleans naval station, he had for an associate a Captain David Porter, of whose career every historian wishes that more could be known, for he saw service in the Revolution as captain, both of a privateer, and of a ship in the Massachusetts navy. He was also at one time in the Jersey prison ship of infamous memory.

It is particularly well worth recalling here that he was in command of the American schooner Eliza, lying in the port of Jeremie, San Domingo, in 1796, when a British press gang tried to board her. The old captain, calling his men to the rail, made a fight for liberty wherein several were killed and wounded on each side, and the men-stealers were finally driven off. This exploit made Captain Porter famous. Because of it Washington appointed him a sailing-master in the regular navy, and he was, in due time, ordered to the naval station at New Orleans. One may well believe that young

Farragut often heard the stories of Captain Porter's adventures, and particularly of that in the port of Jeremie, for the captain and George Farragut, while associates at New Orleans, became warm friends.

It is said that Captain Porter had been ordered south because he was not in good health. He was, at any rate, well on in years. One day while fishing from a small boat on Lake Pontchartrain he was sunstruck and fell unconscious to the bottom of the boat. In this condition he was found by Sailing Master Farragut, who took him home to the plantation on the Pascagoula, where he was assiduously nursed by the hospitable Mrs. Farragut, until she was stricken with the yellow fever. The two died within so brief a time that they were buried on the same day (June 22, 1808).

The kindly work of George Farragut in caring for the captain was to have far-reaching effect upon the fortunes of his son, David Glasgow. For, some time later, the captain's son, Commander David Porter, came to New Orleans to take charge of the naval station. To show his appreciation of the kindness of the Farragut family, he offered to adopt one of the motherless boys and train him for a career in the navy.

At that time the oldest Farragut boy, William, was already a midshipman, and when Porter's offer was discussed during a visit, young David Glasgow, as he writes in his diary, "said promptly" that he would go. The diary adds that he was inspired to make this decision by the commander's uniform, and the uniform worn by young Midshipman William ; but one may believe that this was not a complete statement of all the facts. While the joy of wearing gold lace must have appealed to the boy, the adventurous career for which the uniform stood was not without its influence, even though he was less than eight years old.

Something of what Commander Porter did to earn fame, will appear further on in connection with the War of 1812, and with the *quasi* war that was waged on the Cuban pirates between 1819 and 1825. But as showing the already established character of the man by whom young Farragut was adopted, it should be recalled here that as a lad of sixteen Commander Porter was in the fight for liberty on the Eliza in the port of Jeremie. Later, during West India voyages, he was twice impressed into the British navy, but succeeded in escaping both times. Naturally, as Soley points out,[1] he conceived "a personal antipathy for everything British—a feeling not unlike that which the English sailors of Drake's day entertained for everything Spanish." Having entered the navy as a midshipman, young Porter had a part, during the naval war with France, in the capture of the Insurgente by the Constellation, and he was with Lieutenant Rodgers who, with a dozen seamen, carried the captured ship and two hundred prisoners through a three-days' gale into St. Kitts. Later he was executive officer of the schooner Experiment, and had part in her remarkable series of fights

[1] "Admiral Porter," p. 4.

with the French and the pirates in the West Indies. During the subsequent wars on the Mediterranean pirates he was on the schooner Enterprise when she captured a Tripolitan polacca; he distinguished himself by leading a landing party that captured old Tripoli, and he was finally captured by the pirates when the Philadelphia ran on a reef in Tripoli harbor.

It was by a man who had had that kind of a career that David Glasgow Farragut was adopted when less than eight years old.

Going at once to the commander's home, young Farragut was adopted as a member of the family, and thereafter accompanied him on such boat expeditions as were made on the river and bayous of the vicinity. Some of these were undoubtedly service expeditions, for it was in 1809, that the famous pirates, Jean and Pierre Lafitte, began their notorious career by smuggling slaves from the Gulf across the bayous to the planters of the interior. Young Farragut "soon became fond of this adventurous sort of life," and it was admirably adapted to fit him for the more stirring adventures that were near at hand.

After a time Porter was ordered north, and taking Farragut with him, he sailed from New Orleans in the bomb brig Vesuvius, of 11 guns. Farragut now took leave of his father forever. Sailing Master George Farragut remained in the navy until March 25, 1814, when he left, because he had lost his health. He "died of a cough" at Pascagoula, on June 4, 1817.

The Vesuvius went north by way of Havana,
where it was learned that a British man-o'-war had
recently fired on the United States brig Vixen. It
was during the most humiliating period of American history that Farragut reached Havana. For
years the British authorities, urged on by the jealous British merchants, had made systematic efforts
to injure American oversea commerce, and render
it tributary to Great Britain when it could not be
entirely destroyed. For many years, too, American citizens, afloat in American ships, had been
taken by British press gangs and compelled to
serve without pay on British war-ships. British
frigates had blockaded American ports, firing on
all shipping passing in or out, and in one case
killing an American sailor well within American
waters. And then, to complete the humiliation of
the Nation, as the American frigate Chesapeake was
leaving the capes of Chesapeake Bay on a voyage
to Europe, she was attacked by a British frigate,
several of her crew were killed and wounded, and
finally three of her men, two of whom, it was admitted, were American citizens who had been impressed into the British navy and had recently escaped, were taken from her on the charge that they
were deserters from the British navy.

The attack on the Vixen was but one of a long
series of outrages on the American flag but Farragut mentions it in his log because it aroused his
anger, and cultivated his hatred of the aggressor.

"I looked upon this as an insult to be paid in
kind, and was anxious to discharge the debt with

interest," he wrote afterward. And in comment-
ing on this statement Captain Mahan, speaking as
an American naval officer, remarks:

"It is scarcely necessary to say how keenly this
feeling was shared by his seniors to whom the
Vixen incident was but one among many bitter
wrongs which the policy of their government had
forced them humbly to swallow."

On reaching Washington Porter took Farragut
with him on a visit to Mr. Paul Hamilton, of South
Carolina, then Secretary of the Navy. The lad's
desire to enter the navy was considered, and the
Secretary said he would make him a midshipman
as soon as he should become ten years old.

With this promise to encourage him, Farragut
was placed in a school in Washington, while Porter
returned to New Orleans. In the latter part of
1810, Porter was relieved of the command of the
New Orleans station. Returning north in a gunboat by way of the Mississippi and Ohio Rivers
to Pittsburg, he went to Washington where, on
December 17th, the Secretary of the Navy made
good his promise by issuing a midshipman's warrant to young Farragut who was then just nine
years, five months and twelve days old.

The records of the Navy Department show that
he was appointed from Tennessee, and to Tennessee
he was accredited throughout his life. Although
George Farragut was a resident of New Orleans,
and owner of a plantation at Pascagoula, his love
for Tennessee made him claim it as his home state
so long as he lived.

Born on the frontier of the Nation and bred from his early youth in the navy, it may well be said of the first American admiral that he was a typical American citizen as well as a model American seaman.

CHAPTER III

FARRAGUT AFLOAT AND IN BATTLE

FARRAGUT'S first service afloat was seen in the frigate Essex, a ship of unique history, and one whose good fame in the War of 1812 was exceeded only by that of the Constitution. As Farragut served on her through this war until she was captured, it is worth while to relate that the Essex was built at Salem, Massachusetts, for use in the undeclared war with France which began in 1798.

As the reader will remember, this war grew out of the unreasonable efforts of the French Republicans to compel the United States to join them in their war with Great Britain. These efforts took the shape of piratical aggressions on American commerce, and more than three hundred American vessels were captured and confiscated in a single year. Having no naval ships, save a few that the pirates of the north coast of Africa had nagged us into building, the government was compelled, when war was at hand, to seek ships wherever they could be found. In these straits the people of Salem began to discuss, in the summer of 1798, the project of building a frigate for government use, being incited thereto, undoubtedly, by the losses they had sustained through French aggressions. When the sum of $74,700 had been subscribed, a meeting was held (October 25), and it was resolved "to build a frigate of 32 guns and to loan the same to the government.''

Preble, in his '' Ships of the Nineteenth Century,'' tells how the people of the region about Salem passed the following winter in cutting and hauling timber for the new ship, and that they ''considered it a patriotic duty to cut down the finest sticks of their wood-lots for the chastisement of French insolence and piracy.''

The Essex was launched on September 30, 1799. She was 141 feet long on the gun deck, 37 feet beam, and 12¼ feet deep. She measured 840.21 tons. As indicating the care taken in building her, it is related that her first suit of canvas fitted her so well that she never sailed so swiftly afterward. Her battery, when her flag was hoisted, consisted of 26 long 12-pounders on the main deck, and ten 9-pounders on the quarter deck, but was afterward changed.

In the French war the Essex saw no fighting, but she sailed for Batavia on January 6, 1800, to convoy home a fleet of American merchantmen, and was thus the first American man-o'-war to round the Cape of Good Hope. In the wars on the African pirates (1801 and 1805), the Essex was in the Mediterranean, and a part of her crew landed and helped in the capture of Derne (April 27, 1805), when fourteen of them were killed.

The Essex was then laid up in ordinary, for a time, but in January, 1809, was again commissioned and sent to Europe to carry dispatches which now make a part of an immense mass of dreary reading for the patriotic student of American history. When she returned she brought home William Pinckney, who for five years had represented the American government in Great Britain with unsurpassed ability. By his return diplomatic relations with Great Britain were severed, and the War of 1812 was at hand.

From the day when Thomas Jefferson was inaugurated President of the United States until November 2, 1810, every possible effort had been made by the American government to avoid war with Great Britain. Jefferson, and after him Madison, had believed that every European aggressor could be restrained and brought to reason by what they called "peaceable coercion." In a letter to Thomas Paine, written March 18, 1801, Jefferson said:

"We shall avoid implicating ourselves with the Powers of Europe even in support of principles which we mean to pursue. We believe we can enforce those principles as to ourselves by peaceable means."

In another letter he tells how this was to be done:

"Our commerce is so valuable to them that they will be glad to purchase it when the only price we ask is to do us justice. I believe we have in our hands the means of peaceable coercion."

That is to say, no matter what aggressions a nation of Europe might commit, we had only to withdraw our trade from the aggressor to compel him to end the aggression and pay for the damage we had already suffered.

This policy had been followed with astonishing stubbornness, but the British found it more profitable to prey on American commerce than to "purchase" it by "doing us justice." Confiscation of American ships and cargoes under piratical Orders in Council, and murderous attacks on American crews became matters of as common occurrence as gales of wind at sea. But all these aggressions were met by Non-Intercourse Acts and Embargoes only. To stifle the honest indignation which arose at times, the people were told that to build a navy would necessitate the laying of taxes that had been justly odious under the preceding administration. And with infamous iteration members of Congress said that it would be impossible to succeed on the ocean in a war with Great Britain.

"The idea of our meeting Great Britain on the ocean is too ludicrous to be repelled by serious argument," said Congressman Nicholson in the House, and the assertion was applauded. The work of John Paul Jones was never so much as mentioned in the prolonged debates between 1804 and 1812. The deeds of Truxton were forgotten; the work of Sterrett and Decatur was ignored. And to quiet the clamor of honest manhood which arose at each fresh outrage, the President, with deliberate intent to evade the issue, talked well while he postponed action, and his followers in Congress blinded the indignant, by voting money for gunboats which were known to be useless.

From a contemplation of the supposed impossibility of success in a naval war with Great Britain, some leaders of the people came to believe that it would be impossible to defend our seaports ; and Congressman R. Nelson, on January 23, 1807, stood up in the House and said, " When the enemy comes let them take our towns, and let us retire into the country." In fact a time came when, to compel Great Britain "to do us justice," Congress passed a bill [1] to lay "a line of blocks and chains across New York harbor."

John Randolph, though the greatest of American blatherskites, did not live in vain. For, clothed in riding habit, carrying a whip, and followed by a pack of hounds, he strode into the House of Congress, and facing the cowering representatives of the Nation, told them that they could not be kicked into fighting.

Judged by these open assertions and the acts of the majority of Congress, the American people had become a nation of cowards, their property the "safe booty" of every pirate. And the people of Europe, with hearty contempt, accepted them at the estimate of their Congress.

In the meantime, however, a war party had been springing up in Congress and the Nation, with men like John C. Calhoun and Henry Clay as its leaders. The growing power of this party had impelled President Madison to an unwonted state of mind, and it was carrying the country into its second war for independence.

The last act of "peaceable coercion" by self-strangulation, which Congress passed, was the Em-

[1] See Act of February 10, 1809.

bargo of March 1, 1809, as amended by the Act of
June 28th, of the same year. It was provided in
this act that, for a specified period, no trade should
be carried on between the United States and either
France or Great Britain. In due time this act ex-
pired by limitation, but it was further provided
that in case either party to the offensive measures
against American commerce should relent, after the
expiration of the embargo, the President was to
revive it in reference to the unrelenting nation.

Napoleon, in due time, took advantage of the
situation, and by falsehood and treachery led the
American government and people to suppose that
he had repealed his decrees in restraint of American
commerce. This change of policy was first asserted
in a letter to his Minister of Foreign Affairs
(Cadore), dated July 31, 1810. The deception of the
American officials was not complete, but it was sufficient. In a letter from Cadore to the French minister at Washington, received on September 25th, the
new policy was announced. It was by no means a
satisfactory document. But Madison, pushed on by
the war party in Congress, accepted it as sincere, for
war in some quarter was then seen to be absolutely
necessary. More than once men of this party had
urged a declaration of war against both France and
England. It is easy to show now that we had
ample cause for taking strong measures against
France, but policy demanded that one nation only
be chosen, and Madison therefore revived the embargo against Great Britain. His proclamation of
November 2, 1810, said, "it has been officially

made known to this government " that Napoleon's decrees are revoked. Secretary of the Treasury Gallatin sent orders the same day to all collectors of customs announcing that commerce with Great Britain would end on February 2, 1811.

This proclamation was the first step toward a war with England. In answer to it a British fleet was sent to blockade New York harbor, as it had been blockaded while previous non-intercourse and embargo acts were in force. The President, again spurred on by the leaders of the war party, resented this aggression and an American squadron, under Commodore Rodgers, pitifully small in numbers, but with the men behind the guns eager for a fight, was ordered to sea May 6, 1811, to protect the flag. We can imagine how the blood of Midshipman Farragut was stirred when he heard about this order, especially as it proved to him that his opportunity to see service would soon come.

Late in the evening of May 16th, Commodore Rodgers, who was on the frigate President, overhauled the British sloop of war Little Belt. He supposed her to be the British frigate Guerrier, that had recently impressed an American sailor from a merchantman on the coast, and he intended to recover the man. After a hail or two from each side the Little Belt fired a gun, and a brief battle followed. The conflict is memorable chiefly because the captain of the Little Belt reported afterward under oath, although incorrectly, that he had maintained a fight with the Yankee frigate for about three-quarters of an hour, and that he had forced her "to stand from us," at the end of that time. It was a high honor for a sloop so long to endure the fire of a frigate if she could endure it. This testimony shows how British naval officers then regarded the fighting ability of the Americans. The fight is also to be kept in mind because, although it lasted eighteen minutes, the President did no material damage to the Little Belt. The American sailors had not then learned to shoot.

It was soon after this fight that the Essex returned home from Europe bringing Minister Pinckney. She made port at Norfolk, Va., where orders were at once issued to refit her for immediate service. Captain David Porter (he was as yet in rank only a commander) was ordered to do this work.

It was then that young Farragut, who, since receiving his warrant, had been at school at Chester, Pa., first saw active service. For Porter at once took the lad, who was then just past his tenth birthday, from the school to the Essex. It was his first visit to Norfolk, which was to become the scene of some of the most important events of his life.

Of Farragut's first work as a midshipman, we have one brief glimpse in a letter written by Captain Porter and preserved at the Boston Navy Yard:

August 9, 1811.

"SIR:—I have sent Mr. Farragut and David Tittimary on board, and beg you take them under your particular care. When the wherry is perfectly dry I will thank you to send her over to me every morning at half-past nine, under charge of Mr. Farragut."

The letter was directed to "Lieutenant John Downes, United States Frigate Essex, Navy Yard." Downes was then executive officer of the Essex, and was afterward a commodore in the navy. The notable facts in the letter are that the ten-year-old midshipman was mentioned as "Mr. Farragut," and that in spite of his youth and lack of experience, he had the responsibility of commanding a wherry's crew of seamen.

Another significant glimpse of the young midshipman is found in an anecdote related by Mahan. Farragut, having been sent ashore in charge of the boat one day, was obliged to wait some time at the landing. In the usual alongshore fashion a crowd of dock loungers gathered near the wherry and began to make remarks about the personal appearance of the tiny young midshipman who was dressed in a new uniform and was standing fully erect in the stern sheets, after a manner that remained with him through life. The remarks of the crowd were no doubt exceedingly irritating to the lad, and certainly were still more so to the crew of the boat, who held the honor of their ship and officers in the highest estimation.

But Farragut and his men remained silent and dignified under the chafing until one of the loungers procured a sprinkling pot full of water and began sprinkling the little midshipman, at the same time expressing the opinion that watering would make him grow. At that the bow oarsman with his boat hook caught the lounger in the pocket, and by a jerk tumbled him into the boat, where he was well pounded, while the other members of the crew seized stretchers, oars and boat hooks, and jumping ashore, dashed into the crowd, whom they chased up to Market Square, while Farragut, with his long dirk in hand, followed and cheered them on.

At the square the police interfered, and the little midshipman and his men were haled to court, where they were bound over to keep the peace. It was not a lawful fight, but the incident showed first that though but ten years and a month old the lad had self-restraint, as well as self-respect, and that he would fight when the proper time came.

As Porter said to Lieutenant Downes that night, the lad was made up of "three pounds of uniform and seventy pounds of fight." [1]

In the later years of his life Farragut used to tell how Porter once caught him chewing tobacco on the Essex. Seeing the stains on Farragut's lips the captain clapped his hand on the lad's mouth and made him swallow the stuff. Farragut never used tobacco in any form after that experience.

In some memoranda on "The Two Admirals," furnished by Mr. Richard B. Porter, son of Admiral D. D. Porter to the *Century Magazine*, is an account of young Farragut that illustrates one of his peculiarities while on the Essex.

"He was the life of the midshipman's mess," said Mr. Porter, "full of fun and as agile as a cat. He liked nothing better than to climb to the top of the mainmast and sit curl-legged, gazing out to sea.

[1] Barnes in "Midshipman Farragut."

"'Where's Glasgow?' the commodore would ask, missing him.

"'Up on the mainmast, sir, looking for fresh air,' the quartermaster would reply."

In his diary Farragut says of the Essex: "I was exceedingly pleased with the ship and her officers," and after she had sailed from port he adds the important statement: "We exercised the crew until they were brought into as great a state of perfection as ever existed, probably, in the navy." Moreover, the Essex proved "the smartest in the squadron, and Commodore Rodgers complimented our captain highly."

The time when a British sloop of war could endure the fire of an American frigate for eighteen minutes and escape unhurt was passing. But in this cruise no aggressive enemy was found annoying American commerce, and beyond a narrow escape from shipwreck in a gale off the bluffs at Newport, R. I., there was no incident of interest to record.

In the spring of 1812 we find the Essex in New York harbor, and a letter written by her purser, Melancton W. Bostwick, under date of "17 April, 1812, on board the United States frigate Essex, at the Narrows below New York," shows very well the spirit of her crew. It says:

"We are now, sir, going to sea, in every respect prepared for action, and should we fall in with any of the British cruisers which infest our coast, they will not have a Chesapeake to deal with. The Essex is rated a 32-gun frigate, but mounts 44, and carries about 350 men, as eager for a skirmish with

the British as any set of men you ever saw; I believe that many of them would fast three days for
the sake of a dust."

On June 18, 1812, the long humiliation of the
American people came to an end. Though Madison, as well as Jefferson, by the policy of "peaceable coercion" had invited insult and outrage, it
was literally true, as Madison said in two of his
war messages, that the American people had shown
"unexampled forbearance" and patience under
aggressions that were singularly brutal. To the
astonishment of the world they would fight at last.

It is a curious and memorable fact that, when
war was declared, the administration purposed
keeping such ships as we had (nine in all that were
ready) within the range of the protecting guns of
our forts, lest the British should capture them all.
It was the natural instinct of politicians who for
ten years had talked of "peaceable coercion" to
do this; but the spirit of the American people,
which the politicians could not appreciate, shone
forth in the navy, and two captains, William Bainbridge and Charles Stewart, by spirited remon-
strances prevailed upon the timorous executive, and
the ships were ordered out to try their strength.

A small squadron that included the Essex, had
been gathered at New York under Commodore
Rodgers just previous to the declaration of hostilities, and when the word came, all the ships except
her put to sea. She was detained by the necessity
of making repairs, the need of which was not apparent when Dr. Bostwick wrote his letter. Farra-

gut tells in his journal that while the crew worked at the rigging the declaration of war was read to them on three successive days, and they were told that if any British subject was on board he could have his discharge by asking for it. No one responded, but when all were called to the capstan to swear their allegiance, one man, who was really an American, but who wanted to go ashore for a spree, declined to take the oath. At that his messmates, who knew his birthplace, were so angry that they tarred and feathered him as a coward—a fact that seems worthy of mention to show the conditions prevailing on the Essex during Farragut's first experience aboard ship.

On July 3d, the Essex put to sea in search of the British frigate Thetis, a 36-gun ship reported on her way to South America with specie. The Thetis was not found, but a convoy of British merchantmen were overhauled, and a brig, with 150 soldiers and some general officers on board, was taken out. The frigate Minerva in charge of the convoy, though of equal force, declined to fight the Essex, and the latter, because of the strength of some of the ships of the convoy, could not close in on the Minerva.

On August 13, 1812, Farragut first smelled gunpowder under service conditions. A sloop of war was seen bearing down upon the Essex, and Captain Porter put drags over the side of his ship, and then made sail as if eager to escape. The stranger at once gave chase and the crew of the Essex was sent to quarters, though the ports were kept shut to continue deceiving the enemy until she was alongside.

In due time the stranger arrived within range and fired a gun. The Essex hove to, and then the other ship crossed astern. She was now within "the lion's reach," as Farragut writes, and Old Glory, then contemptuously called by the enemy "the gridiron flag," was flung to the breeze. At sight of the flag the British crew cheered and fired a broadside, but while their smoke was yet in the air, the ports of the Essex were opened, and for eight minutes a steady fire was maintained. The enemy at first tried to run, but was shot to pieces and hauled down his flag. The ship proved to be the British sloop of war Alert, of 20 guns.

The story of the fight, as told by Purser Bostwick, is particularly interesting because it describes the feelings of the crew of which Farragut was a member. A letter he wrote at the end of the cruise says :

"We left New York on the 2d of July, and during the cruise were as far south as 28° north latitude and north as far as 47° north latitude, and as far east as 30° west longtitude. We have captured nine of the enemy's ships and brigs. I presume you have seen an account, as I am informed it has been published, of our first capture, the particulars of which reflect as much honor on the American, as it does disgrace on the British, flag. The next succeeding seven were merchantmen, four of them with cargoes, ordered for the United States —(we have only as yet heard of the arrival of one, a West Indiaman),—two with no cargo, burnt ; one sent into Newfoundland as a cartel for the purpose of effecting an exchange of prisoners; and our last prize captured on the 13th of August, H. B. M. sloop of war Alert of 20 guns, commanded by Captain T. L. Langharne, after an action of eight minutes, without the loss of a drop of American blood; the enemy had 5 men wounded, 3 dangerously, and it is stated by the crew that they had 13 men killed and thrown overboard before we got possession of her, and from examining the course and effect of our shot, it is presumed that at least that number fell a sacrifice to British pride and arrogance; and we are now convinced, notwithstanding Captain Bingham's assertion to the contrary, that a British sloop of war has the assurance to commence an action on an American frigate, within short pistol shot, for such they told us they knew us to be, and when our flag went up, and they under our quarter, they had the impudence to give three cheers, which did us as little injury as their five broadsides which followed it in succession. We returned their fire as fast as our guns could be brought to bear, and in the short space of eight minutes their pride was humbled, their flag was struck to a Yankee, with seven feet of water in her (the Alert's) hold; then it was our turn to cheer. She was much cut to pieces in every part and it was evident that had she not struck the moment she did, but received the broadside which we were on the point of firing, she must most inevitably have gone down, and very probably before our boats could have gotten out to save her crew from a watery grave. When her commander came on board to deliver up his sword, he informed Captain Porter the ship was sinking which we however prevented by wearing her around and bringing her shot holes above water." [1]

[1] Quoted by Admiral George Dewey, United States Navy, in *Navy League Journal*, October, 1904.

This fight, unequal as were the forces, was memorable. For in the action between the President (a much more powerful ship than the Essex) and the Little Belt, a ship of the Alert class, the firing lasted for eighteen minutes, yet the Little Belt was able to go on her way not badly hurt. Now, at the end of eight minutes, the fire of the Essex had cut the Alert to pieces so badly that when an American lieutenant boarded her, he found that she had seven feet of water in her hold. On the ship where Farragut got his first lessons in the art of war the men were trained to aim their guns.

Curiously enough, the prisoners from the prizes were so loosely guarded that some time later they conspired to take the Essex. Arms were secured, and the moment of uprising was at hand, when one of them, with a pistol in hand, went to Farragut's hammock to see if he were asleep. The lad was awake, but seeing the pistol in the man's hand, he pretended that he was not until the man left. Then Farragut hastened to inform Captain Porter, who ran to the berth deck and began to shout:

"Fire! Fire!"

Ever since leaving port the captain had been exercising his men at fire drill. He had sounded the alarm at all times of the night, and he had even built smudges in the hold to give the men the idea that she really was burning. Hearing this cry the crew ran to their stations in perfect order, while the prisoners were so confused and alarmed that they were easily controlled. Thereafter the Essex fell in with the British frigate Shannon and another ship

that gave chase.   The Essex ran until night, when,
seeing the Shannon well separated from her consort, Porter turned.   By swinging a small anchor
to the main yard whence it could be easily dropped
into the rigging of the enemy to hold him fast, and
in other ways, the Essex was prepared to attack the
Shannon by boarding.   It was a most hazardous
enterprise, for the Shannon was bowling along at no
less than ten knots an hour and it was likely that
the Essex would be traveling at least four when
striking her.   A collision like that in the night
was likely to dismast both ships, and might sink
them.   But the Essex failed to find the enemy, and
the attempt is worthy of mention only because it
shows something of the daring of the man by whom
Farragut was first trained in the duties of a naval
officer.

Finally, having run short of food, the Essex returned to the Delaware for supplies.   She had been
out seventy-two days.   Captain Porter expected to
put to sea once more after only a trifling delay;
but on arrival he found that his ship was destined
for a more interesting adventure.   How this cruise
proved of lasting honor to the navy, and was to end
in a battle that served better than any other of
that war to rehabilitate the American people in
the eyes of the world, if not in their own estimation,
shall now be told.

CHAPTER IV

CAPTAIN OF A SHIP WHEN TWELVE YEARS OLD

IT appears from the record that when Captain Porter returned with the Essex to the Delaware for provisions he was disappointed in finding none there. The government at Washington had followed the policy of "peaceable coercion" for so long a time that a small bit of war-like work such as the preparation of provisions for a single ship, could not be attended to properly.

However, the failure proved beneficial in the end. Porter had recommended some time previously, that a squadron be sent to the Pacific Ocean to destroy the enemy's commerce—especially the whale-ships cruising there. It was decided now to follow this advice, and the Constitution, Captain William Bainbridge, and the Hornet (sloop of war), Master-Commandant James Lawrence, with the Essex, were detailed for the work.

Accordingly, after overhauling the rigging and taking in supplies, the Constitution and the Hornet, which were at Boston, sailed on October 26, 1812, for the Pacific. The Essex sailed from the Delaware, two days later, to join them. Porto Praya, in the Cape Verde Islands, off the coast of Africa, had been appointed as the meeting-place, and at this far-away harbor the Essex arrived November 27th.

The Constitution and the Hornet were not there, and the Essex anchored for five days to get in fresh water and provisions. Then she sailed to Fernando de Noronha, the place that had been appointed for meeting in case of failure at Porto Praya. On December 11th, Porter had the good fortune to fall in with the British packet Nocton, having on board $55,000 in coin, which was a prize of material use, as shall appear.

On the 15th Fernando de Noronha was reached and a letter was received from Commodore Bainbridge, directing the Essex to cruise off Cape Frio, and wait for the Constitution and the Hornet, for a certain length of time, after which, failing to meet his consorts, Captain Porter was to go to St. Sebastian's Island and thence to St. Catherine's Island further down the Brazilian coast.

The Essex reached her station off Cape Frio on December 29th. A British ship of the line—the Montagu—was known to be stationed in those waters, but Porter held his place until rough weather and heavy seas so strained the masts and rigging of the Essex as to make it necessary for her to enter port and refit. Accordingly he bore away for St. Catherine's Island, 500 miles down the coast of Brazil, where he found a harbor fit for his purpose, and sufficiently far from the Montagu. He arrived there on January 20, 1813.

As showing the ingenuity of Farragut's instructor it may be worth mentioning that Porter worked the Essex through a dead calm to a good anchorage at St. Catherine's by means of two sea anchors—

sails stretched to small spars that, when hauled aft alongside the ship, stood upright in the water, and when dragged forward to the spritsail-yards for a new grip, floated on the surface. The speed attained with this device was about two knots (or sea miles) an hour.

The refitting was done rapidly in spite of squally weather, and then on January 25th, a small coaster came into port from Rio de Janeiro, the captain of which told Porter that the Montagu had captured an American sloop of war that had been cruising with a frigate on the Brazilian coast. The story was untrue, for in the meantime the Constitution had captured the British frigate Java, and the Hornet was then blockading the Bonne Citoyenne in the harbor of Bahia. But Porter had no reason for doubting it; and he naturally supposed the sloop was the Hornet. It was also reasonable to think that the captain of the Montagu would learn that the Essex was refitting at St. Catherine's, and would come in search of her. Therefore it was necessary for the Essex to leave as soon as possible, and with that necessity the opportunity of a lifetime came to Captain David Porter.

Before nightfall his ship was on her way down the harbor and on January 26, 1813, she headed away for the Pacific. Porter had been waiting for the Constitution and the Hornet to come down to St. Catherine's and to join him in the cruise beyond the Horn. But now, having no longer any hope that either would arrive, he had decided that he would go on the hazardous trip alone. It is a memorable fact that Farragut's earliest training was under a man who could thus promptly and courageously choose a course that involved the greatest responsibility.

As Mahan points out, too, it is a notable fact that young Farragut, along with the others of the crew, was put on short allowance of food immediately after leaving port, although the ship was bound to the stormiest waters of the world. The Essex had been unable to procure either bread or flour at St. Catherine's, and the food supply was so short that when serving only a half a pound of bread per day for each man on board she had enough for but three months.

With the men perpetually hungry the ship entered the fierce cold and storms of Cape Horn. Throughout the month of February, she butted the tremendous seas and squalls found in that region, and then on March 3d, a sea struck her that burst in, from stem to stern, every gun port on one side of the ship. Immense volumes of water flooded in, and many sailors, supposing the ship was going down, fell on their knees and began to pray. But in the midst of the danger, good, profane William Kingsbury, boatswain's mate, ran up from below, shouting to the men :

" Damn your eyes, put your best foot forward. There is one side of the ship left yet ! "

" Long shall I remember the cheering sound of his stentorian voice, which resembled the roaring of a lion rather than that of a human being," wrote Farragut in his diary.

Good courage proved as contagious as panic. The men followed Kingsbury on deck where all hands got the ship before the wind, patched up the broken ports, and then drove her on her way. The disastrous stroke proved the last of the storm. A fair wind came next day and carried the Essex up to the island called Mocha, on the Chilean coast, where the crew were glad to land and shoot wild horses in order to get a supply of fresh meat. Then on the 11th Valparaiso was reached and a good supply of provisions was purchased with the money taken from the captured Nocton.

On going ashore for news, Captain Porter found that the Essex was needed in those waters to protect American commerce as well as to destroy British trade. For Chile had revolted against Spain, and the Spanish viceroy in his efforts to subdue the Chilenos, had fitted out several privateers to prey on their commerce ; and these privateers, on the plea that Spain was an ally of Great Britain, had begun to capture American whalemen.

Accordingly, the Essex, as soon as supplies could be brought on board, sailed north along the coast, and on March 26th fell in with the privateer Nereyda, of 15 guns. The Essex was flying the British flag, and a lieutenant of the Nereyda boarded her and talked with the utmost freedom. He boasted of having captured two Yankee whalers already, the crews of which were then held on the Nereyda as prisoners.

Thereupon Porter seized the Nereyda, but, not caring to send her to the United States, he threw her guns and ammunition overboard, took off her topgallant masts to cripple her speed, and sent her to her own home with a message to the viceroy that " was calculated to insure peaceable treatment to American vessels "

The two whalers captured were the ship Barclay, Captain Gideon Randall, of New Bedford, and the Walker, Captain West, of Nantucket. The Walker had been taken from her Spanish prize crew by the British whaler Nimrod, carrying a letter of marque, and she was sent to England. On March 27th, the Essex fell in with the Barclay, as her prize crew were taking her into Callao, and captured her.

To begin the work of clearing the sea of the British whalers the Essex now sailed for the Galapagos Islands, a whaler resort lying 500 miles off shore, and just south of the Equator. The islands were reached on April 17th, and the Essex cruised around them until the first of June when she was obliged to head for the mainland for water. During this time six British whalers were captured. Three of these were taken on April 29th.

The first,—the Montezuma, Captain Baxter—was overhauled by the Essex, early in the forenoon. The other two were then from seven to nine miles off and the wind dying out entirely, a boat expedition, under First Lieutenant John Downes, was sent in pursuit, and young Farragut was placed in charge of Downes's boat. The sailors worked the oars from 11 to 2 P. M., when though the Americans were yet out of range, the whalers opened fire ; for the British boats were armed, and had letters of marque. Downes divided his flotilla into two divisions, and approaching one of the whalers at bow and stern, hailed and asked the crew if they surrendered, at the same time displaying, for the first time, the American flag on a boarding pike instead of a flag-staff. At sight of the flag the whalemen began to cheer, and Farragut notes that they were for the most part American seamen who had been carried on board by press gangs. Many of them were glad to seek revenge by shipping on the Essex. The other whaler surrendered a little later.

On June 8th, the Essex sailed for the coast and arrived at Tumbez on the 19th. It is to be noted that she first made the coast well to the south of the port ; that is to say, to the windward. Then she ran alongshore, in order to have the weather guage of any of the enemy's ships she might find in port.

At Tumbez (on the bay of Guayaquil), the swift-est of the captured ships, the Atlantic, was armed with ten 6-pounders and ten 18-pounder carro-nades and commissioned as a cruiser, with a crew of sixty men, under the name of Essex Junior. The new cruiser was then ordered to convoy four of the prizes to Valparaiso, among the four being the New Bedford whaler Barclay, Captain Gideon Randall, though Randall was no longer master of the ship. As a lawful prize of the Essex, Captain Porter had the right to designate her crew and officers, and he did so by sending Midshipman Farragut to com-mand her, with a faithful crew from the Essex to handle the sails.

On June 30th, the fleet (nine vessels all told) sailed from Tumbez and reached off shore until July 4th, when, having arrived within the trade winds, the Essex Junior proceeded to head for Valparaiso with her convoy, while the Essex, with the other ships reached on toward the Galapagos Islands. At that point Farragut's ability and courage as an officer were put to their first great test. Captain Randall, who had been sent along as navigating officer on the Barclay, wished to go whaling, and was determined to do so, once he could get clear of the Essex Junior. Having commanded ships for many years, he was in no humor to take orders from a youngster of a midshipman, Farragut at this time being less than twelve years old.

One day Captain Randall had been blustering around the deck in a way calculated to overawe the whole crew, including Farragut.

"You will find yourself off New Zealand," he said to them, "to which," as Farragut remarks in his diary, "I decidedly demurred." The Barclay had her main yards aback at that time.

"We were lying still, while the other ships were fast disappearing from view, the commodore's going north and the Essex Junior with her convoy, steering to the south for Valparaiso," continues Farragut. "I considered that my day of trial had arrived. The time had come, at least, for me to play the man; so I mustered up courage and informed the captain that I desired the maintopsail filled away, in order that we might close up with the Essex Junior. He replied that he would shoot any man who dared to touch a rope without his orders.

"'I will go my own course,' he said. 'I have no idea of trusting myself with a damned nutshell.'

"Then he went below for his pistols. I called my right-hand man of the crew, and told him my situation. I also informed him that I wanted the maintopsail filled. He answered, 'Ay, ay, sir!' in a manner which was not to be misunderstood, and my confidence was perfectly restored. From that moment I became master of the vessel and immediately gave all necessary orders for making sail."

Farragut also told Captain Randall not to come on deck with his pistols unless he wished to go overboard, and Randall remained below.

On arriving up with the Essex Junior, young Farragut went over to her and made report to Captain Downes of what had occurred. Randall also went over, and tried to persuade Downes that it was all a mere practical joke, intended to frighten the youngster. "I replied by requesting Captain Downes to ask him how he succeeded; and to show him that I did not fear him, I offered to go back and proceed with him to Valparaiso," says Farragut in his diary. Accordingly Downes sent both Farragut and Randall back to the Barclay, with Farragut still serving as master, and thereafter "everything went on amicably."

On reaching Valparaiso, Captain Downes found important news for the Essex. The American consul at Buenos Ayres had written to say that on July 5th the British frigate Phœbe, of 36 guns, in command of Captain James Hillyar, "a vessel in every way of superior force to the Essex" as Mahan notes, and two sloops of war, the Cherub and the Raccoon, each of 20 guns, had sailed from Rio de Janeiro for the Pacific, to capture the Essex and destroy the American ships on the whaling grounds.

With this news in hand the Essex Junior made haste to the Galapagos Islands, carrying along the officers and men who had handled the prize ships, and on arrival there found that the Essex had captured four more British whalers, all valuable.

The work of the Essex as a commerce destroyer now came to an end. She had captured ten British whalers, which with their cargoes were worth $2,500,000. There was but one other British whaler in the region, so far as Porter could learn, and she was laid up in port. The New Bedford whaler Barclay had been taken from the enemy and other American whalers worth $2,500,000, had been protected from destruction at the hands of the British armed ships and Peruvian privateers.

The Essex—a ship that had cost but $154,687.77, fully armed and equipped for war—had earned in damage done to the enemy and in property saved for her nation, at least $6,000,000 in one cruise that was not a year long.

CHAPTER V

THE ESSEX AND THE BRITISH SQUADRON

ON learning that the enemy had sent a vastly superior force to meet him, Captain Porter sailed from the Galapagos Islands to the Marquesas, far to the westward, where he anchored in a port called Nukahiva. For the moment he was running away. His object in doing so, however, was to seek a safe harbor where the Essex and the Essex Junior could be thoroughly refitted for battle.

For six weeks they both remained at anchor, during which time landing parties from the ships went ashore to defend the natives near at hand from the tribes in other parts of the island, and establish peace. Farragut and the other boys on board were not permitted to go on these expeditions because Porter thought they were too young for such work. To keep them usefully employed, they were put on one of the prizes where the chaplain was established as a schoolmaster. But after four o'clock, each day, they were allowed to go ashore, and there Farragut learned from the natives how to swim. In his journal he speaks with enthusiasm of the prowess of the savages in the water, saying that he often saw mothers go into the sea with children no more than two years old, and that the little ones "could swim like young ducks."

As for the refusal to let him join the war parties,

he says he and his mates "were indignant." But when a strange sail appeared in the offing, and the Essex Junior was sent under Captain Downes to learn her character, with the possibility of a sea fight ahead, Farragut was sent along as aide to Downes. The stranger proved to be an American East Indiaman called the Albatross.

In the meantime the prisoners, having been allowed considerable latitude, took advantage of it to plan an uprising to capture the Essex Junior, but they were betrayed, and were thereafter confined. At the end of six weeks, the Essex and her consort had been thoroughly refitted for battle, and on December 4, 1813, they made sail for the South American coast.

It is to be noted here that previous to this war the guns originally mounted on the Essex had been replaced. She now carried only six long 12-pounders, and for the remainder of her battery had 40 32-pounder carronades—a short, thin-barreled gun that used two pounds of powder to throw a 32-pound shot. A long 32-pounder used from five to six pounds. The extreme effective range of these light guns was a little over three hundred yards. At a greater range than that the 12-pounders she had carried were much more effective because they could penetrate an enemy's ship where the short guns could not. But if the captain were able to lie alongside the enemy, yard-arm to yard-arm, then the short guns might prove slightly more effective. On the whole, considering the fact that our naval ships of that day were obliged to fight

an enemy with a vastly superior navy, and that
one of our ships could rarely hope to choose her
own position in time of battle, it was as serious a
mistake to arm a ship with short-range instead of
long-range guns, as to fritter away the nation's
resources on harbor-defense (that is to say, short-
range) gunboats; but it is a mistake not repeated
in the twentieth century, for, caliber to caliber, our
modern guns are the most powerful afloat.

The Essex was fit for battle in hull and rigging
though not in guns. Her crew were fore and fit.
Every man was armed with a cutlass, kept as sharp
as a razor, a dirk that had been forged from a file,
and a pistol. Day after day the men were drilled
at the great guns, with muskets and with wooden
swords called single sticks, the use of sharpened
cutlasses being wholly impracticable in drill.
Their skill became so great that Farragut wrote
in after years : "I have never been in a ship where
the crew of the old Essex was represented but that
I found them to be the best swordsmen on board."

"With a crew thus perfectly drilled," says Mahan,
"Porter had done all that in him lay in the way
of preparation for victory. If he did not win he
would at least deserve to do so." Mahan adds that
Farragut thus had before him, in his earliest training, a most admirable captain—one who was "daring to recklessness, and yet leaving nothing to
chance,"—one who was a rigid disciplinarian and
yet in full sympathy with the peculiarities of his
men—a captain who was able to infuse his own
spirit into the entire crew.

The story of all this work of refitting the ships and drilling the men is an important part of the history of the Nation as well as of the life of Admiral Farragut. For let it be said again for the sake of emphasis that the War of 1812 was forced upon the American people because the English knew we were not prepared for hostilities, and fully believed that we were a nation of cowardly traders who could not be kicked into fighting. To secure peace and maintain it we had to change these conditions; it was especially necessary to demonstrate that we could and would fight. That Porter realized the necessity resting upon the navy seems apparent, but whether he did or not the venture of the Essex alone into the Pacific to do what a squadron of three ships had been assigned to do was of itself a fair indication of the spirit of American sailors. The destruction of the British whaling fleet showed something of the thoroughness of their work, while the training of the American crew indicated their fitness for service conditions.

But what was of still more importance for the future peace of the young republic is yet to be considered. The British had already acknowledged that a change had come over their opinions by sending three war-ships, aggregating much more than twice Porter's force, to drive him from the sea; while Porter was to exhibit his own spirit and that of his people by deliberately going, after thorough preparation, in search of this powerful enemy when without dishonor he might have sailed for

home. The work which followed is not exceeded
in interest by that done by any American ship of
war ; though this is not to say that Porter, with all
his ability and care, made no mistakes.

To make sure of meeting the British fleet, he
headed for Valparaiso, since that squadron, after
rounding the Horn, would be sure to look in there
for refreshments. But in order not to be caught to
leeward of a superior force, Porter laid his course
so that he reached the South American coast several hundred miles south of his objective. The
reason for doing this was that the wind usually
blows from the south up along the coast. On his
passage along shore Porter would sail with the
wind ; and it would be in his favor if he found the
enemy's squadron in any port.

However, on February 4, 1814, on reaching Valparaiso, Porter learned that the enemy had not yet
arrived. Accordingly, the Essex Junior was stationed out at sea to give warning of the approach
of any sail. While Valparaiso was a neutral port,
and the Essex was by law safe from attack when
within three miles of land, Porter knew very well
that neither the British nor the French in the war
then raging would have regard for any right of another people that was not fully protected by well-
manned guns.

Moreover, as Mahan points out, Commodore
James Hillyar had already grossly violated neutral
rights in a boat attack on Spanish frigates in Bar-
celona harbor. He had sheltered his flotilla behind
a Swedish vessel that was standing into the port

until the over-patient Spaniards began to fire on the sheltering ship. Porter, therefore, had every reason to suppose he would be attacked if he were caught napping in Valparaiso harbor.

Knowing, as he did, the British contempt for neutral rights; knowing further the character of Hillyar (for he was personally well acquainted with the British flag officer), the story of Porter's subsequent forbearance, when the British ships might have been, and by right should have been, taken, stirs the blood of the patriot.

On the evening of February 7th, Captain Porter gave a little hop or dance on the Essex. Many of the ladies and gentlemen of Valparaiso came off to the ship, and in order to give opportunity to the officers of the Essex Junior to enjoy the evening she was brought in from the sentinel station. At the same time one watch of the men before the mast (that is, one-third of the crew, for because of their efficiency, the Essex men were divided into three watches instead of the usual two), went ashore for a frolic.

The ball ended at midnight, and after helping to carry away the guests the crew of the Essex Junior got up their anchor and reached out to the lookout station. No sooner had they passed the cape at the south side of the harbor than they signaled to the Essex that two ships were coming with the wind from the southward. The bunting that had decorated the Essex for the ball had not yet been taken down, and a third of her crew were still on shore. Porter ordered a recall signal set and a gun fired to bring the liberty men on board, and then he went off in a small boat to take a look at the strangers. Satisfied that the enemy was at hand, the Essex Junior was sailed into port and anchored where she could support the Essex, while Porter returned to his ship. He had been gone an hour and a half only, but he found all the shore party on board and every man sober except one, while even that one was not so drunk that he could not accomplish something, as he almost did at a critical moment.

Some time after daylight, the two strangers appeared in the offing with colors flying. They were, as Porter supposed, two of the enemy's squadron—the Phœbe and the Cherub. The third ship had gone north to destroy the American fur-trading station on the Columbia. In the meantime the mate of a British merchantman at anchor in the harbor, seeing from the signals on the Essex Junior that the British squadron was coming, manned a yawl and, pulling off to the British flag-ship, told Hillyar about the ball, and that one watch of the Essex was on shore.

What Hillyar thought, or said, on receiving this information is not a matter of record. What he did was to clear his ship for action. With every man ready for battle he steered into the harbor, heading directly for the weather quarter of the Essex. When there he put down his helm and luffed up within fifteen feet of the weather side of the Essex precisely as if he supposed he had caught the Yankee crew napping, and intended to attack them, then and there. Every intelligent person

familiar with the facts believes that this is what
Hillyar meant to do.

As the Phœbe ranged forward, a powder-boy,
stationed with slow match ready to fire one of the
guns on the Essex as soon as Porter should give the
command, was peering through the port-hole at the
gun crews of the enemy.   This lad was the only one
of the Essex men who had taken too much liquor
while on shore leave the night before, and he was
still feeling the effects of his dram, when he saw
one of the Phœbe's crew grinning at him.

"My fine fellow, I'll stop your making faces," he
said, and leaned forward with his match to fire the
gun, but Lieutenant McKnight saw the movement
and knocked the boy down before the fire reached
the powder.

"Had that gun been fired," says Farragut in his
diary, "I am convinced that the Phœbe would
have been ours."

In this opinion Hillyar unquestionably concurred.
As his ship weathered the Essex he climbed on
a gun carriage.   He had seen that the American
ship was ready and he had no longer any desire to
force the fighting.   He said :

"Captain Hillyar's compliments to Captain Porter, and hopes he is well."

Porter replied :

"Very well, I thank you ; but I hope you will
not come too near, for fear some accident might
take place which will be disagreeable to you."

"And with a wave of his trumpet," says Farragut, "the kedge anchors went up to our yard-arms,

ready to grapple the enemy.'' In fact, Porter
called his boarders to the rail, where they stood
with sharpened cutlasses in hand ready to board
the enemy under cover of the smoke of the first
broadside, '' as was our custom at close quarters.''
At that Hillyar braced aback the yards of the
Phœbe so that she drifted astern, and said, in an
agitated voice that ''if he did fall aboard he
begged to assure Captain Porter it would be entirely accidental.''

'' Well,'' said Porter, '' you have no business
where you are. If you touch a rope yarn of this
ship I shall board instantly.''

With that he let the Phœbe go, and she anchored
half a mile astern—well out of range of Porter's
short guns, but where her own long eighteens could
be used with effect. '' We thus lost an opportunity
of taking her, though we had observed the strict
neutrality of the port,'' says Farragut.

'' The British frigate was unquestionably in a position where a seaman should not have placed her
unless he meant mischief,'' says Mahan. In short
the approach of the Phœbe was lawfully an attack
on the Essex and Porter would have been fully
justified in every way had he opened fire on her.

He was '' the pink of chivalry,'' and therefore let
her go. But his chivalry cost him his ship and
the lives of nearly a hundred of his men, not to
mention the sufferings of his wounded. If another American naval captain is ever guilty of
such folly a court martial will give him the pun-
ishment due him for neglect of duty in the presence

of the enemy. Nevertheless, in the long run, the battle that followed, if it be rightly considered, was perhaps as good for the peace of the Nation as the capture of the Phœbe would have been.

In the days thereafter, Captain Porter did all that he reasonably could to induce Captain Hillyar to meet the Essex, ship for ship ; but Hillyar very plainly said that he had been sent to the Pacific to destroy the Essex, and he should not give up any advantage which his superior force gave him. This was not chivalric, but it was sensible ; and when, on one occasion, the Essex started out to meet the Phœbe, which was at the moment unsupported by her consort, Captain Hillyar promptly ran away to obtain aid.

On another occasion, the sea being calm, Porter and his crew (with Farragut along as aide) pulled out in small boats intending to try surprising the enemy by boarding at night on the high seas. But on getting alongside he learned that the British were at quarters waiting for him, and the attack had to be abandoned.

Finally he heard that other British frigates were coming and he determined to sail out and take his chances against the superior force, whenever he could see a reasonable hope of getting to windward of the enemy. While waiting for such an opportunity a squall came up (March 28, 1814), and drove him from his anchorage in a way that brought on the final battle.

As already noted, the wind usually blows from the south along the South American coast. In

March there are many squalls and one of them that
came in a gale parted a cable by which the Essex
was anchored.   Captain Porter, seeing sufficient
room between the enemy and the south point of
the harbor, immediately made sail and stood out to
sea.   The Essex was doing well, and should have
weathered the foe in fine style, but when the point
of the harbor was close aboard another fierce
squall came down off the lofty promontory there
and carried away her maintopmast, together with
several men who were at work aloft.

After cutting away the wreckage Captain Porter
turned around and tried to regain the anchorage.
He did this because Hillyar had promised, in return
for Porter's generosity when the Phœbe was in jeop-
ardy, to respect the neutrality of the port.   What
Farragut thought of the attempt to return to the
harbor is recorded in his diary and he let it stand
in his mature years.   He wrote :

"I consider that our greatest error was in at-
tempting to regain the anchorage ; as, being greatly
superior to the enemy in sailing qualities, I think
we should have borne up and run before the wind.
If we had come in contact with the Phœbe, we
should have carried her by boarding ; if she avoided
us, as she might have done by her greater ability to
manœuvre, then we could have taken her fire and
passed on, leaving both vessels behind until we replaced our topmast, by which time they would have
been separated, as, unless they did so, it would
have been no chase, the Cherub being a dull sailor."

Thus at thirteen years of age Farragut was of the

opinion that it was better for a crippled ship to fight than to trust the enemy to observe the laws of nations.

When the Essex reached back for her anchorage, she was unable to make it. She anchored, therefore, on the leeward side of the harbor, a quarter of a mile from the beach. Captain Hillyar now felt under no obligation to keep his word, and with colors flying the Phœbe and Cherub swooped down on the cripple.

" I well remember the feeling of awe produced in me by the approach of the hostile ships," says Farragut in his diary ; "even to my young mind it was perceptible in the faces of those around me, as clearly as possible, that our case was hopeless. It was equally apparent that all were ready to die at their guns rather than surrender."

At 3:54 o'clock in the afternoon with the whole population of Valparaiso standing on the bluff to watch the battle, the Phœbe opened fire. She had taken station under the stern of the anchored Essex (where not one of the guns of the Essex would bear), and coming to the wind, broadside to, she began to work her broadside of 13 long 18-pounders, one long 12-pounder and one long 9-pounder. Porter had only six long guns on board and they were 12-pounders. Three of these were brought aft, and pointed through the cabin ports ; that is, three 12-pounders were pitted against the whole great broadside of the enemy. They threw 36 pounds of shot where the Phœbe threw 255 pounds. At the same time the Cherub took a position off the starboard bow of the Essex where her two long guns would bear. And the long guns only are mentioned because the British ships were carefully held beyond range of the short guns of the Essex.

Nevertheless, in spite of the overwhelming odds on the British side, and because of the excellent marksmanship of the Essex gunners, both the Phœbe and the Cherub were compelled, after a half hour of firing, to haul off for repairs.

After a little while the Phœbe returned to the fight, and taking a position off the port quarter of the Essex, where none of the American guns could reach her, she anchored broadside to, and opened fire. Lieutenant William Ingram, the executive officer of the Phœbe said "it was deliberate murder" to lie off there and fire at the Essex as if she were a target, but he was thinking of the chivalry, rather than the business, of war. It was Hillyar's object to destroy the Essex with as little loss as possible to his own crew and he was doing it.

In the meantime Porter had put springs on his cable three times to swing the Essex so that his guns would bear, but each time that they were hauled taut, they were cut by the enemy's shot. The Essex thus became at last literally a mere target, and moreover a target in flames. But at the moment when the last spring was shot away, and all hope of making another effective shot at the enemy seemed gone forever, the supreme moment of the battle was at hand.

A gentle breeze came drifting from the shore to waft the smoke of the burning Essex out to sea.

She was a wreck aloft. Her halliards and sheets were shot away. Her sails were torn and cut to pieces. Many of her guns had been dismounted. Her decks, in spite of sanding, were slippery with blood because nearly a third of her crew had been shot down. But with this crew—even those dying under the surgeon's care—shouting on all sides, "Don't give her up, Logan," and "Hurrah for Liberty!" Porter hoisted a jib—the one sail that could be spread to the breeze, and with the square sails hanging ragged, loose and fluttering, from the yards, he slipped his cable and headed the Essex for the Phœbe, determined to lead his men to the enemy's deck.

Hillyar had been trained under Nelson—trained in the school wherein ship commanders were told that " no captain can do wrong if he places his ship alongside an enemy."   But when he saw the Essex coming with her ragged sails flapping in the air, and the blood of her crew running in streams from her scuppers, he slipped his cable, brailed in his spanker as a whipped dog sticks its tail between its legs, and fled. As for the Cherub it had already been beaten off so that it was no longer of much consequence.

Times had changed since the crew of a British sloop of war would cheer for joy, as did the crew of the Alert, at the prospect of a battle with a Yankee frigate.

As the Phœbe fled, she continued firing, and her gunners being safe, their aim was good. Porter once more anchored the Essex, hoping the Phœbe would drift out of range. But when Porter anchored, Hillyar ceased to flee. An effort to run the Essex on the beach failed because the wind threw her flat aback. In the meantime fires that had been started in the hold of Porter's ship were spreading rapidly, and were nearing the magazine. The shot of the enemy were still splintering the hull and slaughtering the crew. It being no longer possible to fire an effective shot in return, it was manifest to all that the Essex must surrender at last ; "passive resistance" was no longer worth the growing losses. Accordingly men came to Porter to beg that he would save the lives of those who remained by surrendering the ship. Among the suppliants were sailors with their clothes on fire.

In reply to these petitions Porter gave permission to all who wished to do so to jump overboard and swim ashore, and many, supposing the ship would soon blow up, did so. Then he called for his officers to get reports as to the condition of the various parts of the vessel, but only one lieutenant was able to respond, and after a brief consultation with him, Porter at 6:20 o'clock ordered the flag hauled down. With batteries that threw 273 pounds of metal where the Essex could throw less than 72, it had taken the British two hours and a half to gain the victory.

The Essex lost 58 killed and 66 wounded. After the battle there were 31 men found missing, nearly all of whom, it was learned, had been drowned in the effort to swim ashore when Commodore Porter gave his crew permission to jump overboard to escape the flames. The British official report acknowledged a loss of but four killed and seven wounded on the Phœbe, and one killed and four wounded on the Cherub. The Phœbe went into battle with 300 men, the Essex with 255. When the Phœbe fled for fear that Porter would board her she had 289 men on board, while the Essex had less than 150.

The Essex was at last conquered but the objects for which the War of 1812 was necessarily waged had been attained as in no other battle of the war, afloat or ashore. By endeavoring to board the Phœbe, by driving an enemy of vastly superior force before him, Commodore David Porter compelled the British to admit, in the most humiliating way, that the American people were not the cowards they were supposed to be. As a test of American pluck and persistency this battle was most convincing. From this standpoint even Porter's "pink-of-chivalry" refusal to fire on the Phœbe when she came alongside to attack him on the day of her arrival in Valparaiso was, perhaps, as good for the Nation, as the capture of the frigate would have been.

It may seem absurd, at first thought, to dwell upon this view of the Essex affair, now that the United States has attained unquestioned prominence as a world power, but it is necessary to do so in order to emphasize these facts. It was the substitution of "peaceable coercion" for line-of-battle ships that invited the outrages and spoliations which at last compelled us to fight. The war was fought to secure a respectful hearing from the nations of the world, and such a hearing never could have been obtained in any other way. How well the war succeeded is evidenced by the fact that the enunciation of the "Monroe Doctrine," within ten years after hostilities ended, peacefully effected its purpose of protecting Spanish America from European aggression. It will be remembered too that British war-ships, when cruising afterward on the African coast for the destruction of the slave trade, did not dare to interfere with slavers which sailed under the American flag, even though they knew they were engaged in this illicit commerce.

In describing his work during the battle between the Essex and the British ships, as he had part in it, Farragut says, "I was like Paddy in the cat-harpins, a man on occasions." He was, first of all, the captain's aide, and his station was beside Porter on the quarter-deck. But as aide there was not enough work to keep him busy, and he turned to the guns near at hand for employment. He hauled on the side tackles, ran as a powder monkey for ammunition, and, perhaps, trained a gun now and then. Although the shot fell short the carronades were fired as often as possible. It was while working thus that he saw, for the first time, a man killed in battle. A boatswain's mate was cut to pieces by a cannon ball.

The sight of the mutilated corpse "staggered and sickened me," he wrote afterward, "but they soon began to fall around me so fast that it all appeared like a dream, and produced no effect on my nerves."

Even when a shot came through the bulwarks, at the waterways, and glancing upward killed four men and scattered the blood and brains of the last of the four all over Farragut and the captain, the effect was by no means as trying as the sight of the slaughtered boatswain's mate had been.

"I neither thought of nor noticed anything but the working of the guns," he says. After a time Midshipman Isaacs reported to the captain that a sailor named Adam Roach had gone skulking to the berth deck. Turning to Farragut, the captain said:

"Do your duty, sir."

Farragut took a pistol in hand and went hunting the man to kill him. But a sailor named William Call, even though he had a leg shot off, had been dragging himself, pistol in hand, about the deck in chase of the skulker and, thus warned, Roach had been able to hide himself so well that Farragut was unable to find him.

Farragut says that Roach had been considered a leading man of the ship. At the time the Phœbe came into the harbor to attack the Essex, he was seen at the head of the line of Americans who stood ready to board her, standing on the cat head, a most exposed position, with sleeves rolled up, and sharpened cutlass in hand, ready to leap among the sailors on the British deck. But when the Essex became a target for the enemy without a chance for effective reply his courage fled. Farragut says: "Roach was brave with a prospect of success, but a coward in adversity."

After his failure to find the skulker, Farragut

was sent below by Porter to bring up some gun primers. While he was on the ladder leading down to the wardroom deck a shot struck the captain of the gun standing opposite the hatch. The man was knocked down the hatch and fell upon Farragut. Fortunately he landed across the boy's hips and he escaped with bruises, whereas he might have been killed; for the man weighed nearly two hundred pounds. Though not much hurt the shock knocked from the lad's mind the thought of what his errand was, and he ran on deck.

"Are you hurt?" asked Porter, as he saw the lad was covered with blood.

"I believe not, sir," replied Farragut.

"Then where are the primers?" asked Porter.

"This brought me completely to my senses," says the diary, "and I ran below again and carried the primers on deck."

One of the greatest charms of the diary of the admiral is its entire frankness. He even tells us in one place how the executive officer of the ship, Lieutenant Downes, found him asleep when on watch. He was reclining on a gun carriage. The lieutenant covered him with a greatcoat, so that he would not catch cold, and let him sleep on, but did not fail to tell him afterward what sleeping on post meant in a man-o'-war.

After a time Farragut saw Porter knocked to the deck, and ran to ask if he were wounded, but learned that the captain's fall was probably due to the wind from a shot passing over his head, for "his hat was somewhat damaged."

When the surrender of the ship was determined on, Farragut was sent to see that the signal book was thrown into the sea. Having found and thrown it overboard, he and Midshipman Isaacs ran along the deck tossing small arms into the water to keep them from falling into the hands of the enemy. Finally, Farragut went to the lower deck where the wounded were laid out. "When I saw the mangled bodies of my shipmates, dead and dying, groaning and expiring with the most patriotic sentiments on their lips, I became faint and sick; my sympathies were all aroused," he wrote.

But the shock passed away quickly, and he hastened to help the surgeon. He found, dying, one of his best friends, Lieutenant J. G. Cowell, and gained a lesson in unselfish manhood that was not lost. A shot had taken off Cowell's leg just above the knee, and he was carried to the surgeon. But when the latter proposed to attend to him at once, the lieutenant replied :

"No, doctor, none of that; fair play is a jewel. One man's life is as dear as another's; I would not cheat any poor fellow out of his turn."

When Cowell's turn came it was too late. Farragut observed that "many of our fine fellows bled to death for want of tourniquets," also a lesson that he did not forget.

Another glimpse of Boatswain Kingsbury, who with a lion's voice led the men on deck in the fight for life when the sea knocked in all the ports on one side of the ship off Cape Horn, is found in the story of the battle. He came from the Essex Junior in a small boat while the contest was raging, and in the fighting that followed was so badly burned that there was scarcely a square inch of his body that did not show marks of the flames. Yet, at the word, he jumped overboard and swam ashore— three-quarters of a mile. The Essex Junior had been unable to join in the action because the wind did not serve.

In his official report of the battle, Commodore Porter wrote as follows : "Midshipmen Isaacs, Farragut and Ogden, as well as acting Midshipmen James Terry, James R. Lyman and Samuel Duzenbury, and Master's-mate William Pierce, exerted themselves in the performance of their respective duties, and gave an earnest of their value to the service ; the three first are too young to recommend for promotion ; the latter I beg leave to recommend for confirmation."

It was equivalent to saying that the lads had served as well as possible, even though yet too young to carry a lieutenant's commission ; but the words always nettled Farragut, for in later years as well as at that time he found himself doing duties usually performed by older officers, and yet was unable to secure promptly the recognition that such work seemed to demand.

As a prisoner Farragut was sent to the Phœbe, on the morning of the 29th. He was so mortified by the defeat that, on reaching the steerage, tears streamed from his eyes. Just then, however, a British midshipman came along with a young pig in his arms, and shouted :

" A prize ! a prize ! Ho, boys, a fine grunter, by Jove ! "

It was a pig that had been a pet in the steerage of the Essex, where it was called " Murphy," and Farragut at once claimed it as private property.

" Ah," replied the young Britisher, " but you are a prisoner and your pig also."

" We always respect private property," said Farragut, and he grabbed the pig, determined to hold on until forced to surrender. The oldsters present, liking his pluck, sided with him so far as to say :

"Go it, my little Yankee ! if you can thrash Shorty you shall have your pig !"

A ring was then formed, and " Shorty " came at Farragut, "hammer and tongs." There was no lack of strength or pluck in "Shorty," but Farragut was a well-trained pugilist, for one of his years, and he very quickly won the pig. It is a small matter but it shows, as shall yet appear more fully, that Farragut, like John Paul Jones, "was every kind of a fighting man there was."

A little later Captain Hillyar sent for the lad and asked him to eat breakfast in the cabin, where Captain Porter was entertained. It is not unlikely that Hillyar had heard of Farragut's fight for "Murphy," and liked his pluck. At any rate, when he saw how the lad was cast down by defeat, he said in a very kind manner :

" Never mind, my little fellow, it will be your turn next, perhaps."

Farragut replied that he hoped so, and then with

tears in his eyes once more, he hurried from the cabin. Defeat was a heavy burden for a lad who was made up of three pounds of uniform and seventy of fight.

Having arranged with Captain Hillyar for the parole of the prisoners and their return on the Essex Junior to the United States, Porter took all hands ashore, where Farragut served faithfully as surgeon's assistant until all except two of the wounded who were necessarily left behind were ready to embark.

The Essex Junior sailed from Valparaiso on April 27, 1814, rounded Cape Horn with all sails set, and on July 5th was stopped ten leagues off the Long Island coast by the British razee Saturn, one of the blockading fleet. Captain Nash, on learning how the Essex Junior happened to be there, held her over night. Under the terms made with Hillyar this absolved Porter from his parole, and the next morning he launched a whale boat and pulled to the Long Island beach, landing near Babylon, where, when recognized, he received an ovation from the people, and was conveyed, as a hero, to New York City.

In the meantime, after an examination of the prisoners, the Essex Junior was allowed to go on. She was twice mistaken for an enemy's ship, and fired on for some time by shore batteries in New York harbor, but was not struck by a single shot —a fact that caused Farragut to think "it was not such an awful thing as was supposed to lie under a battery." Apparently the memory of that experience came to him in a most critical time of his life in later years. On July 7, 1814, the Essex Junior anchored in the upper bay at New York. The ship was sold, and the crew, being on parole, were dispersed to their homes to await exchange.

For Farragut the fighting of the war was ended. But that the injustice of the British, especially in their battle at Valparaiso, made a lasting impression on his mind, appears from a remark he uttered when at New Orleans during the Civil War. Speaking of the men who saved the Nation in the War of 1812, he said : "We have no better seamen in the service to-day than those gallant fellows. . . . *If I only had their chance and could lay the Hartford alongside an English ship*, I should like it better than fighting our own people."

CHAPTER VI

STUDY AND TRAVEL

AFTER landing under parole in New York City, young Farragut went to Chester, Pa., with his adopted father, and was there sent to school to "a queer old individual named Neif." Neif had been one of Napoleon's guards. In his school he used no books but relied entirely upon lectures and oral instruction. The pupils were taken for long rambles across the fields where Neif gave them lectures in geology, mineralogy and botany. They were also drilled like soldiers. One may well believe that they were duly instructed in the languages, meantime, and that the school was in some respects far in advance of others of that period. Farragut himself says that what he learned there was "of service" to him "all through life."

On November 30, 1814, the boy was exchanged, and was ordered to the brig Spark, then fitting out under Lieutenant Commandant Thomas Gamble to join a small squadron with which Commodore Porter was to go cruising against the enemy's commerce in the West Indies. While the work on the Spark was in hand, Farragut was quartered on the John Adams, a receiving ship, and thus for the first time since entering the navy, he was removed from the immediate influence of Commodore Porter.

The lad was not yet fourteen years old, but for four years he had been trained as few men of the sea have been. Whenever an opportunity for a fight had offered, or had seemed to offer, Porter had been careful to put him in the battle line. At every opportunity for exercising authority, as in the command of single boats, and of the captured whaler, he had been called on to accept the responsibility, and in the meantime he had been taught by schoolmasters whenever possible. It seems certain, therefore, that at this time David Glasgow Farragut, in spite of his youth, was one of the best equipped midshipmen in the world.

In connection with this fact it is apparent from the records that he was thoroughly well-liked by all his associates. While dignified as an officer—he never forgot that he had need to hold erect every inch of his small frame—he yet combined the frankness and good-nature of the Tennessee woodsman with the hearty and wholesome manners of the typical American sailor.

It is small wonder, then, that the midshipmen's mess on the John Adams made him welcome. And because they were a wild set of youngsters—doubtless, boys who were, in some cases, uncontrollable at home—they at once led him into some kinds of dissipation of which he had learned nothing. While Farragut joined with the gang for a time, he no sooner saw the trend of the life they were leading than he abandoned it, and this is one of the most important facts in the life of the first admiral of the American navy. In this determination Farragut was greatly assisted by the advice and encouragement of Lieutenant William H. Cocke, the executive officer of the Spark, of whom something is to be said further on.

Before the squadron could be made ready for sea, peace with honor was obtained and the day when American sailors could be taken from beneath their flag by a foreign press-gang was gone forever. Farragut was then ordered to the Independence, a ship of the line rated at 74 guns commanded by Captain William N. Crane. War had been declared against Algiers, to which nation of pirates the United States had paid tribute for many years, and a squadron commanded by Commodore Bainbridge was under orders to sail for the Mediterranean. Captain Crane chose Farragut for his aide. The squadron arrived out too late because Commodore Decatur had already "thrashed the Algerines and made peace with the Bey." However, the fleet went to Carthagena, and thence to Tripoli and the Barbary coast, across to Malaga, and finally back to Gibraltar where, as Farragut notes in his diary, he saw fifteen American warships, carrying 320 guns, all gathered in one foreign port. It was the largest fleet of Yankee men-of-war ever seen abroad, and it was an impressive sight to a boy. The real greatness and power of this assemblage, however, were found in the spirit and ability of the crews, since as fighting machines the ships were all small, save only the Independence, though two were 36-gun frigates.

Returning home with the fleet in 1815, Farragut

sailed once more for the Mediterranean in the ship-of-the-line Washington, Captain John Orde Creighton. Farragut here served again as captain's aide. Creighton had entered the navy as a midshipman in 1800, and obtained his commission as captain on April 27, 1816. The Washington was therefore his first ship under his new rank. He was naturally proud of commanding a ship-of-the-line so soon after attaining battleship rank, especially since the Washington was to be the flag-ship of the Mediterranean squadron, and she was to carry Hon. William Pinckney, Minister to Naples, to his post. Under such circumstances, Captain Creighton's highest ambition was to put his ship into perfect condition, and to bring his crew into an unequaled state of discipline and ability. To do this, being by nature a martinet, he kept all hands on the jump, day and night, and "it was no uncommon thing with us for the officer of the deck to call up the whole watch and give them two or three dozen strokes with the cat-o'-nine-tails apiece for the fault of one man, or perhaps an accident. All hands were sometimes kept out of their meals for eight or ten hours, and once, at Algiers, the whole crew was kept on deck all night for several nights in succession."

The captain had his wish. The Washington was called the "crack" ship of the squadron, and of those seas. Work was done with a precision and celerity unsurpassed. But the life they led was ruinous to the peace and to the health, as well, of the crew.

All of this is particularly worth telling because of its effect upon Farragut. He saw and appreciated the desirable qualities of a "crack" ship, but he was able to note that these qualities were not worth the sacrifice of the comfort of every one on board. He determined, therefore, to consider the welfare of his crew, whenever he should attain commanding rank, and the loyalty and affection of his men, in later years, proved the wisdom of his course.

Nevertheless, when the facts are considered now, one cannot help feeling a sympathy for a captain like Creighton. He saw that the American navy numbered only a few ships, as compared with other navies, and that those few were on parade before hostile and "gimlet-eyed" critics. It was for the honor of the flag that they made their ships outshine and outsail all others afloat. On one occasion a party of British naval officers were conducted around the decks of the Constitution. They were silent or yielded grudging praise, until they came, at last, to the wheel on the quarter-deck, when one of them, with manifest pleasure, pointed to it as an object of scorn. To this the American officer in charge of the party had ready a reply. He admitted that the wheel was not above criticism and said :

"We lost our own wheel in battle, and took that one from the Java." [1]

[1] The Java was the British frigate captured by the Constitution off Bahia (or San Salvador), Brazil, while Porter and the Essex were cruising off Cape Frio waiting for the Constitution and Hornet to meet him for the proposed cruise in the Pacific.

The squadron of which the Washington carried the flag wintered at Port Mahon, and in 1817 made a cruise around the Mediterranean, visiting many places of interest. During this trip Farragut showed the bent of his mind by making ample notes, none of which, however, have been published because his journal of that cruise was lost. But he recalled in after years the visit of the Emperor of Austria and the King of Naples, along with Prince Metternich, to the Washington while she lay in the Bay of Naples. Farragut, as the best linguist present, was interpreter for the Emperor. He excited the derision of Prince Metternich by addressing the Emperor as "Mister." The Emperor was ridiculous, in Farragut's eyes. "He seemed to be a mere puppet, and he took short, mincing steps, presenting to my youthful mind altogether a silly appearance."

While the royal guests wandered around the decks "one of the Emperor's chamberlains mistook a wind-sail for a mast, and leaning against it, was precipitated to the cockpit." The fall broke his leg. As the chamberlain fell an American quartermaster faced aft and in a loud voice reported to the officer of the deck: "One of them kings has fallen down a hatch, sir," and his words are related at navy mess-tables to this day.

The Emperor and the King seemed to think that the accident, though due to the stupidity of the chamberlain, was in some way a manifestation of evil designs against their persons, and they left the ship hastily.

Another incident illustrating the service in those days is noted in connection with the passage of the Washington through the Straits of Messina. A file of marines with loaded muskets was stationed in the gangway to shoot the pilot in case he ran the ship aground.

In the fall (1817), the squadron returned to Port Mahon, where the discontent due to the rigorous discipline culminated in two memorials, one of which was signed by the lieutenants and was sent to the Senate, while the other was signed by midshipmen and sent to the President. The chief point of complaint was that junior officers had been struck by captains of the fleet. Not only were midshipmen treated in this fashion, but Captain John Heath, of the marine corps, was knocked down in the cabin of the Java by Captain O. H. Perry, the hero of Lake Erie—an affair that led afterward to a duel on the Hoboken ground where Alexander Hamilton had been killed by Burr.

Farragut did not sign the memorial prepared by the midshipmen; he had left the squadron before it was written. But he notes with satisfaction that it was "highly approved by the Navy Department," while that sent by the lieutenants and marine officers was disapproved because they threatened to use force in resenting the attitude of the captains. It is further noted in the diary that as a result of these memorials "the powers assumed by the post captains were moderated, whereas, before this event, with the exception of life or death, the absolute authority which they assumed was but little inferior to that of the Czar of all the Russias."

Farragut left the squadron at the end of the season of 1817 in order to study. The chaplain of the Washington was Mr. Charles Folsom, and he was also the schoolmaster of the midshipmen. It appears that Farragut was the most studious of all the boys. He was what later-day midshipmen would call a "boner"; midshipmen who are not "boners" would have called him a "chaplain's favorite." He attended to such studies as could be pursued instead of joining the roysterers of the steerage in more or less demoralizing sports ashore.

Accordingly in the fall of 1817, when Mr. Folsom was appointed American consul at Tunis, Farragut was anxious to go thither with him and pass the winter in study. A petition to Commodore Isaac Chauncey, the flag officer, was favorably considered, and Farragut left the Washington at Gibraltar, going to Tunis by way of Marseilles.

While waiting at this place the boy showed his entire willingness to fight a duel, according to the notions of honor prevailing at the time, although, like John Paul Jones, he never did fight one. He was frequently invited to the house of an American merchant named Fitch, while in the French city, and although he had "no fondness for cards" he felt obliged to take a hand at whist. The arrogance with which good players of this game usually treat those who have small interest in it, was carried far by Farragut's partner. He threw his hand on the table as a mark of contempt when the young Amer-

ican naval officer made an error in playing. But
Farragut at once resented the indignity by throwing his hand into his partner's face, and then, after
an apology to Mr. Fitch, left the house. If the
partner had been a fighting man, as well as a whist
player, a duel would have followed ; but nothing
came of it.

At Tunis, Farragut devoted his time for nine
months chiefly to the study of the Italian and
French languages, mathematics and English literature. As this was his last schooling it may be
worth while to note for the encouragement of those
similarly afflicted, that he was never able to learn
to write or spell in his own language correctly. His
autobiographical letter, written to Dr. Lyman C.
Draper on September 20, 1853, and published in the
American Historical Review for April, 1904, is of a
character to make a modern sophomore shiver.
" On one occasion our house was surrounded by some
stragling Indians," he writes, while telling of the
time his mother guarded the house door with
an axe. Further on in the same letter he says,
speaking of Commodore Porter—" When he was
releived I embarked with him." Then his father
is referred to as "a man of great *wrecklessness* of
character." Nevertheless his letters and diary both
show that he could think clearly, and express his
thoughts on paper in a way not to be misunderstood. That his orders, as expressed on the quarter-
deck, or when lashed to the futtock shrouds during
battle, were not misunderstood, has never been
doubted. As for the rest it appears that he was

well-read in general literature and possessed a fund
of information that was certainly remarkable. But
it was of the knowledge of his profession that he
had most notable mastery—an example for all naval
men who shall come after him.

Of his life at Tunis a number of facts are memorable. He became very popular with the foreign
colony. He studied so hard that at the end of three
months his health gave way. Partly in consequence of this, and for their own pleasure, the
Danish, the French and the American consuls determined to visit the ancient ruins of the region,
and particularly those of some old Roman works
built by Julius Cæsar, after the capture of Carthage.
The site of ancient Carthage is only a short distance
from Tunis. Farragut's notes on this journey
show that he was a good observer—he would have
been beyond question an excellent newspaper correspondent. But he was so venturesome that he
"received a stroke of the sun which caused a par-
tial paralysis of the tongue." The effects of this
accident were felt for many years afterward.

On the ninth day out from Tunis the "splendid
amphitheatre of El Jem" appeared in view, but the
pleasant anticipations of the party were somewhat
modified by the scowling of the natives who very
plainly showed their dislike for the Christian "sons
of dogs." In fact, every one of the excursionists
went well armed while exploring for fear of an attack. Farragut got tired of carrying a gun, and
went wandering about the old ruins alone, with
small pistols only. Seeing him apparently un-

armed, a Bedouin went after him with a club.
Farragut let the fellow approach within a few feet
and then drew the pistols, the sight of which sent
him flying.

One of the Sheiks of the region, however, proved
to have a very friendly temper, for he invited the
excursionists to dine with him and gave them not
only an excellent meal but an abundance of good
wine. He invited them to drink freely by setting
an example, swallowing a bottle of wine and "four
solid glasses of brandy, which seemed to have no
bad effect on him." The Sheik showed a special
regard for the midshipman by giving him a gazelle.

In all, Farragut was under the instruction of Mr.
Folsom for nine months, and would have remained
longer still but for the fact that a plague broke out
in the city. This spread so alarmingly that Mr.
Folsom thought Farragut ought to leave, and early
in October he sailed with the Danish consul, Mr.
A. C. Gierlew, for Leghorn. It is pleasing to note
that, when Farragut became a vice-admiral, Mr.
Folsom was still alive. He was residing in Cam-
bridge, Mass., and Farragut, to show his appreciation of his old-time instructor, sent him a painting which "set forth two great epochs of our connection," as the admiral wrote. An artist had
been employed to make the painting from sketches
drawn by Farragut, "to portray our landing at
Tunis" from the United States ship Erie, Folsom
as United States Consul receiving a salute while
"accompanied in the boat by Midshipman Farragut." The other epoch is illustrated by the old

Hartford "gracefully lying at anchor, bearing the flag of the Vice-Admiral."

The passage to Leghorn was made in a Genoese brig. Off Corsica one evening, a dead calm fell on the boat, and the captain went to sleep, leaving orders that he should not be awakened. Farragut, going on deck, saw that the brig was drifting ashore. No one of the crew dared call the captain, so Farragut did it himself. The former, on seeing the danger, lost his head, but when the Danish consul threatened him with a sword he recovered a little sense and the danger was, by a narrow margin, averted.

After forty days in quarantine at Leghorn, Farragut went to Pisa where he attended a grand ball, but with no great pleasure. He managed to catch his shoe-buckle in the dress of an archduchess, to tread on the toe of a duke, and finally he found that a countess was using his cocked hat as a foot warmer. In the meantime the host spread out a number of gold table dishes and invited the guests to gaze upon them and wonder at his immense wealth. Farragut was disgusted with the whole entertainment.

Nevertheless life at Pisa had not been without amenities. In a letter to Consul Gierlew (January 27, 1819), he says, "I am happy to inform you that I had a pleasant ride out last evening with a young Jewess, who was very easy and agreeable in her conversation, so that I did not repent in the least my late ride, as we contrived to make the time pass."

Going from Pisa, late in January, Farragut re-

ported on the flagship Franklin, and was assigned
to duty as the aide of Captain John Gallagher. The
squadron remained at Messina during the remainder of the winter. It is noted in Farragut's diary
that the younger officers of the fleet went to the
arsenals, of afternoons, where they engaged in ath-
letic exercises, "in which," says he, "I always held
my own." He was not large in frame, but was wiry
to an extraordinary degree; and he never lost an
opportunity for improving himself.

The summer of 1819 proved an important one in
Farragut's career because he was then, though only
eighteen years old, made an acting lieutenant and
sent to the schooner Shark, on which in due season
he became executive officer. Farragut notes in his
diary that he was at times the actual commander
of the schooner, and his words in connection there-
with ought to be printed in large type and kept on
the desk of every secretary of the navy. He says:

"I consider it a great advantage to obtain command young, having observed as a general thing
that persons who come into authority late in life
shrink from responsibility, and often break down
under its weight."

After serving in the Shark until the spring of
1820, Farragut was ordered home for the regular
examination preceding his confirmation in the rank
of lieutenant. For the encouragement of ambitious
young men who may be unfortunate in some way,
it is worth while anticipating the event by saying
that when he first tried to pass this examination he
failed and was greatly discouraged. But after a

voyage to the coast of Mexico, he tried once more and was successful. He acquired fame through his determination to succeed in spite of failures that to some observers might have seemed to indicate a certain degree of mental deficiency.

In going home Farragut took passage in the merchant ship America along with two invalided man-o'-war sailors, and while on the way across had an interesting adventure.

When approaching the United States coast the weather one day became perfectly calm, while a brig that was seen to be armed was approaching. As the wind failed, the crew of the brig manned sweeps and began rowing her toward the America —an act that with good reason made every one on board the ship believe that the stranger was a pirate. The captain and mates of the America became panic-stricken. No thought of resistance entered their heads. They begged Farragut to put on citizen's clothing because they supposed that the uniform of an American naval officer might incite the men to greater ferocity.

To such talk Farragut not only refused to listen but he called on the two man-o'-war sailors to stand by him in resisting the attack of the pirate. The two promptly obeyed, and when the brig was seen to be sending a boat with an armed crew to board the America, a grindstone and a barrel of tar were brought to the starboard gangway ready to drop down through the bottom of the coming boat and sink it alongside. The courage of the man-o'-war's men proved as contagious as had been the panic of the captain ; the crew of the ship came to the aid of Farragut, who assumed command of all hands.

When the boat came within hail, and Farragut asked if its mission were friendly, the officer in charge said "yes" in English, and a little later announced that he was from Baltimore and bore the unpiratical name of Smith. He added that the armed brig, of which he was lieutenant, was a Colombian man-o'-war, instead of a pirate. He boarded the America, leaving his arms in his boat at Farragut's suggestion, and delivered a bundle of letters to the captain, to whom he offered any supplies that might be needed. Farragut refers to the incident in his diary in order "to remark how easily men may defend themselves against pirates if they do not become panic-stricken at the beginning." And he adds, speaking of the two man-o'-war's men that *"men trained to arms will never fail*, if properly led."

Whether this particular brig was a pirate or not cannot be definitely learned at this late day, but it is fair to suppose that she was one of a fleet of armed vessels that had been fitted out in American ports to sail as privateers under various Spanish-American flags and prey on Spanish commerce. The story of this privateer fleet has never been, and very likely never will be, written. But the vessels of which it was composed were, without exception, sent to sea in violation of the laws of the United States. According to the treaty existing between Spain and this country, every one of them was a pirate. By their outrages they raised up a host of pirates in the West Indies against whom the American navy waged a most remarkable undeclared war. This campaign deprived the navy of two of the most famous captains of the War of 1812, caused the addition of more than a dozen vessels to the navy's list of ships, and cost the lives of scores of sailors and officers.   In this work of pirate hunting an important part was taken by David G. Farragut.

CHAPTER VII

IN THE WAR WITH THE WEST INDIA PIRATES

ONE of the most interesting episodes in the history of American commerce is that of our war with the Spanish West Indian pirates from 1819 to 1826. And yet our writers of school histories do not mention the war, and other historians have failed to set forth the one feature of it best worth consideration.

In our naval histories these piratical aggressions are said to have been merely the outgrowth of the spoliations committed by the French at the end of the eighteenth century. But the fact is that while some of the French pirates of the eighteenth century may have been found among the later gangs, the piracies that brought on the war were the direct outgrowth of the work of sundry predatory ships fitted out in the United States and England to prey, under the flags of the Spanish-American insurgents, upon Spanish commerce.

During the War of 1812, many American privateers were commissioned to cruise in search of British merchantmen, and some of them were so successful that the owners became very wealthy. Their success, instead of satisfying them, did but stimulate a number to greater exertions. This was also true of the officers of other privateers. In fact it created a form of greed that became, when the war ended, not unlike the hunger of wolves. These privateersmen looked around for an opportunity to continue their predatory work and they found it awaiting them.

Beginning in 1810, a number of Spanish-American colonies had thrown off the yoke of Spain. At the end of 1815, the insurgent leaders had succeeded so well that several ports on the Spanish main were found under their control. To these ports came the plunder-hungry privateersmen who had failed to get rich during the War of 1812 and with them were some who had captured much British property and were yet eager for more. Commissions were there easily obtained and then the ships went cruising against Spanish commerce. The pirates of Barataria, under Pierre and Jean Lafitte, had already done some plundering before the War of 1812 ended, but the number of armed vessels of the kind was greatly augmented after the war.

The laws of the United States explicitly declared these cruisers to be pirates, and they were pirates in other points of view, as well. The commissions were often issued by men not legally competent to do so ; the vessels gave no bonds for the indemnity of ships that might be wrongfully captured ; the prizes were not taken before any court of admiralty for judicial examination. In short there was no restraint on the captain of such a cruiser stronger than his own conscience, or the fear that he might bring some naval ship, belonging to a power other than Spain, in chase of him.

For a time these privateers marketed a part of their plunder in the United States, but the ships captured from the Spaniards were more difficult to handle. Some of these were sold in the United States also, but Spanish consuls were prompt to appeal to the courts in behalf of the original owners, and it was there made plain that the privateers were without standing before any just judge.

To overcome the difficulty thus arising, the pirates established (1816–1817) a resort on the island where Galveston, Texas, now stands, and went through the forms of organizing a new republic whereof their community was to be the capital. A similar resort was created on Amelia Island (Fernandina), Florida, and it was called the capital of the Two Floridas Republic. A court of admiralty was established at each place first of all, and to these courts came the predatory cruisers with their captures.

That these privateers in some cases were remarkably successful is a matter of record in the " American State Papers." Havana and Santiago, Cuba, were blockaded for days at a time, even when Spanish naval ships of superior force were lying within. The cruisers also hovered off Cadiz, and the various ports of the Spanish main under Spanish control. They even sailed as far as Manila and captured prey on the waters where Dewey won fame in later years. Millions of dollars' worth of Spanish cargoes were taken. But while some of these predaceous vessels enriched their owners, a much greater number failed to secure a single

Spanish cargo. With the crews they carried, some kind of plunder had to be secured, or a mutiny would sweep the officers over the rail. This is not to say that a mutiny was necessary to induce the average captain to seek plunder wherever it could be found, for with few exceptions the officers were more greedy than their men.

No flag could protect a ship at that time and in those waters, but American commerce suffered from the depredations more than that of any other nation. The Wait edition of "State Papers and Public Documents" contains several tales of American ships that were robbed by American-owned privateers. Niles's Register supplements these with many others. Perhaps the most notable instance of an attack upon an American merchantman was the capture of the schooner Evening Post by the brig Brutus, Captain Jolly, who sailed under the Venezuelan flag. For the capture of the Evening Post led directly to the death of Commodore Perry as told further on.

The depredations committed by these American and English privateers under Spanish-American insurgent flags, in time compelled the authorities at Washington to send our naval ships to cruise in West Indian waters for the protection of American commerce. Neither the French nor the Spanish pirates of the preceding century were even remotely involved when, on November 5, 1819, the naval schooner Lynx, commanded by Lieutenant J. R. Madison, appeared off Lafitte's resort on Galveston Island and began sounding the channel preliminary to an attack. This work of the Lynx was due solely to the depredations of the privateers that had made Galveston harbor their home port. But Lafitte, by hanging one of his gang who had been stealing slaves in Louisiana, warded off the attack, and continued to hold his place as a pirate's "fence" for many years. The sloop of war Congress and the brig Boxer were also cruising in the Gulf of Mexico to restrain these pirates under insurgent flags at the time the Lynx went to Galveston Island.

Meanwhile a still more important expedition had been fitted out. On March 29, 1819, Commodore Oliver Hazard Perry, then recently home from his cruise in the Mediterranean, was sent with a squadron of three vessels to the Caribbean Sea, with orders to sweep the pirates from those waters; but first of all he was to go up the Orinoco, and visit Bolivar to obtain a list of privateers that had been commissioned under the Venezuelan flag, and to demand compensation for their attacks on American merchantmen. Perry went up the river, as directed, but he died of a fever in consequence of the trip—the first notable loss of life in the campaign.

It is to be noted further that the Act of March 3, 1819, was especially designed to meet the exigencies of such a case. The President was " requested " to employ the navy in protecting commerce by sending into port as good prize all armed vessels that might attempt "piratical aggression, search, restraint, depredation or seizure," upon American merchantmen, or "any other vessels." The plain meaning of the act was that American men-o'-war were to protect the commerce of all nations including Spain's. The courtesy of the Colombian armed brig toward the captain of the merchantman on which he found Midshipman Farragut was, very likely, inspired by this act.

Finding that such ships as the navy already possessed were unfit for pirate hunting because of their great draft of water, Congress, by the act of May 15, 1820, appropriated $60,000 for building "any number of small vessels of war (not exceeding five)." These were named Porpoise, Alligator, Dolphin, Shark and Grampus, and ranged in size from 177 to 198 tons. They carried ten guns in broadside batteries and a long pivot gun amidships, mounted on a kind of disappearing carriage that could be lowered to the deck when not in use and raised above the bulwarks' level in time of battle. The last of the five was launched in August, 1821. The work had been done deliberately, but after the last launching, it was hastened because an American merchantman was plundered, at about that date, just south of Chesapeake Bay.

By the time these five schooners were put in commission, however, the situation had changed. When the Spanish-American privateers first went hunting Spanish merchantmen, the sympathy of the American people was with them. Their successful battles were applauded everywhere. But by the increasing number of piratical acts committed by them on American as well as European shipping, they for-

feited almost all the favor our people had earlier
exhibited for them.

This sympathy, however, had endured too long.
The loyal Spanish knew very well the hailing ports
of the privateers, and they knew too that the American people were, or had been, favorable to the
piratical crews. The Spanish minister kept the
State Department at Washington very busy reading
his complaints, and while he complained the prejudices of his countrymen grew. When the Spanish-American cruisers began capturing American
merchantmen the Spanish of the Cuban ports openly
taunted the Americans resident there. "It is so
much for so much" was a common expression when
the capture of an American ship was reported—
meaning, "it serves you right for allowing those
pirates to fit out in your ports."

This state of public mind having been attained
in Havana, it was but a short step easily taken to
the manning of piratical vessels that should seek
vengeance on American commerce for the injuries
received from the American-owned privateers, and
at the same time make good profits on the transac-
tion. The measures of the American government
for the destruction of the Spanish-American pirates,
such as the building of the five schooners named,
were taken much too late to save it from the indignation of the loyal Spanish. In fact, because the
earlier acts of our Government to this end were
inadequate, the Spaniards were the more deeply
angered by what was done at Washington.

The work of the Spanish vengeance-seeking pirates

soon startled the world. Their armed boats and vessels appeared, in 1821, off all the coasts of Cuba. When on October 16th, of that year, the United States war brig Enterprise arrived at Cape San Antonio, at the western end of Cuba, in search of lawless privateers under Spanish-American insurgent flags, she found a gang of Spanish pirates there, together with one American and two British vessels and the cargo of another American vessel, which they had captured. The plunder was taken by the Enterprise, but the pirates escaped. On November 8th, following, the Porpoise found another cargo of plunder there, and seized it, but the pirates got away as before. On December 21st the Enterprise returned to the cape and captured a fine schooner that the pirates had fitted out for cruising. This was thought to be a serious blow to them, but when the Porpoise came again a little more than two weeks later (January 7, 1822), the pirates were found afloat with six smart schooners. These were all captured, and five of them were burned, but the gang was by no means broken up, for they were backed by rich merchants who made their headquarters at Regla, on Havana Bay, within sight of the palace of the Captain-General, the Governor of Cuba, and there they openly fitted out pirate schooners and small boats for the capture of American merchantmen.

Because of the activity and ferocity of these Spanish pirates (they murdered and tortured many of their prisoners in a shocking fashion), the whole available strength of the American navy was concentrated in Cuban waters in 1822. Even the big square riggers Macedonian, Congress, John Adams and Cyane went cruising there, the whole force being under command of Commodore James Biddle. Biddle had some correspondence with the Captain-General (Don Nicholas Mahy), that is still interesting, because the Don said unmistakably, though with much politeness and diplomatic circumlocution, "We have done at least as much to restrain our pirates as you have done to restrain yours."

Neither by diplomatic correspondence nor by actual war was Biddle able to accomplish anything of consequence. Thirty pirate vessels, big and little, were captured; five merchantmen that had been taken by the pirates were released; but so secure did they feel in the support received from the Spanish authorities that when a gang of them were attacked (November 9, 1822), in Cardenas Bay by Lieutenant William Howard Allen, commanding the schooner Alligator, they made a fight in which Allen and four of his men were killed, and several others were wounded. In fact, the work of the navy during 1822 served only to increase the ferocity of the pirates, and President Monroe was impelled to send a special message to Congress, saying that there was needed a "peculiar kind of force . . . effectually to suppress" them.

This "peculiar force" when procured, included a side-wheel steamer that was purchased in New York. She was renamed the Sea Gull, and was the first steamer to see actual service in the American navy. The sloop of war Peacock, the schooner

Shark, the store-ship Decoy, and eight smart little
Chesapeake Bay schooners, each drawing no more
than seven feet of water and carrying three guns,
one of which was a "long Tom," were added to the
squadron. And then to perfect the scouring of the
shoal-water harbors, five big barges or rowboats,
each propelled by twenty oars and fit to carry forty
men, were built to order and sent along. The total
number of vessels added to the navy especially to
suppress piracy was thus brought up to twenty.

To command this fleet the Secretary of the Navy
selected Commodore David Porter; and David Glasgow Farragut, who had meantime passed his exam-
inations for promotion, but was yet a midshipman,
was assigned to one of the newly purchased schooners—the Greyhound, commanded by Lieutenant
Commandant John Porter.

In the course of a banquet tendered the officers of
the fleet by the citizens of Norfolk, where the vessels were assembled, Commodore Porter declared
that the rallying cry of his men should be "Remember Allen." The expedition sailed from the
Chesapeake on February 14, 1823. Commodore
Porter had the sloop of war Peacock for his flagship, the steamer Sea Gull for use in calm weather,
nine shoal draft schooners for patrolling the coasts
and giving convoy, and the five big barges for
scouring the shoaler waters, besides the store-ship
Decoy. On March 2d, the fleet reached St. Thomas,
and sailed thence to the vicinity of San Juan, Porto
Rico.

Off San Juan the fleet hove to and the schooner

Greyhound, Lieutenant Commandant Porter (with Farragut as deck officer), was sent into harbor with a letter to Governor Miguel de la Torre asking for an official list of the privateers that had been authorized to cruise from Porto Rico, and for a set of blank papers such as had been filled out for these cruisers in order that all lawful privateers overhauled by the fleet might be recognized.

This request was made because, during the previous year (1822), a half dozen privateers had been commissioned in Porto Rico, and sent cruising, ostensibly for vessels bound to or from a 1,200 mile strip of the Spanish mainland that had been declared under blockade but was not actually blockaded even by one ship. These privateers had taken every American vessel that came within their range, regardless of the port of departure or destination. One of them (the Palmyra, alias Pancheta) had fired on the American war schooner Grampus (August 15, 1822), had been badly damaged and was then sent to Charleston, S. C., for adjudication. Because the Palmyra had a commission she was released, in spite of the fact that she had robbed American vessels on lawful cruises. The Spanish of Porto Rico, and notably those of San Juan, where the Palmyra belonged, took this release as an admission that she had been fully justified in her attacks on American commerce, and were eager to avenge the drubbing she had received from the Grampus.

The opportunity to obtain such a revenge as they desired came after Porter sent the Greyhound into

San Juan on March 4th. The "Naval Affairs" volumes of the "American State Papers" contain the correspondence in connection with this affair, and it is there conclusively shown that the Spanish authorities deliberately planned to fire on the first American vessel to follow the Greyhound into port, and they did so. The vessel was the little schooner Fox, commanded by Lieutenant Commandant William H. Cocke, who had been Farragut's friend and counselor on the John Adams in New York harbor, late in the year 1814.

As the Fox reached in toward the fort (March 5), five guns loaded with solid shot and scrap iron were fired at her, and Cocke was struck in the shoulder. He died ten minutes later. The gunner who fired this shot saw that his aim had been good, and shouted exultantly that he had avenged the Palmyra.

As Porter wrote to Governor Torre, it was "an act of most unpardonable cruelty and barbarity," done "by the hand of a dastard whose aim was the more sure from a confidence in his own safety and the defenceless condition of his object."

A number of effusive letters were written by the Governor, but Porter got neither a list of licensed privateers nor a set of the papers he had asked for. Accordingly, the American fleet was divided and one part was sent to examine the south coasts of San Domingo, Haiti and Cuba, while the commodore himself with the other part hunted along the north coasts.

This search was made in the most thorough manner, especially on the Cuban coasts, but nowhere was a pirate found. For the Captain-General of Cuba, Don Nicholas Mahy, had sent to all ports notice of the approach of the American fleet.

In writing in his diary about his cruise in the Greyhound, Farragut notes that but few of the American officers of the fleet had ever sailed in a schooner-rigged vessel. They left the Chesapeake in a northeast gale. Lieutenant John Porter, commanding the Greyhound, carried sail in a way that ran his vessel out of sight of the squadron very quickly and was but little short of driving her under the waves. As she labored along, Farragut, who was officer of the deck, and had had experience in driving the schooner Shark across the Mediterranean, called Porter's attention to the fact that the Greyhound did not "rise to the sea," but Porter who was sitting well aft replied: "If she can't carry the sail, let her drag it." It was great sport for a captain to outsail a squadron, as the Greyhound did. But at eight o'clock Porter went below, leaving Farragut to handle her as he pleased. She was then put under a foresail, "when she scudded through the gale like a duck."

Before again joining the fleet, the Greyhound met a British squadron, and a brig carrying twenty guns sent to intercept the American ship, fired a gun to bring her to the wind. Porter merely called his crew to quarters and kept on. At that the brig fired another shot and Porter said to the gunner in command of the pivot gun :

"Fire, but don't hit her."

The gunner obeyed. He did not hit her but he

sent the shot only a few feet above the heads of the
officers on the brig's poop deck. The Greyhound
had her colors flying and no American naval officer
would take orders from a foreigner after the War of
1812. This reply to his second shot satisfied the
British captain. "None but a Yankee would have
done that," he said. He had now arrived within
hail, and after asking for the nationality of the
Greyhound, made a proper apology.

In the meantime the crews of brig and schooner
were "furious." The English captain, hearing
that Porter was sick, sent a boat with some fruit.
As the cockswain of the boat passed it over the
Greyhound's rail he said :

"Here is some fruit for the shot you sent us."

To this the Yankee boatswain's mate who received it replied :

"We are always ready to fight or eat with you."

And a careful consideration will convince any
student of American history that this boatswain's
mate expressed a sentiment not unknown among
American naval men ever since that day.

After cruising along the Cuban coasts the fleet
gathered at Key West, where a naval station had
been established the previous year. A deal of
shifting among the crews followed in order to make
a still more thorough search for the pirates. Commander Lawrence Kearney, who had already done
excellent work on the Cuban coast with the brig
Enterprise, took command of the little Greyhound,
and with the Beagle, commanded by Lieutenant
J. C. Newton, explored the southern shores of Cuba.

The numerous islands there were carefully searched but no pirates were found until Cape Cruz was reached—July 21, 1823.

At this point Kearney and Newton went ashore partly to look for signs of pirates and partly in search of game. A man crossed their path, and one of the sailors was going to shoot him, but was stopped by Kearney. The sailor said he knew "by his rig" that the fellow was a pirate, and the party therefore returned to the boat. When they prepared to pull off to the schooners the ruffians opened fire with muskets from the brush. The sailors returned the fire, aiming at the smoke (forms could not be seen in the bushes), but no one was hurt on either side.

In order to exterminate this gang a landing party under command of Acting-Lieutenant Farragut was ordered ashore at three o'clock next morning. The party numbered seventeen, including two acting-lieutenants. The Greyhound was to warp in close to the beach in order to cover them, and once landed they were to keep back in the brush, out of sight of the vessels, and march toward the higher land near the point of the cape.

On landing, Farragut found himself on a long narrow island. To make headway on their course it was necessary for the men to hew a path through the brush with their cutlasses. After a time they arrived at the end of the island and saw that an unfordable strait lay between them and the rocky cape. They were therefore obliged to show themselves on the beach. When they appeared the

crew of the Greyhound were about to fire on them,
for they were covered with mud and looked like
natives, rather than sailors in uniforms. But
Kearney saw Farragut's epaulette in time, and then
sent boats to ferry the party across the channel.

The crews of these boats, on seeing the party so
fully covered with mud, dropped discipline for the
moment, to laugh heartily at their ridiculous appearance. It is pleasant to note that Farragut enjoyed the scene as much as any one.

Captain Kearney, after transporting Farragut's
party to the mainland, pulled boldly alongshore
until close under the bluffs of the cape when the
pirates opened fire on him with a four pounder and
so great a number of muskets that he was obliged
to retreat. Then, after ordering Farragut to work
through the brush to the rear of the pirate stronghold, Kearney returned to the Greyhound and with
sweeps drove her and the Beagle within range when
he opened fire with the great guns.

In the meantime the task assigned to Farragut
was proving to be one of the most laborious of his
life. The bushes were thickly covered with thorns
and well intermingled with cacti. The ground was
covered with sharp rocks and bits of iron ore that
cut the shoes from the feet of the men with most
painful rapidity, and every inch of the way had to
be opened by stroke of cutlass. Worse yet the sun
had climbed well up, and the heat of the motionless
air had become intense. One officer was overcome
and fainted, while several of the sailors were greatly
exhausted.

When half a mile from the beach a tremendous clatter was heard in the thicket behind the toiling party, and after listening a moment, Farragut became convinced that a large number of pirates were coming to attack him. He therefore made a most stirring speech to his command, and then charged the enemy, only to find that it was a great host of land crabs migrating through the brush.

A little later they heard the schooners firing on the pirate stronghold, and with renewed energy worked on only to find, upon reaching the more open country near the cape, that the enemy were already in flight. They chased the retreating pirates as well as they could. "Now and then a fellow would be seen in full run, and apparently fall down and disappear from view"—crawling through the brush. Only two were taken, and they were "old and decrepit beings." Farragut captured a big black monkey that bit him through the arm, "but had to surrender at discretion."

The pirate haunt consisted of one large, well-thatched house and three smaller ones that were well concealed from view—structures made of poles and covered with palm leaves. Near by were "numerous deep and intricate caves," as Kearney says in his report. The settlement was defended by a "4-pounder, two swivels mounted on the heights" and numerous muskets and blunderbusses. In the caves were found considerable plunder including goods with English labels on them "but of no value." One woman and several children were

among the outlaws.   The houses were burned and
the guns were carried away.

The party also destroyed a quantity of fishing
tackle and all the boats but one, which was given
to the "old and decrepit" prisoners, who were
allowed to go, even though they had lighted signal
fires to announce the approach of the Americans.

On returning to Key West for provisions, Farragut was transferred to the steamer—the Sea Gull
—of which he was made the executive officer.
Commodore Porter was using her as his flagship,
while searching the Cuban coast, and was willing
to give Farragut an opportunity to learn how to
handle what was then a wondrous innovation—a
steam war vessel.

But a great and fearsome peril was now hanging
over the fleet.   When the Sea Gull returned to
Key West with Farragut, he found the yellow fever
raging there.   Of twenty-five officers who had been
attacked at this time, twenty-three died, and Farragut says that the enlisted men had suffered in
the same proportion.   During 1823 and 1824, taken
together, a half of the officers and men employed
in the fleet were stricken with the disease, and one-
fourth of the entire force died of it.

Though he might have obtained a transfer to
another station at any time, Farragut faced the
yellow fever on the West India coasts for two years
and a half; for there, and nowhere else in the
world, he had a chance to smell burning gunpowder
—to see active service.   It is interesting, now, to
recall the fact that the men who were cruising

nearest the beach suffered most from the fever. The surgeons supposed that this was due to the influence of the "night air," but Farragut noted that "night air" was not injurious in all cases. He says:

"On board the Greyhound we all slept on deck. For myself I never owned a bed during my two years and a half in the West Indies, but lay down to rest wherever I found the most comfortable berth."

Yet Farragut escaped the dread disease until he was ordered north near the end of the pirate war. Among the twenty-five officers stricken with the fever, when it first came to the fleet, was the commodore himself. He was one of the two that recovered, although he was so much debilitated that he went north in the Sea Gull, taking Farragut with him. But the latter soon returned to the West Indies and was sent on a cruise that was extended to St. Kitts and St. Bartholomew.

On reaching the Florida Keys after this cruise Farragut found a schooner, loaded with brick, bound for the Mississippi, and obtained leave of absence for one month to visit his relatives in Louisiana. This schooner, as the diary notes, carried the first cargo of brick used in building Fort Jackson which was designed, as no one could foresee, for the defense of New Orleans against Farragut and his men nearly forty years later. Commodore Daniel T. Patterson was in command at New Orleans when Farragut arrived there, and a letter written by him on May 20, 1824, contains this sentence:

"We have been gratified by the visit of young Farragut, of whom we have formed a high opinion."

The young man returned to the fleet just in time to obtain an independent command. The captain of the Ferret was going north, and Commodore Porter had established the rule that the passed midshipmen should be chosen for command in the order of the dates of their warrants. Farragut's warrant had an earlier date than any other midshipman within reach, but Porter for a time hesitated lest he be accused of partiality in giving his ward the schooner. Like many a young man afloat since his day, Farragut found that an influential father, even though an adopted one, might be an impediment to his advancement. However, Fleet Captain W. B. Finch interceded and Farragut got the schooner—"another important event in my life," he writes. It was his first naval ship. He was then twenty-three years old.

Going to sea within a few hours, Farragut entered upon the search for pirates with the eagerness of a youth most ambitious to accomplish something; but the previous work of the fleet had been so thorough that they no longer went afloat, save at night and in rowboats when they saw a merchantman becalmed offshore, though they were not wholly suppressed until 1825. However, the young captain found employment in convoying merchantmen "through the Gulf and as high as the Double-Headed Shot Keys," and in handling his crank little schooner in the squalls that frequently swept those waters.

"It required great vigilance, but it was an admirable school for a young officer," he wrote afterward, "and I realized its benefits all my life. I have never felt afraid to run a ship since, generally finding it a pleasant excitement."

During this period we get one glimpse of the young midshipman in a personal encounter with two men supposed to be pirates. In arranging for convoys, Farragut had frequently to go ashore at the ports to consult with the merchants and captains. In this way he became well-known personally to the alongshore people. Accordingly when he was sitting on his hotel veranda, in Havana, one evening, two men took seats near him, where they abused the whole American nation in general, and then insulted Farragut personally. It was tolerably certain that they were "looking for trouble"; and whether they were or not, they found it.

As it happened, the two were sitting close to a stout iron railing that guarded the front edge of the veranda. Noting this fact, Farragut left his seat, grabbed the two men by the throats, jerked them from their chairs, and whirling them around backed them over the rail and held them with their heads down toward the pavement until they begged him to let them go. It was a striking exhibition of the young officer's strength and skill as an athlete, and of his courage as well; for every member of the piratical gangs carried a knife. In fact, Farragut was soon warned that the pirates would waylay and murder him, if he were found ashore at night, thereafter. But they apparently had had enough of fighting with him, hand to hand, for he came and went as usual, and was never again molested in any way.

It appears from what he told his son (Captain Loyall Farragut of New York, from whom the above story was obtained), that he learned to know some of the pirates by sight.   There was one in particular, named Domingo, whom he mentions in his diary as a man who had "something chivalric" about him.   In 1823 or 1824, a schooner was built in Baltimore, which under the name of Pilot, became noted for her speed.   She was put in the Havana trade, where she attracted much attention among seafaring people.   To secure this schooner for piratical uses Domingo gathered a crew, and awaiting her approach, went off in a rowboat one night and captured her within gunshot of the Morro.   In addition to a rich cargo, the Pilot carried a great amount of mail for the naval men under Commodore Porter.   Domingo carefully preserved this and sent it all to Porter's fleet, "with a message in which he said that the Yankees were a gallant set of fellows, and he had no wish to keep them out of their letters ; but that he would retain the miniature of Lieutenant G.'s wife, in case he should meet the original.   He thought if she looked like the picture he should make love to her."

Later, while cruising in the Pilot, Domingo fell in with two of the big barges manned by the Yankee sailors.   These chased him ashore, shot him through the arm, killed one of his men, and retook the schooner.   Farragut afterward saw Domingo loafing around the mole in Havana with his arm in a sling waiting for another chance to go afloat.

Farragut writes in his diary that he was ordered to Nassau, N. P., on August 23, 1823, but he was writing from memory, and the date must be wrong, because in a report of the Captain of the Squadron, W. B. Finch (Finch afterward changed his name to Bolton), dated July 20, 1824, an event of this trip is described much as Farragut describes it, though the report is dated July 10, 1824.[1] The report says:

"Acting Lieutenant Farragut, commanding the Ferret, reports that while at Nassau, about the 10th inst., one of his crew, of the name of James Fredenburg, stated himself to be a deserter from H. B. Majesty's ship Pandorn ; and that in consequence he gave him over to Captain Du Maigue, commanding H. B. Majesty's ship Kangaroo. The grounds on which Lieutenant Farragut acted are that no foreigners were wanted in our service, and moreover Captain Du Maigue had recently returned an American deserter to the Wild Cat." Captain Finch was especially careful to add that Farragut was "not constrained thereto by any act of the British officer."

Farragut gives more details in his diary. The sailor hailed the British ship, announced himself as a deserter, and asked to be taken from the Ferret. As soon as Farragut heard what had been done he got up his anchor, sailed outside the harbor, and

[1] State Papers, Naval Affairs, Vol. II, p. 301.

tricing the offending sailor up to the rigging, gave him a thorough application of the cat, returning then to the anchorage. There he waited two days to see whether the British officers would demand him, being fully determined, meanwhile, that he would not surrender the fellow under any circumstances. But the days of insolent foreign demands had ended with the War of 1812, and having heard that the British had promptly given up an American deserter from one of their ships in Havana, Farragut thought to return the courtesy. The deserter was therefore sent to the ship he had hailed.

On leaving Nassau, Farragut sailed under orders for Washington, and when within sight of that city was stricken with the yellow fever. He recovered in due time, but remained in delicate health for several months. Moreover, his eyes troubled him through the lingering effects of the sunstroke received in Tunis. In consequence the Ferret was placed under the command of Lieutenant Charles H. Bell, who capsized her off the north coast of Cuba, and lost many of her crew.

The fact that another took the schooner seems to have made a deep impression on Farragut, for he says in connection with the event:

"I had always to contend with the burden first imposed on me by Commodore Porter's saying that I was 'too young for promotion.' Although that remark was made just after the action of the Essex, I never appeared to get any older in the eyes of the government, or my commander, and consequently had to contend, inch by inch, as opportunities presented, with men of riper age and apparently more entitled to the places sought."

This reference to the competition "with men of riper age" is explained by an examination of the old naval registers. Boys who were older, and who had had much better schooling than the backwoods Farragut, came into the navy just before and during the War of 1812. Their warrants were of later date than his by years, but where he failed to pass his first examination for promotion, they succeeded. No less than ninety-eight midshipmen who entered the navy after Farragut, received the lieutenant's commission ahead of him. Moreover, in the register where his name appears for the first time as a lieutenant, twenty-one names stand ahead of his with their commissions of the same date, and nearly all of the twenty-one entered the navy after him.

In his experience in battle, and in his ability to handle men and ships, Farragut was undoubtedly superior to nearly every one of those promoted over him, as we can easily see now. Few officers of the American navy have had such an experience in this regard as Farragut. It is a most interesting fact for the reason that he was never soured by his ill-fortune. He never lost pluck or ambition, and he worked all the harder to fit himself to embrace the opportunities to which he ever looked forward.

With the attack of yellow fever Farragut's service in the West Indies came to an end, although he was nominally attached to the fleet some months longer.

However one other incident of the war should be related here, briefly. On the night of October 23, 1824, pirates from the little village of Foxardo, in the east end of Porto Rico, landed at St. Thomas and robbed the store of two American citizens of a large quantity of goods which were carried to Foxardo. Lieutenant Charles T. Platt, commanding the schooner Beagle, sailed to that place, landed and asked the Alcalde and other officials to help him recover the property. But they, being in partnership with the pirates, not only refused to do so, but imprisoned the lieutenant and otherwise grossly insulted him. On November 12th, this matter was reported to Commodore Porter, who went to Foxardo with a competent force and compelled the Alcalde to make a proper apology to Lieutenant Platt.

This act did more to make the Spanish of Porto Rico respect the American navy than anything ever done in that region theretofore. As documents in the case show, every American naval officer who landed in the island thereafter was treated with marked courtesy and consideration. But when the Spanish minister complained at Washington, Porter was ordered home, and was tried by a court-martial that declared his conduct "censurable." The blood of Lieutenant William H. Cocke, deliberately shot to death at San Juan, was forgotten, and Porter, unable to endure such treatment, resigned his commission, August 18, 1826—the second of the heroes of the War of 1812 that were lost to the navy through the pirate war.

When Jackson became President he offered to restore Porter to his place, but the latter declined to return to an association with officers who could censure a man for showing an excessive regard for the honor of the Nation and the naval service. Afterward Porter was sent to represent the United States at Constantinople, where he remained until his death on March 28, 1843. His body was brought home and buried in Woodlands Cemetery, West Philadelphia.

Farragut was a witness before the court that tried Porter but his testimony was not important, for he was not in any way connected with the Foxardo affair.

CHAPTER VIII

AFTER recovering from the fever which he had contracted in the West Indies, Farragut went to Norfolk, Va., where on September 2, 1824, he was married to Susan Caroline, the daughter of Jordan and Fanny Marchant. Naval officers are known the world over as good husbands, but Farragut was especially noted in this respect. His wife lost her health and was an invalid who suffered intensely until December 20, 1840, when she died. During the years of her sickness Farragut was stationed at Norfolk, much of the time, and how he cared for her may be inferred from the remark made by a Norfolk lady :

"When Captain Farragut dies," she said, "he should have a monument reaching to the skies, made by every wife in the city contributing a stone to it."

As for his work during the years following the pirate war it was on the whole merely the routine life of a naval officer in time of peace. Nevertheless there were incidents in it worth recalling.

On January 13, 1825, he became a lieutenant in the navy. His pay was then forty dollars per month with three rations added. As a midshipman, and when married, he had received nineteen dollars a month, with one ration.

When the frigate Brandywine was sent to carry Lafayette home (she sailed from the Potomac on September 13, 1825), Farragut was ordered to her as a deck officer. His pride in his profession is shown by his diary wherein he notes that the Brandywine was one of the fastest vessels in the world, and was able to keep up with the other ships in the Mediterranean squadron, which she joined, while spreading from twelve to sixteen sails less than any of them.

Between 1826 and 1828, being at Norfolk once more, he observed that but few of the apprentices on the station knew so much as their letters. Seeing very clearly, what few officers saw then, that the education of the apprentices would promote their efficiency as seamen, he established a school on the sloop of war Alert for their instruction, and was so successful with it that the secretary of the navy on visiting the yard was moved to compliment him. It is a matter that ought to be remembered. If Farragut were living now we may believe that he would favor giving all apprentices of the navy as good an education as is given to the midshipmen.

After that (1828), he made a cruise to the South Atlantic station in the old Vandalia, wherein the late Rear Admiral Benjamin F. Sands was a midshipman. Sands in his autobiography recalls a squall that struck the ship off Cape Frio, Brazil. It was so severe that even Captain John Gallagher, a well-tried officer, "became somewhat excited." But Farragut, who had the deck, "gave his orders through the trumpet calmly and distinctly; and with no confusion the ship in a little while was under snug sail." "Young as I was," continues Sands, "I was struck with admiration, and breathed a hope that I would some day make just such an-other sailor and officer—as he was my beau-ideal."

On the South Atlantic station, Farragut was present at some of the proceedings in one of the oft-recurring revolutions in the Argentine, but his eyes having failed him he was sent home. On December 4, 1832, he joined the Natchez as her executive officer (first lieutenant), and on January 5th sailed for Charleston, to which port the ship had been ordered by President Jackson to quell with force, if necessary, the troubles that were expected to arise in connection with the "nullifica-tion" of the national revenue laws by the state of South Carolina. The only work done by the naval force was when Farragut with fifty men went ashore and helped the citizens extinguish a fire that threat-ened to sweep the city. The Natchez was the largest ship (700 tons) with which Farragut had been con-nected as executive officer, and she carried a crew of 140 men. One of the officers who sailed in her wrote afterward :

"Never was the crew of a man-of-war better dis-ciplined, or more contented and happy. The mo-ment all hands were called, and Farragut took the trumpet, every man under him was alive and eager for duty."

When at Rio, on one occasion, he "box-hauled" a ship out of port, although the wind was ahead, the passage was narrow, and many good seamen thought "the manœuvre could not be successfully accomplished."

On August 7, 1838, Farragut got his first square-rigged ship, the Erie, a vessel of 509 tons, and carrying 140 men. France was, at that time, at war with Mexico, to compel the payment of damages for injuries done to French citizens during the unending revolutions that prevailed in that country, and the Erie was sent down to the Mexican coast to look after the rights of American citizens, and presumably to see that the provisions of the Monroe Doctrine were not impaired.

There is a significant entry in the diary of the young captain, during his stay on the Mexican coast. Having leisure at one time, he says, "I occupied myself in sounding around the reefs and islands of Sacrificios." Farragut had been in these waters in 1822 as a midshipman in the sloop of war John Adams, and he was now continuing the work of studying the coast that he had begun in his first cruise thither.

But a much better opportunity for increasing his knowledge was found in connection with the French fleet, under Admiral Baudin. For Baudin being unable to secure the satisfaction demanded of Mexico determined to capture the huge fort of San Juan de Ulloa, guarding the harbor of Vera Cruz. The French fleet included two steamers brought out for use as tugs. On November 27, 1838, these tugs placed the frigates, sloops and bomb vessels where their fire would be most effective, and at 2 : 30 o'clock the action began. The firing was continued during the daylight hours until nine o'clock the next morning, when the fort capitulated. About 200 shot a minute were hurled into the works during that time.

Farragut had already carefully noted the armament of the ships and now he had an opportunity to see the effect of the shot. As early as 1825, guns to fire shells horizontally—as distinguished from the high-thrown shell-fire of mortars—had been introduced into the French navy, and the frigates in this fleet each had either two or four 80-pounders for throwing shells. No other navy then mounted such guns, the best in the American navy being a long 32-pounder firing a round six inch solid shot with a charge of five or six pounds of powder.

His examination of the French ships led Farragut to declare in a letter to Commodore Barron, that "the English and ourselves may affect to despise the French by sea, but depend upon it, sir, they are in science far ahead of us both. Of all this I know you have seen much in theory, but I have seen it tested in practice."

The attack on this fort was the first practical trial of the value of guns for firing shells instead of the solid shot that had been used theretofore, and it was also the first comparative test with mortar fire. Fully alive to the occasion, Farragut noted that "the French threw almost entirely shell-shot, which entered the wall twelve or eighteen inches and then exploded, tearing out great masses of stone, and in some instances rending the wall from base to top. The damage done by these [horizontally-fired] shell-shot was inconceivably greater than that by the shell from the bomb vessels. I am satisfied that they might have bombarded with bomb vessels for a month without success, while the frigates would in four hours more, with their shell-shot, have reduced the fort to a heap of ruins."

In modern days a Bureau of the Navy Department has been established to collect just such information about foreign ships and their work as was then gathered by Farragut, and sent to Commodore Barron. Moreover the peculiarities of every officer are now recorded in the Navy Department so that when one like Farragut shows a special interest in gleaning information, and a special aptitude for such work, the facts about his abilities are all written down to his credit, in order that his services may be obtained in case of need.

But in those days no records were kept, either of the officers of the American navy or of the progress made by foreign navies. The success of the navy in the War of 1812 had been in one way injurious to it. Splendid victories had been gained with such inadequate preparation that the American people came to think their "valor" was sufficient for every emergency. Indeed as late as in 1884 a famous New York orator said, in a public address, in that city, that if a foreign war squadron should attempt to blockade New York the population would rise up *en masse*, board the great fleet of harbor steamers, rush down to the bar and mob the enemy off the face of the ocean. And yet every European power had ironclads a-plenty in 1884,

and it was the well-equipped battleship that the
orator thought to mob with wooden river steamers
and ferry boats. Said Farragut in his letter to
Barron :

"If we who wander about the world do not keep
those at home informed of the daily improvements
in other navies, how can we hope to improve, particularly when we see men impressed with the idea
that, because they once gained a victory, they can
do it again ? So they may, but I can tell them that
it must be with the means of 1838, not those of
1812."

In the meantime Farragut was relieved of the
command of the Erie by an officer of superior rank,
and he returned to his home in Norfolk. Thereafter he was not afloat again until February, 1841,
when he was ordered to the battleship Delaware as
executive officer. The activity of "the little luff,"
as he was then called, is well shown by the fact that
he devised improved machinery for hoisting ammunition from the magazine to the various gun decks,
and then drilled the crew until they could fire three
aimed broadsides in four minutes—a speed that was
astounding to the gunners of that day.

Farragut was promoted to the rank of commander
on September 8, 1841. In the following two years
he was attached to the South Atlantic station, from
which he returned to Norfolk once more in command of the sloop of war Decatur. He arrived
there on February 18, 1843. On December 26th,
the same year, he was married to Virginia, the
daughter of Mr. William Loyall, of Norfolk. He

remained in that city, being employed on the Pennsylvania (ship-of-the-line), or at the navy yard, until the outbreak of the war with Mexico. During this period of comparative ease, Farragut wrote much of the material that has been incorporated in his published diary, using the log books of his various cruises when he had them, and writing from memory of periods for which they had been lost.

When war with Mexico was at hand, Farragut made every possible effort to obtain command on the Mexican coast. In a letter to the Secretary of the Navy, Hon. J. Y. Mason, dated November 3, 1846, he wrote saying that although two letters previously forwarded had accomplished nothing, "I now take the liberty of addressing you, sir, in much the same language, with the sincere hope, that, should anything like an attack on the Castle of San Juan de Ulloa be contemplated, at some future day, I may be allowed to participate in the glorious achievement, for such I believe it will be whenever it is undertaken.

"I served in the Gulf in 1822, '23, and '24, under Commodore Porter, and in 1838, '39 under Commodore Dallas. I was present in command of the sloop of war Erie when the castle was taken by the French in 1838, and was in the castle a few minutes after its surrender, and I therefore know how vulnerable it is to ships. I was intimate with the French officers, and saw daily all their preparations and plans of attack; all of which might be serviceable. I am proud to say I learned a good deal.

The French were prepared to attack by escalade. This I also considered feasible, and at, perhaps, much less risk than by bombardment; but it would have been executed under cover of night. My intimate knowledge of the localities and these arrangements induces me to hope that I may have a position under whoever has the good fortune to command the squadron."

In his diary Farragut tells of the outcome of his efforts: "I finally obtained command of the sloop of war Saratoga, after much difficulty. I had urged my claims on the ground that I had taken great pains to inform myself as to the local advantages of attacking the place, measured the depth of water all around the fort, and marked the penetration of *every shell from the French ships;* and that in so doing I had not at the time looked forward to a war with Mexico, but I had made it a rule of my life to note these things with a view to the possible future. I had labored much in this way, and it was the first opportunity I had ever had of reaping a reward. I urged that I could take the Castle of San Juan with the Pennsylvania and two sloops of war like the Saratoga, for which declaration I came near being ruled out as a monomaniac. I was willing to take the inferior position of executive officer on board the Pennsylvania that I might have the duty of organizing her crew for the fight; but it was not permitted, and I did not obtain command of the Saratoga until February, 1847."

Once in command of this ship, Farragut made such haste as has been rarely seen on a naval vessel. To gather his complement of men he took servants, boatmen—any one that could haul on a rope—and two days after receiving his orders, he sailed with a crew that was ten per cent. short of the necessary number. He had just one man that was rated as an able seaman. But he drilled the crew every day on his way down, and when he engaged in target practice off the Bahama Banks, "they made pretty good practice," and he had them "in fair trim" when they reached Vera Cruz.

In the meantime the fort had surrendered to General Scott. The navy did not enjoy the honor of taking it and why it did not do so Farragut thus explains :

"Unfortunately the officers then in the Gulf, who did not understand the condition of the fortifications or know the people, were not willing to attack, because an English officer had said that the castle 'could sink all the ships in the world.' It is now known, and sadly felt, that they were imposed upon. The navy would stand on a different footing to-day if our ships had made the attack. It was all we could do, and it should have been done at all hazards. Commodore Conner thought differently, however, and the old officers at home backed his opinion ; but they all paid the penalty—*not one of them will ever wear an admiral's flag*, which they might have done, if that castle had been taken by the navy."

The significance of these words is observable when one remembers that it was the gallant feats of

the navy in the Civil War which induced Congress
to create the rank of admiral, and Farragut was the
leader in this work. But "of all the service I had
seen since entering the navy," he writes, "the
cruise during the war with Mexico was the most
mortifying. I have little to look back to with satisfaction or pleasure at that time, except the con-
sciousness of having done my duty. I had the ill-
will of my commodore [M. C. Perry]. I was not
permitted to participate in any of the expeditions
or more honorable duties, but was placed under a
reef of rocks off Tuxpan, to blockade that port.
When I could bear the imposition no longer, I reported the facts to the Navy Department, and asked
to be relieved from under his command, or from
command of his ship."

Farragut was accordingly ordered home, where
he learned that his letters "were considered improper by the Secretary of the Navy." In the meantime he had passed through another attack of yellow fever that well-nigh ended his life.

On returning from the Mexican War (he reached
New York on February 19, 1848), Farragut was
made second in command at the Norfolk Navy
Yard, a position showing that the Department
still had confidence in his ability. His first
work of importance was an assignment in
October, 1850, in company with four officers
of lesser rank, to write a book of ordnance
regulations. The value of this work, which occupied him for a year and a half, was never fully
recognized because the ordnance of the navy was

soon to be revolutionized by the inventive talent
of Lieutenant John A. Dahlgren. The old style
32-pounders were to be thrown aside and 9-inch,
10-inch and 11-inch smoothbores of improved design were to be substituted. Farragut's work involved a thorough study of the gunnery systems of
the world, and that was something to his taste.
While engaged in it he regularly attended the lectures at the Smithsonian Institution, a fact worthy
of mention as showing his habit of acquiring
knowledge.

It was now, after forty years of unwearied toil for
self-improvement, that Farragut came to be recognized at the Department as an officer of special at-
tainments, and when he was done with the ordnance regulations, he was sent to Norfolk and
ordered to give a series of lectures on gunnery to
his fellow officers on the station. In 1852 it was
determined to test the endurance of all the various
kinds of guns in the navy and Farragut was chosen
to fire one or two of each class until they were finally
worn out and bursted. He says that by the results
obtained "many preconceived opinions of the service were entirely overturned."

But when on April 12, 1854, Farragut asked the
Department to send him to the Crimea that he might
render a report on the advancement that had been
made by the British and French in naval affairs,
"no action was taken" in the matter. Although
armored batteries were used in the Crimean War,
and novelties in guns such as a cannon with a grape-
vine shaped bore, were to be seen, the Navy De-

partment thought it not worth while to possess a knowledge of the improvements then made and making in Europe. The fact that our success on the ocean during the War of 1812 was due to superior guns, as well as to valorous and well-trained men, had been forgotten.

However, Farragut was sent on a mission that was considered important. The government had decided to establish a navy yard near the growing port of San Francisco, California. A site had been selected on Mare Island, thirty miles up the bay from the young city, and Farragut was ordered in August, 1854, to create the yard. He was four years on the station, and while there, he was promoted to the rank of captain on September 14, 1855.

At the Mare Island Navy Yard it has been said that "he reserved the ornamental work until everything of importance had been accomplished." And it is not a little pleasing to read that "the poorest laborer could approach him with any complaint or grievance, without awe or inferiority of manhood, and feel that he would receive equal and exact justice without respect to person. He inspired and preserved the confidence, respect, and esteem of all his subordinates."

It was while Farragut was in command at Mare Island that the celebrated Vigilance Committee of 1856 was formed in San Francisco. The blacklegs of the city obtained control of all official machinery and created a reign of terror from which there seemed no escape but by lynch law methods. It was a trying time for Farragut because the Vigilance Committee on the one hand, and the city and state officials calling themselves the Law and Order Party, on the other, steadily besought him to interfere by landing an armed force. To add to his difficulties a sloop of war, the John Adams, of the Pacific squadron, came into port, and the city officials begged her captain, Commander E. B. Boutwell, to fire on the town in order to compel the Vigilance Committee to release one of their prisoners, the notorious Judge Terry. Thereupon Commander Boutwell wrote a letter threatening to "use all the power" at his command to save Terry from the committee.

Farragut was then obliged to interfere so far as to require Boutwell not to take sides with either party ashore. It is very plain that Farragut appreciated the evils which had goaded the citizens to form the Vigilance Committee. He would have sanctioned any efforts short of anarchy for ousting the blacklegs who were supported by the so-called Law and Order Party. But he was very far from countenancing lynch law, or what may be called the American cross-lots route to a supposed natural justice. His course had the approval of the Department.

On his return to the east, Farragut was given command of the Brooklyn, one of a new squadron of steam frigates that had been built because it was thought that trouble with England impended. At any rate, the Secretary of the Navy said to Commander John A. Dahlgren, on the evening of February 7, 1856, that such a war would break out "in a twelvemonth," and Dahlgren's plans for arming the new ships were adopted for that reason. The broadside guns of the Brooklyn were 9-inch Dahlgren smoothbores, then the most efficient broadside guns in the world.

Farragut took the new steamer on her trial trip, and afterward in 1859 on a cruise through the West Indies and along the coast of Mexico, which country at the time was in a rather worse state of anarchy than usual.

It was fortunate for Farragut that he obtained this command. He had been trained to the handling of a sailing ship, and had shown himself able to take a sloop of war out of the harbor of Rio de Janeiro against both wind and tide. But his profession had "materially changed since the advent of steam," as he said at the time. There were many officers in the navy who had a strong prejudice against steam ships of war, but Farragut was not one of them. On the contrary, he found as much pleasure in handling the Brooklyn "as ever a boy did in any feat of skill." And he showed his unvarying interest in the work of the ship by constantly drilling the crew—particularly by target practice, and boat expeditions.

Farragut did not know it, but on this cruise he himself was in training; he was receiving the final schooling that was to fit him for the great work that lay but a short distance away.

In her cruise on the Mexican coast the Brooklyn was acting most of the time as a transport for the use of Robert M. McLane, United States Minister

to Mexico.   Our government had recognized Benito
Juarez, a liberal, as the legitimate executive at the
time that Mexico City was in the hands of the con-
servatives.   McLane traveled up and down the
coast, visiting the American consuls wherever he
could find them, and looking after the interests of
American citizens resident in the country.   But
during these visits he was also lending his influence
to the Juarez party.   The size and power of the
Brooklyn undoubtedly strengthened the influence
he constantly exerted, and it is not too much to
suppose that Farragut, with his perfect command
of the language, and superior knowledge of the
character of the Spanish-American people, was
able to give the minister great assistance.

Eventually the ministers of England, France,
Germany and Spain united with Minister McLane
in recognizing the Juarez government.   The special work of the Brooklyn then came to an end,
and McLane was taken to the Mississippi and
landed at a plantation below New Orleans.   As it
happened Farragut's older brother, Lieutenant
William Farragut, whose state of health had for
years prevented active service, was at the point of
death in New Orleans, when the Brooklyn entered
the river.   Farragut though unaware that his
brother was in a critical condition hastened to the
city, but arrived too late to find him alive.

The cruise of the Brooklyn came to an end in
1860.   The government was then, as now (1905),
interested in plans for an interoceanic canal, and a
naval expedition was sent out in this ship to sur-

vey the Chiriqui route. The expedition, however, was under the command of Captain Frederick Engle, who was lower on the list than Farragut, and thus the latter was obliged to take orders from a junior officer.

Farragut put the ship in trim for the expedition, and sailed with it from Hampton Roads on August 13, 1860; but he had in the meantime made a protest to the Secretary of the Navy, who, on perceiving the abnormal condition of affairs, relieved him from the embarrassing situation by ordering him back to Norfolk.

CHAPTER IX

FARRAGUT AND SECESSION

It was in October, 1860, that Farragut returned
to Norfolk after his cruise to the Isthmus of Panama,
and within a month (November 6th) Abraham Lincoln was elected President of the United States.
South Carolina seceded from the Union at 12:45
o'clock on December 20th; Mississippi followed on
January 9th; Florida on the 10th; Alabama on the
11th; Georgia on the 19th; Louisiana on the 26th,
and Texas on February 1st.

The origin of the secession movement cannot be
considered in the biography of a naval officer who
had no part in it. But one may recall that it was
the most appalling period in the history of the
American people; and that no man in the Nation
maintained his poise and self-possession better than
did David G. Farragut. He was born in Tennessee.
His home, so far as a naval officer could have a
home, had been in Norfolk, Va., for nearly forty
years. His friendships and affections were formed
south of Mason and Dixon's line, and so far as
he had prejudices, they were those of a Southern
man.

But he had begun to wear the uniform of the Nation's navy before he was ten years old. At thirteen he had borne an honorable part in one of the

most important battles ever fought for the honor of the flag and the unity of the Nation. For if the navy had not done such triumphant work in the War of 1812, New England might have left the other states. One may well remember here the blue-light traitors of 1812, for while they strove to divide the Nation, they did but arouse the indignation and strengthen the patriotism of every man who fought under the stars and stripes. Farragut learned on the bloody decks of the Essex to revere the flag as the emblem of a Nation, not of a conglomerate of petty communities. For no one need doubt that though but a boy, he knew about the secession movement in New England, and shared the patriotic indignation expressed against the men of the Essex Junto and the Hartford Convention.

Then, too, he was of the naval force sent by "Old Hickory" Jackson to quell the South Carolina nullification movement. It was a small matter in his experience but it was an incident that must have strengthened the national sentiment of every naval man engaged in it.

It is apparent from his diary that Farragut was familiar with the arguments for and against the division of the Union, as they were used in the period before the Civil War, and that he fully understood the principles on which the Union had been maintained. Thus, in his correspondence with Commander N. B. Boutwell, who, during the San Francisco Vigilance Committee troubles, threatened to use the guns of the John Adams on the city, Farragut not only pointed out the attitude that the

National government had always maintained toward individual states, in cases of domestic troubles, but he quoted Kent and Story in the matter.

When South Carolina seceded, Farragut had already determined that he would remain faithful to the flag under which his life had been passed. As Mahan says, "Those appeals to affection, to interest or to prejudice under which so many succumbed," could never move him from his position.

But the real test of his devotion to the Nation did not come when South Carolina seceded. Virginia did not follow the cotton states immediately. Efforts were made by the Virginia legislature to preserve peace, though on a basis where it was impossible; and when on February 15th, a state convention, urged by the more radical element, assembled at Richmond to consider the proposition to join the states that had already organized a confederation, a vote showed (April 4th), that eighty-nine delegates were against secession while forty-five favored it. The Union men came chiefly from the section that was afterward organized as West Virginia, the least influential section of the state; but some were from Norfolk, as Farragut said in a speech after the war, which will be mentioned farther on.

In spite of the majority that favored the Union on the first vote, the hope of keeping Virginia out of the secession movement rapidly faded. Lincoln's official assertion that he would "hold, occupy and possess property and places belonging to the government," and "to the best of my ability repel force by force," turned some of the Union delegates. The excitement following the attack on Fort Sumter alienated more. Then, according to the statement of one of the members of the convention (Annual Cyclopedia, 1861), ten members were intimidated by threats of personal violence into remaining away from the hall when the next vote was taken, and thus the ordinance of secession was passed (April 17th), eighty-five to fifty-five.

Whether this particular statement is true or not, Farragut believed it. He said, and the facts seem to justify him, that the state was "dragooned" from the Union. How the ardent secessionists tried to dragoon him from the Nation's navy can be told only in part because the facts were never fully recorded. In lieu of a club the naval officers in Norfolk and their friends were in the habit of meeting at a certain store to discuss the news, and it was there that the question of allegiance was argued out. The secessionists appealed to Farragut's love for his friends, to his pride in the state where he had made his home, to such prejudices as he held against the "fanatics" of the North, and finally to his ambition by offering him any place in the Confederate service that he might name.

Discussion came to an end when it was learned at Norfolk (April 18th), that the secession ordinance had been passed at Richmond. It is a pity that the talk of the naval officers at the meeting-place on that day was not fully reported, for it was then Farragut asserted that the state had been "dragooned" from the Union. It is certain, too, that the bearing of the secessionists soon became

menacing, for by one report Farragut then said to
them :

"Gentlemen, I would see every man of you
damned before I would raise my arm against the
flag."

Whatever he said, the others quickly told him
that a man holding his sentiments "could not live
in Norfolk," and to this he replied :

"Well, then, I can live somewhere else."

Farragut's own account of the event was given in
a brief address at Norfolk, after the fall of Richmond, where at a public gathering he met some old
friends and many naval officers. He then said :

"I wish that I had the language to express myself as I have heard others very near four years ago,
in this place, when we had our best speakers standing forth for the Union, and striving with all their
rhetoric to persuade the people to desist from their
unholy resolution, and cast their votes for the
Union. This meeting recalls to me the most mo-
mentous events of my life, when I listened in this
place till the small hours of the morning and returned home with the feeling that Virginia was safe
and firm in her place in the Union. Our Union
members of the convention were elected by an overwhelming majority, and sent to Richmond, and we
believed that everything was right. Judge, then,
my friends, of our astonishment in finding a few
days later, that the State had been voted out by a
miserable minority for the want of firmness and
resolution on the part of those whom we trusted to
represent us there, and that Virginia had been
dragooned out of the Union.

"What was the reason for this act? The President's call for 75,000 men? Why, our arsenals,

navy yards, money in the mint at New Orleans, had been seized, Sumter bombarded. Was it, then, remarkable that the Government of the United States should call for troops to sustain itself? Would Jackson have submitted to this? No ; for I recall that I myself had the honor to be sent to South Carolina to support his mandate that the Union must and should be preserved.

"I was told by a brother officer that the state had seceded, and that I must either resign, and turn traitor to the government which had supported me from my childhood, or I must leave this place. Thank God! I was not long in making my decision. I have spent my life in revolutionary countries and I know the horrors of civil war, and I told the people what I had seen, and what they would experience. They laughed at me, and called me 'granny' and 'croaker.' And I said, 'I cannot live here, and will seek some other place where I can live ; and on two hours' notice !' I suppose they said I left my country for my country's good —and thank God I did !

"I went from here with the few valuables I could collect. I was unwilling to believe that this difficulty would not have been settled ; but it was all in vain. And as every man must do in a revolution, as he puts his foot down, so it marks his life. It has pleased God to protect me thus far, and make me somewhat instrumental in dealing heavy blows at the rebellion. I have been nothing more than an instrument in the hands of God, well supported by my officers and men, who have done their duty faithfully."

When Virginia seceded, Farragut had reached the parting of the ways. For the love of the flag, he was willing to abandon home and friends and lifelong associations. He was ready to do even more, for on returning home he told his wife that he should at once leave Norfolk to go North. He then pointed out to her that if she went with him, she was likely to be separated from her home and friends for years, and told her to make her choice.

Having taken an oath that he would support the Constitution he was ready to stand by it, even though he was obliged, when doing so, to leave his wife among his enemies until after the war. And he reached that determination too, when he knew that as an officer of Southern birth he would be an object of suspicion among the people of the North, and that he could have, on account of this suspicion, but little hope of obtaining a command suited to his rank and abilities. The greatest sacrifice short of life itself that man can make for his country was made by David Farragut, and he was ready to sacrifice his life also.

Happily Mrs. Farragut was a woman worthy of such a man, and at night, on April 18, 1861, the captain, his wife and his son Loyall, went by steamer to Baltimore. They found the city in a state of turmoil following the attack that had been made that morning (April 19th), by a furious mob on the Sixth Massachusetts Regiment. The bridge on the railroad line to Philadelphia had been destroyed and no trains were running north. The mob was still in possession of the city and the lives of known Union men were in danger. Under these conditions Farragut and his family, with a lot of other Union refugees, took passage on a canal boat through the Delaware and Chesapeake canal for Philadelphia, and so the North was reached.

Going to Hastings on the Hudson, Farragut made his family as comfortable as possible in a little cottage there. Then he applied to the Navy Department for an active command, and on failing to get it, he settled down to wait. He had a tedious time there among strangers—most tedious. To pass the long months he took walks over the hills and fields round about the village, and thus excited a suspicion among the people of the region that he was an emissary of the Confederacy seeking an opportunity to destroy some part of the Croton Aqueduct in order to create a water famine in New York City.

CHAPTER X

To understand fully the part taken by Farragut in the Civil War it is necessary first to consider what was done by the sailors and ships that were engaged in the war before he entered it.

The most important feature of this work is to be found in the order repeatedly issued by the Navy Department to commanders of ships and expeditions, to "act strictly on the defensive." Moreover, fear was often expressed that officers might act "on the defensive" with too much energy. On January 12, 1861, Captain James Armstrong surrendered the Pensacola Navy Yard with all its arms and military supplies to Confederate troops without making any resistance whatever, lest a fight there should "precipitate a conflict" and bring on "all the horrors of war." On January 21st, when the warship Brooklyn carried supplies to Fort Pickens, on Santa Rosa Island, off Pensacola harbor, her orders were to "act strictly on the defensive," and these orders were so interpreted that Lieutenant Adam J. Slemmer, U. S. A., who held the fort for the Union with splendid heroism, was not relieved until April 1st. And, when D. D. Porter came down to Fort Pickens in command of the steam warship Powhatan, as shall be told further on, thus increasing the Federal forces to a degree amply sufficient for retaking and holding Pensacola, he was stopped on his way into the harbor (April 17th) by the same act-on-the-defensive policy. Then on April 12th, when a relief expedition reached the channel leading to Fort Sumter, and the Confederate forces were found bombarding the fort, the expedition remained in the offing instead of making a dash to help the overmatched soldiers of the Nation.

In spite of the infinite national shame, degradation and loss that had come, before 1812, through the porcupine policy inaugurated by Thomas Jefferson, that President's theories had a mighty influence on the minds of the whole American people, in 1861. While the Confederates with splendid energy reached out for Pensacola, Fort Sumter and the Norfolk Navy Yard, even Lincoln and his cabinet were uncertain what to do because of the feeling that whenever Americans were compelled to fight they ought always to act "on the defensive."

It is a most important matter. For the hardest lesson that the American people have had to learn is that the best means of self-defense is the most vigorous possible attack upon the enemy. To "act strictly on the defensive" is to bring the enemy and the "horrors of war" upon our own homes, while vigorous offensive action, when war is necessary, keeps the enemy at his home and the horrors of war upon his borders. The fact is, the American people have not yet learned the full value of offensive action at the very beginning of a war. Many a congressman, in recent years, has pointed with silly satisfaction to the Atlantic Ocean as something that would weaken an attack upon our shores, while our naval officers, in working out their war games, have been employed in considering means for defending Long Island Sound, or Delaware Bay, or Cheesequake's Creek.

The first aggressive work for the Federal navy in the Civil War was laid out when, on April 19 and 27, 1861, proclamations were issued for blockading the Confederate ports. Then in August an expedition under Flag Officer Silas H. Stringham was sent to Cape Hatteras and on the 28th, Fort Hatteras, at Hatteras Inlet, was captured. This was the first victory obtained by the National forces in the Civil War.

In November, 1861, Port Royal was taken. A base for the Atlantic blockading fleet was thus established, and in the meantime the Gulf blockading squadron had made a base at Ship Island, which lay near the mainland, northeast of the mouths of the Mississippi. Key West with its harbor was also kept under National control.

On the whole, something had been done, but in after years Gideon Welles, who was Secretary of the Navy throughout the war, felt impelled to write,[1] regarding the National naval work of 1861 : " But for some redeeming successes at Hatteras and Port Royal, *the whole belligerent operations would have been pronounced weak and imbecile failures.*" Nevertheless it was at the end of 1861 that the most impor-

[1] Galaxy, February, 1871.

tant naval expedition of the war—the expedition against New Orleans—was projected, and command of it was given to David G. Farragut.

Before entering into the details of this campaign, it is advisable to relate the story of the blockade of the Southern ports which had been established before the expedition was planned. For the work of the blockade served to reduce the Confederate forces precisely as a well managed siege reduces the garrison of a beleaguered fort. Moreover, a consideration of the blockade will help to an understanding of Farragut's great naval movement.

President Lincoln's first proclamation (April 19, 1861) covered all the Confederate states except Virginia and Texas, which had not then seceded. The second covered those two states, having been issued after they had left the Union. From the beginning of its existence, the American government had stood for the doctrine that a blockade to be legal must be actual; a sufficient force to stop commerce must be stationed off every blockaded port. This doctrine had been accepted by the maritime governments of the world, and they were quick to apply it to the United States. It was therefore necessary to station an adequate force off the Confederate ports.

To appreciate how great a task had thus been assumed, one must remember that there were one hundred and eighty-five harbor and river openings in the Confederate coast line. Nor was that all. In pleasant weather merchandise could be landed at almost any point on the whole long coast line of the Confederacy, and many cargoes were landed where no harbor existed. This coast line extended from Alexandria, Va., to the Mexican port of Matamoras which lies forty miles up the Rio Grande. The Continental line so measured was 3,549 miles long. The shore line including bays and sounds was 6,789 miles long, and if to this be added the beach lines of the various islands the total length to be guarded was 11,953 miles. The alongshore waters were almost everywhere too shallow for the warships of the day, but were admirably suited to shoal-draft vessels of various kinds— another fact which greatly contributed to the safety of all kinds of smugglers.

To guard this great stretch of coast line the National government had just three ships at the time the President's proclamation was issued. There were in commission twenty-six steamers and sixteen sailing ships, but all except three were scattered around the world where they could not be made available immediately. To add to the embarrassments of the situation no one at Washington, or at the ports of the North, for that matter, had any adequate idea of what force would be needed for the work. When the Secretary of the Navy held a consultation with leading ship merchants of New York in regard to the matter, one of them informed him that "at least thirty armed sailing ships" would be needed. The number actually employed in the work was above 600, of which nearly all were steamers, and even then the blockade runners were able to slip through with almost the regularity of packet lines to both Charleston, S. C., and Wilmington, N. C.

How the 600 blockading vessels were provided by purchase and building need not be told here. As to their crews the clippers, the coasters, the fishing smacks of the sea, and the boats of the Great Lakes supplied an able host. The increasing force of ships and men soon stopped short the employment of the great fleet of European merchantmen that had been running to the Southern ports, and it deprived the manufacturers of Europe of the supplies of cotton, tobacco and naval stores that they had been obtaining from the South, and could obtain nowhere else. The shock which the commerce of the world then received is not easily appreciated in these prosperous days of the twentieth century.

But the flow of commerce is much like the flow of a stream of water. Dam it and the flood will rise so high that it will find every crevice in the dam. The price of cotton fell in the Southern states and rose amazingly elsewhere. The prices of some goods that the South had been accustomed to buy rose amazingly there. A bale of 500 pounds of cotton when smuggled through the line, could be sold in Europe for a price that would pay all risks and expenses and yet yield a net profit of $250. The arms, ammunition, medicines and clothing needed by the Confederates, paid profits equally great on delivery.

A contraband trade at once sprang up, and those engaged in it found the ports at the Bermuda and Bahama Islands most convenient for their unlawful operations. The distance from the Bermudas to Wilmington was 674 miles; from the Bahamas to Charleston, 515 miles. Havana was within a day's run of a good landing place on the Gulf coast, and Matamoras, Mexico, was just across the Rio Grande from Texas. The trade that developed through the blockade lines was almost entirely in the hands of British merchants and sailors. The British merchants had been so badly beaten in their competition with Yankee clippers that they added to their love of great profits a strong dislike for the North. At first they loaded their goods into vessels of the cheapest classes, sail or steam, in order that the loss might be less in case of capture. The risk on the cargo was covered by insurance at a premium of twenty-five per cent. The risk on the lives of the crews did not worry the merchants, save only as the wages rose to unheard-of heights. The ships were loaded in England and sent thence under regular papers to Nassau in the Bahamas, to the Bermudas, or to some other foreign destination where they again cleared for whatever Confederate port had been decided on.

The touch at a neutral port was to give safety to ship and cargo thus far on the journey, but the courts soon held that if the ultimate destination of the goods was a Confederate port, they were contraband no matter where they were captured. In this emergency goods were ostensibly sold to merchants in the neutral ports, and on arrival were landed. They were then reshipped, of course, to the Confederate coast.

The papers of the ships showed that merchants on the barren coral reefs of the Atlantic were buying ship-loads of cannon, muskets, ammunition, blankets, medicines and other military supplies. Of course the papers were mere blinds. There was no real sale, and every person engaged in making the papers was guilty of perjury each time he swore to one of them. Every blockade runner found perjury as easy as drinking wine. But one should remember that the pilots were citizens of the Confederacy and must be excepted. The foreigners were an infamous gang, ready at any time to sacrifice honor and risk human life for gold ; the Confederate pilots were engaged in what they believed was a righteous cause—they were fighting or were risking their lives for principle, and were as honorable as the foreigners were degraded.

To show the runners' standard of honor one may quote from Thomas E. Taylor's account of how he got rid of the Will-o'-the-Wisp, a vessel that was "a constant source of delay and expenditure." [1] "After having her cobbled up with plenty of putty and paint," he opened "negotiations with some Jews with a view to her purchase." A trial trip was arranged, with "a sumptuous lunch" to precede it, and then with steam bottled up to the last gasp the vessel was driven over a measured mile. "She logged seventeen and a-half knots. The Jews were delighted, so was I ; the bargain was clinched." Thus the blockade runners would boast of how they swindled others even in the

[1] "Running the Blockade," p. 110.

books which they wrote publicly describing their adventures.

When preparing to run from a near-by neutral port, such as Nassau, in the Bahamas, the vessel was painted a dirty white, and the crew were required to wear clothes of a similar color. The hold was crammed full of cargo, and such quantities were stowed on deck that the men dreamed of capsizing. The crews received their money in advance. The captain got $5,000 for the trip, the mate and chief engineer $1,000 each, the second mate $500, the firemen eighty dollars and the deck hands forty dollars.

From the beginning, swift vessels were in demand. The famous yacht America was a blockade runner. But even the best of the sailers were soon found to be too slow, and then the swiftest steamers that the ship yards of England could turn out were built for the purpose. Feathering paddle wheels, that were as nearly noiseless as possible were in favor, but some double screw propellers were used. The frames and plating were of the lightest possible kinds. For fuel the runners bought the anthracite of New York (because it was smokeless), until the export of that kind of coal was forbidden.

On the passage from the Confederate to the neutral port the runner always avoided every sail and every pillar of smoke that was seen, and there was a bright lookout on each ship. Very rarely was such an outlaw caught on the high seas. The run was timed, of course, so that the vessel arrived off her port at night—at the dark hour just before day, if possible. The lone light always displayed on the flagship served the runner as well as a light-house, and on seeing it she ran around the end of the line of blockaders, or else steered boldly through under the guns of the big ship whose light had been detected. It was work to make the crews feel as if they were walking on air, but that was a part of the inducement to some of them. If seen, they had to run; it was piracy to resist. It was piracy for the crew of a captured vessel to rise upon the prize crew, but one of them did so with success, and the act was rewarded and applauded by the Liverpool Board of Trade.

An itemized account printed in Scharf's " History of the Confederate States Navy," shows that one blockade runner in one voyage incurred expenses amounting to $80,265, and received for freight $160,000 and for passengers $12,000, all in gold. The net profit of the round trip was $91,735, or about twice the cost of the steamer. The Banshee on her first trip in was paid $250 per ton in gold for her cargo of war materials. How high this was will be understood by landsmen when it is said that within a week of this writing (November, 1904), a cargo of coal sent from Baltimore around the Horn to San Francisco cost the owner but $5.50 per ton for freight. On her outward trip the Banshee carried 100 tons of tobacco at $350 per ton and 500 bales of cotton for which she received $250 each—all in gold.

Between November 1, and December 6, 1864, forty-three steamers sailed from Charleston and Wilmington, N. C., for various neutral ports.

Between November, 1861, and March, 1864, eighty-four different steamers were engaged in blockade running between Nassau and various Confederate ports, of which thirty-seven were captured, twelve were wrecked with all cargoes, eleven were lost with parts of their cargoes, and one foundered at sea. A record of 425 runs from Nassau shows sixty-two failures. Between March 1, 1864, and January 1, 1865, the Confederate authorities shipped out cotton that sold for $5,296,000. They imported in return, among other things, 1,507,000 pounds of lead, 1,933,000 pounds of saltpetre, and no less than 8,632,000 pounds of meat—a most significant matter. The importation of meat shows that the Confederacy was starving to death, while the other articles on the list are proof that the blockade deprived the Confederate armies of all war-making material. If the blockade runners did ply with almost packet-like regularity they were in all cases small vessels, and with all their activity and success they could not bring in more than a small part of the great amount of supplies needed by the Confederacy.

There was an element of bitter cruelty in the effect of the blockade ; many a woman and many a little child died for want of the medicines that it kept from them. On the other hand, by its severity the barrier of vessels shortened the period of war.

The work of the National fleets is soon described. Each important port like Charleston, S. C., Wilmington, N. C., and Mobile, Ala., was blockaded with a squadron—a sufficient number of vessels to form a line, each almost within hailing distance of another, from beach to beach. The line was established as close to the beach and the mouth of the harbor as the Confederate guns would permit. Charleston was further obstructed by sinking a line of old hulks in the channel. Once formed the blockade was maintained steadily. At small inlets one or two vessels only were stationed. At unimportant inlets, such as Sabine Pass, Texas, was supposed to be in those days, sailing ships took the place of steamers.

For the men the service was the most monotonous and wearisome known to the history of the navy. To lie, month after month, just out of reach of the shore guns, and do nothing but keep a bright lookout, was trying to the soul. It was all the worse when an ambitious officer learned how some brother officer had had opportunity to win renown elsewhere. Irritability followed on stagnation. Food spoiled. The water was never fresh. The heat of the stoke-hole varied from 110 to 150 degrees. Many of the vessels had been built by contractors who were thieves at heart, and they were constantly in need of repair. The wonder is not that runners slipped through, but that the blockade service was half as efficient as it was.

To show in a way how successful the blockaders were, it is only necessary to cite the fact that in all over 1,000 runners were captured. The Memphis paid her captors in prize money $510,914.07, and whole fleets of prizes yielded upward of $100,000 each.

As already noted, Port Royal was captured by the National forces late in 1861, for use as a supply station for the Atlantic blockading fleet. Earlier still the Federals had captured the forts at Hatteras Inlet and occupied the sounds within the long sand bar. While these advances gave shelter to the blockaders it was seen that in occupying a port it was closed in a way that no fleet off shore could close it. The best way to blockade a port was to occupy it; and it was after this fact had been clearly demonstrated that a young officer of the navy came to Washington with a plan for the capture of New Orleans.

CHAPTER XI

THE expedition under Farragut against New Orleans had a curious origin. In the course of the early naval operations of the Civil War, which Secretary of the Navy Gideon Welles afterward called "weak and imbecile failures," the war steamer Powhatan was placed under the command of Lieutenant D. D. Porter and ordered to Pensacola to assist in the relief of Fort Pickens and the maintenance of the National authority over Pensacola Bay. The Powhatan was still off Fort Pickens when, on May 12, 1861, the senior officer on the station received the President's proclamation blockading all Confederate ports, and on May 30th, Porter was ordered on blockade duty off the Southwest Pass of the Mississippi.

The hull of the Powhatan was rotten and it leaked. The boilers had been thinned by rust. The machinery was in need of many repairs. Her supplies were so far reduced that she had no rope from which to make braces, sheets or halliards ; no paint or whitewash with which to cover her well-worn planks—not even a nail or a board with which to repair a small boat. The condition of affairs while this ship lay at the mouth of the Southwest Pass was enough to make any officer thoughtful,

and more especially such a resourceful man as
Lieutenant Porter.

Accordingly when the Confederate cruiser Sumter
came down to the head of the Passes, preparing for
the dash that finally took her to sea, Porter observed
that she had for a tender an armed tug called the
Ivy, which frequently lay at the telegraph station. A crew of thirty-three picked men, under
Lieutenant Watson Smith, was therefore sent by
night to seize the telegraph station and capture the
Ivy. The station was occupied but the tug was
seen no more. A mail steamer came, however, and
landed at the opposite bank of the pass. Then
Smith with his men under the hatches of a little
schooner went drifting over to take her instead of
the Ivy, but the character of his force was discovered just one minute before he could arrive within
boarding distance, and the steamer escaped up the
river. Had she been taken, Porter intended to put
200 men on her, and use her to get alongside of
and capture the Sumter by boarding. With the
Sumter he purposed proceeding to New Orleans to
destroy whatever Confederate shipping he could
find there.

While Porter failed in carrying out this plan he
accomplished something of greater worth, for it was
then that he conceived the idea of an expedition
for the capture and permanent occupation of New
Orleans. In reporting his failure to Flag Officer
William Mervine (July 4, 1861), he said, "There is
a field here for something to do." And to Midshipman John R. Bartlett, of the warship Mississippi,

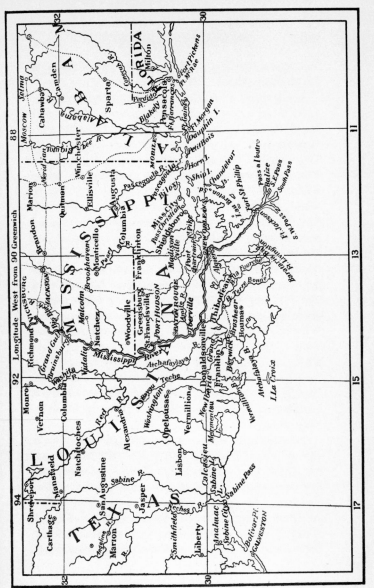

The Gulf States, Showing the Scene of Farragut's Engagements

who visited the Powhatan at this time, Porter said
that if he "had half a dozen good vessels he would
undertake to run by the forts and capture New Orleans."

Until August 13th, Porter contemplated this un-
worked field and then went in chase of the Sumter
that had, in the meantime, escaped through the
Pass a l' Outre. The chase was unsuccessful, and
finally the rotten and pitted Powhatan had to head for
New York, where she arrived on November 9, 1861.
While chasing the Sumter Porter had kept in mind
the "something" that might be done in the Mississippi, and on reaching New York he went to Washington to lay before the Navy Department a plan
he had evolved for the capture of New Orleans.
Fortunately, while waiting for an interview with
the secretary, Porter met Senator Hale, of New
Hampshire, and Senator Grimes, of Iowa, to whom
he unfolded his scheme. Their good judgment approved it, and they took him at once to the secretary who also thought favorably of it.

"In general and desultory conversation with military and naval men and others, the passage of the
forts and the capture of New Orleans was spoken of
as desirable, but not a practicable naval undertaking," wrote Secretary Welles, in connection with
the "weak and imbecile failures" of the first seven
months of the war. The hope of the Department
and of the President had been to open the Mississippi by means of an armed flotilla that had been
preparing in the upper waters of the river. The
tremendous strategical advantages to be obtained

by wholly dividing the Confederate States along the
line of the Mississippi, as the British strove to divide the colonies on the line of the Hudson, in the
War of the Revolution, were so manifest, and the
success so far attained in the upper river had been
so great, that neither the authorities at Washington
nor those at Richmond had given any considerable
attention to New Orleans as an object of attack by
a naval force from the Gulf.

But with the plans evolved by Commander Porter (who had meantime been promoted), Secretary
Welles was readily convinced that the scheme was
practicable. He was the more easily persuaded,
perhaps, because he was in a very comfortable state
of mind on the day the matter was presented to
him. It was the 12th of November, and the news
of the capture of Port Royal had reached the Department that morning. Moreover the scheme
fitted in well with what was then called the "ana-
conda" plan of "strangling the rebellion." With
the National armies on the north, the navy blockading all ports, and the whole Mississippi in the
power of the Union forces, the Confederacy, it was
thought, would soon be "strangled."

Porter's plans as first submitted to the Secretary
of the Navy were of course tentative and incom-
plete. Accordingly after the matter had been presented to the President, and his approval of the
general scheme was obtained, a conference was held
for the purpose of working out the details. At this
conference there were present, Secretary of the Navy
Welles, Assistant Secretary Fox, Commander D. D.

Porter and General George B. McClellan (then at the head of the army).

With Ship Island for a base (the Confederates had evacuated the island on September 17, 1861), it was proposed that a National fleet should enter the river, pass the two forts that guarded the river's lower reaches and anchor before the unwalled city of New Orleans. The army was to furnish 20,000 men to hold the place after the navy captured it.

So much was approved by McClellan, and Major-General Benjamin F. Butler was selected to command the troops. Then the conference considered whether the squadron should make a dash past the forts, leaving the Confederates in possession of them, or should first reduce them, and then go on to New Orleans. Assistant Secretary Fox, it appears, was in favor of the first method. To aid the squadron in passing up the river, Porter suggested that a mortar flotilla, carrying the most powerful mortars of the day, be sent along in order to bombard the forts while the squadron should be passing them. This seemed to be a good idea; McClellan agreed to it, and appointed Major J. G. Barnard to represent him in future conferences. Barnard, who, like McClellan, was an engineer and had a strong confidence in the power of forts, thought those on the Mississippi ought to be reduced, and Porter fell in with this suggestion quite naturally. Porter's rank was not high enough to entitle him to command the expedition, but he could take charge of the mortar flotilla, and if the forts were captured his own hope of winning favorable notice would be increased.

In the meantime, the choice of an officer to command the expedition had to be considered, and it was now that the work of a lifetime met its due reward. The records of the Navy Department did not show what Farragut had done, but all naval officers well knew his natural abilities, of his experience and the training he had given himself—a training that had long included daily physical exercise. It is asserted by officers who knew him that Farragut at this time often took a broom in his hands and then, while retaining hold of the handle, leaped up and passed his feet between his hands and over the handle, either forward or backward, or both in succession.

Because of the reputation that he had gained by prolonged hard work, Farragut was suggested by Porter for the command of the expedition. It is true that Farragut was Porter's adopted brother, but the latter's interest in the expedition was too great to allow any such family ties to influence him in the choice of a commander.

Soley in his " Admiral Porter " relates that Secretary Welles was not easily convinced of Farragut's abilities, and was particularly doubtful as to his loyalty. Porter himself says that Assistant Secretary Fox " named several but I opposed them all, and finally urged the appointment of Captain D. G. Farragut so strongly that I was sent to New York to communicate with him on the subject." For the man who had been hoping against hope during eight long months of idleness at Hastings, work was now at hand, though Secretary Welles considered the matter until the middle of December before ordering Farragut to Washington.

Farragut reached the National capital on December 21, 1861, and was taken to the home of Montgomery Blair, where Assistant Secretary of the Navy Fox (Blair's brother-in-law) laid the plans before him and asked his opinion of them.[1] "Farragut unhesitatingly answered that it would succeed." Fox then showed him a list of the vessels assigned to the squadron, and Farragut said, "he would engage to run by the forts and capture New Orleans with two-thirds the number."

This remark is significant, for while the plans contemplated the reduction of the forts, Farragut said "he would engage to run by" them and capture the city. But neither Fox nor Secretary Welles seems to have fully appreciated what was said. In fact, after the command was offered to Farragut, Mr. Fox thought that he showed rather too much enthusiasm over the prospect; for Farragut, with all his ability, courage, determination and persistence, was a boy at heart.

On January 9, 1862, he was formally "appointed to command the Western Gulf Blockading Squadron" and to hoist his flag on the Hartford, the geographical limits of the area under his authority extending from St. Andrew's Bay, Florida, to the Rio Grande; and including too all the coast of Mexico and Yucatan. Then on January 20th, he received instructions for the capture of New Orleans.

[1] United Service, January, 1881.

"When the Hartford is in all respects ready for sea," said the letter, "you will proceed to the Gulf of Mexico with all despatch. . . . There will be attached to your squadron a fleet of bomb vessels, and armed steamers enough to manage them, all under command of Commander D. D. Porter, who will be directed to report to you. As fast as these vessels are got ready they will be sent to Key West to await the arrival of all, and the commanding officers, who will be permitted to organize and practice with them at that port.

"When . . . you are completely ready, you will collect such vessels as can be spared from the blockade, and proceed up the Mississippi and *reduce the defenses which guard the approaches to* New Orleans, when you will appear off that city and take possession of it under the guns of your squadron, and hoist the American flag therein, keeping possession until the troops can be sent to you. If the Mississippi expedition from Cairo shall not have descended the river, you will take advantage of the panic to push a strong force up the river to take all their defenses in the rear.

"As you have expressed yourself perfectly satisfied with the force given to you, and as many more powerful vessels will be added before you can commence operations, the Department and the country will require of you success. . . . There are other operations, of minor importance, which will commend themselves to your judgment and skill, but which must not be allowed to interfere with the great object in view—the certain capture of the city of New Orleans." [1]

Rear Admiral W. S. Schley, who was a lieutenant on the Potomac, one of the Gulf Blockading Squadron, in relating his experience on blockade duty, says in his memoirs :

"It was surprising in those days to observe how accurately the men knew and gauged their officers. It often happened in the long hours of the watch that the deck officer would consult with the quartermasters, always old and experienced seamen, about the weather or matters touching the qualities of the ship, etc.   In one of these confidences James Barnes an old and competent quartermaster said that 'the men for'd had heard that the Commodore (McKean) was ill and had to be sent home.'   Almost immediately he volunteered the suggestion that if he had anything to do with it, he 'would pick out Cap'n Davy Farragut' to take his place. He added that if 'Davy Farragut' came down there, it wouldn't be long till the fur was flying."

The steam sloop of war Hartford (a ship with a single deck devoted to guns was a sloop of war) was one of the newest ships in the navy when Farragut took command of her.   Like the Constitution, that was made famous by good fighters in the War of 1812, the Hartford was built of wood at Boston. She was launched in 1858, and was one of four somewhat similar ships built at that time, the Richmond, the Pensacola and the Brooklyn being the other three.   A peculiarity of the hulls of these

[1] Sen. Ex. Doc. 56, 37th Cong. 2d Sess.

ships was seen in the location of the gundeck high above the water, so that they could fight well on the ocean even in a gale of wind. It is a matter of record that they were designed thus because the administration, as already noted, was expecting a war with England at the time they were authorized.[1]

The Hartford was 225 feet long, by 44 wide, and she drew 16.25 feet of water. She was ship rigged, with full sail power, and had engines that could drive her eight knots an hour in still water. With all sail set and steam up she could make eleven knots, provided wind and water were just right. Her battery was excellent for a ship of her size—perhaps the best in the world, for she carried twenty-two 9-inch Dahlgrens (smooth bore), in broadside, and two 20-pounder rifles. A third rifle was mounted later. At the suggestion of Farragut, rims of boiler iron were erected around the foretop and the maintop in such fashion as to protect the men stationed there from musket fire, and then brass howitzers were mounted within the rims.

The howitzers were mounted aloft in order that they might pour grape shot into the gun crews on top of the two Mississippi River forts—Jackson and St. Phillip. And it has been noted by various writ-

[1] From the "Memoir of John A. Dahlgren," p. 176, giving quotation from diary dated February 7, 1856 : "Saw Secretary at his house in the evening. Talked ordnance. He said the chances were war with England in a twelvemonth." See also discussion of a bill for "Additional sloops of war" in United States Senate, March 3, 1856.

ers that the position of the broadside guns on the Hartford, being well above the water line, brought them where they could fire directly into the gun ports of the forts.

Farragut sailed from Hampton Roads on February 2, 1862, bound for the Mississippi, via Key West, and he arrived at Ship Island, the rendezvous 100 miles north and east of the mouth of the river, on the twentieth, after having been detained somewhat at Key West by hard winds. At Ship Island he took formal command of his district. Thereafter the vessels of the expedition assembled rapidly, until the following were found gathered for the work : The flagship Hartford, Flag Officer David Glasgow Farragut, Fleet Captain Henry H. Bell, Commander Richard Wainwright ; Brooklyn, 24 guns, Captain T. T. Craven; Richmond, 26 guns, Commander James Alden ; Mississippi, 17 guns, Commander Melancton Smith; Pensacola, 24 guns, Captain H. W. Morris ; Cayuga, six guns, Lieutenant Commander N. B. Harrison ; Oneida, nine guns, Commander S. P. Lee ; Varuna, ten guns, Commander Charles S. Boggs ; Katahdin, four guns, Lieutenant Commander George H. Preble ; Kineo, four guns, Lieutenant Commander George M. Ransom ; Wissahickon, four guns, Lieutenant Commander A. N. Smith ; Winona, four guns, Lieutenant Commander E. T. Nichols ; Itaska, four guns, Lieutenant Commander C. H. B. Caldwell ; Pinola, four guns, Lieutenant Commander Pierce Crosby ; Kennebec, four guns, Lieutenant Commander John H. Russell ; Iroquois, nine guns, Commander John De Camp ;

Sciota, four guns, Lieutenant Commander Edward Donaldson.

The big frigate Colorado, 50 guns, Captain Theodorus Bailey, and the sailing sloop of war Portsmouth, Commander S. Swartwout, were also brought to the mouth of the river, but the Colorado drew so much water that she could not cross the bar, and the sailing vessel was, of course, unfit for the work of passing the fort. The Colorado's guns, however, were distributed among the other ships.

What may therefore be called the available naval squadron was made up of the seventeen steamers enumerated above, of which the Hartford, Pensacola, Brooklyn and Richmond were screw sloops of about 2,000 tons each, and armed with 9-inch guns in the broadside, besides pivot guns; the side-wheel steamer Mississippi was of 1,700 tons, armed with a 10-inch pivot, fifteen 8-inch smoothbores, and a small rifle; the Oneida, Varuna and Iroquois were screw corvettes, armed with guns that varied from a 32-pounder to an 11-inch smoothbore; and nine members of the squadron were 500-ton gunboats, each of which carried one 11-inch smoothbore, one 30-pounder rifle, and two smaller guns.

The mortar division, under Commander D. D. Porter, included twenty merchant schooners, each of which carried a 13-inch mortar. To these were attached three ferryboats, from New York harbor—the Clifton, Westfield and Jackson; the revenue steamer Harriet Lane; the gunboat Owasco, and a double-ender called the Miami. These steam vessels were armed with guns that varied from a

32-pounder to an 11-inch shell gun, the most useful of all the flotilla being the ferryboats, because they made excellent tugs, and good gun platforms.

When the expedition was planned, it was supposed that all the ships named could readily enter the Mississippi, but after the blockade had stopped the commerce of the river, the mud rapidly accumulated on the bar, and it was only by taking from the Pensacola and the Mississippi every pound of weight that could be spared—guns, spars, provisions and some coal—and then using every available steamer as a tug, that they were at last (April 7th), floated over the bar.

CHAPTER XII

CONFEDERATE DEFENSES AT NEW ORLEANS

WHILE the expedition to the mouth of the Mississippi was in hand, a most remarkable state of affairs prevailed among the Confederate forces in and about New Orleans. From the month of May, 1861, when the Federal government purchased three river steamers at Cincinnati, and began making armored gunboats of them in order to descend the river, the Confederate authorities had seen that an effort was to be put forth to sever the Confederate states on the line of the Mississippi, and capture and hold the important cities from Memphis to New Orleans. Every possible effort was made therefore to meet this attack from the north.

It had been foreseen by some Confederate officials, however, that an attack might come from the direction of the Gulf. On September 6, 1861, Major-General D. E. Twiggs, in reporting the lack of ammunition at New Orleans, said, "There is not in my mind the slightest doubt that this city will be attacked early in the autumn." General Twiggs was too infirm from age to prepare the city for such an emergency and, during the last week in September, he was succeeded by General Mansfield Lovell.

Lovell found that New Orleans had "been greatly

drained of arms, ammunition, medical stores, clothing and supplies for other points," and addressed a
remonstrance to the War Department at Richmond.
In the meantime he worked with energy to complete
a line of fortifications for the protection of the city.
This line included forts on all the bayous that cut
through the lowlands round about, and particular
attention was given to the two forts, Jackson and
St. Phillip, that stood on the banks of the great
river.   On October 25, 1861, he was able to report :

"We have now at the various forts and approaches 210 guns in position, and about 100 more
that we shall soon have in place, giving in all 310
guns of a calibre of 24-pounders and upward."

The forts on the navigable waters constituted an
outer line of works, of which St. Phillip and Jackson were of chief importance.   An inner line of
earthworks began on the river four miles below the
city (where General Jackson beat off the British),
and extended around the east and north as far as
Lake Pontchartrain.   This line was intended to repel a land attack such as the British had made at
the end of the War of 1812.   It was a matter of no
consequence to Farragut's fleet.   In fact, the only
work that had any effect whatever on the National forces was done at the two forts, St. Phillip
and Jackson, ninety miles below New Orleans.
As already noted, Fort Jackson was begun in
1824.   Both forts had been designed to prevent
any fleet, no matter how strong, from passing up
the river.   When taken in hand by the Confederate
authorities, on January 26, 1861, they were armed

with smooth-bore guns ranging from 24-pounders
to 42-pounders and there were a few short guns
(Columbiads) of still larger calibre. Of one hundred and nine guns in the two forts, fifty-six
were 24-pounders. To repel sailing ships of the
style of 1824, the forts were very good. But the development of steam warships carrying Dahlgren
guns of 9-inch and 11-inch calibre had changed
the conditions, and General Lovell, on November
19, 1861, wrote that he felt "satisfied that ships
under steam can pass forts in an open channel."

To strengthen the forts, therefore, Lovell obtained
three 10-inch Columbiads and a few mortars, and
borrowed two 7-inch rifles from the Confederate
navy—a most excellent weapon, designed by Lieutenant John M. Brooke and made of cast iron
strengthened by a double series of wrought bands
over the breech. However two days before the first
attack on the forts one of these excellent 7-inch
rifles was, by order of the Confederate War Department, sent north to Island No. 10.

Each of the forts had a sufficient number of men
in garrison—not far from seven hundred—but many
of them were foreigners. "The party that seized
the forts early in 1861 was a company of German
Yagers." There were also some Northern men in
the forts, most of whom had "volunteered, hoping
in that way to avoid suspicion." General Johnson
K. Duncan commanded Fort Jackson, and Colonel
Edward Higgins commanded Fort St. Phillip.
Higgins was a lieutenant of the old navy whom the
Confederate authorities had placed in the army.

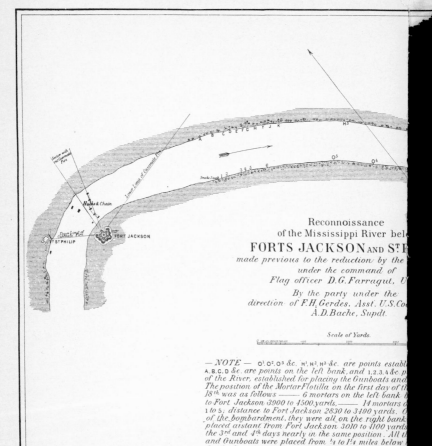

Reconnoissance
of the Mississippi River bel[ow]
FORTS JACKSON AND St. [PHILIP]
made previous to the reduction by the [fleet]
under the command of
Flag officer D.G.Farragut, U[.S.N.]

By the party under the
direction of F.H.Gerdes. Asst. U.S.Co[ast Survey]
A.D.Bache, Supdt.

Scale of Yards.

— *NOTE* — O¹,O²,O³ &c. H¹,H²,H³ &c. *are points establi[shed]*
A,B,C,D &c. *are points on the left bank, and* 1,2,3,4 &c. p[oints]
of the River, established for placing the Gunboats and [Mortars]
The position of the Mortar Flotilla on the first day of th[e]
18th was as follows ——— *6 mortars on the left bank* [between]
to Fort Jackson 3900 to 4500 yards, ——— *14 mortars o[n]*
1 to 5; *distance to Fort Jackson 2830 to 3400 yards. O[n the 2nd day]*
of the bombardment, they were all on the right bank [and were]
placed distant from Fort Jackson 3010 to 4100 yards
the 3rd and 4th days nearly in the same position. All th[e Sloops]
and Gunboats were placed from ¼ to 1¼ miles below [the forts.]
On the first day the small steam sloops and the Gunb[oats went up]
of the Smokestack, where they engaged the forts and th[e]

SALT WORKS.

ILIP

S. Fleet

V.

Survey

d by triangulation,
s on the right bank
rtarboats in position.
ombardment, April
ren c & s. distance
e right bank from
e 19th, the 2nd day
t 20 mortars were
hey remained on
rge armed steamers
owest mortar vessel
went up to abreast
my's steamers.

Of the ability and energy of these two commanding officers there was never the slightest doubt. But it appears that the Confederate War Department, urged by men of influence, had detailed for service under these commanders, some "very young and entirely inexperienced officers who were placed in command of others much their superiors in knowledge." The effect on the men of such an improper disposition of their commanders appeared later on.

Of more interest than the added guns was a raft or boom built across the river at Fort Jackson. Cypress logs, forty feet long and four feet or more in diameter were mortised in two places, on one side and near each end, so that they could be strung like beads, side by side, upon two long iron two and one-half inch ship cables that were stretched across the river. They were placed three feet apart on the cables, and held in place by iron staples. When this boom was completed, a man could run across the river on it, stepping from log to log. Then timbers (4x6 inch) were bolted down on top of the logs so that they were thoroughly well braced, and supported each other. In fact the boom might have been called a floating bridge, although it was more like a truss lying flat down on the water. On the left bank of the river the chains were secured to trees; on the Fort Jackson side to heavy anchors. To take the weight of the current from the end fastenings of the boom, some thirty anchors were placed in the bed of the river above, and chains were secured from them to the boom. Finally a flanking boom was stretched diagonally across the river above the main boom to shed or shunt the driftwood over toward Fort Jackson.

With the current against them it seemed certain that such a fleet as Farragut's, with its best ships able to travel only eight sea miles an hour in slack water, would be detained by this boom, under the short-range and direct fire of the forts, for a very long time. Because the boom was laid at right angles to the current from Fort Jackson, the fire of that fort would strike the ships at a range not to exceed five hundred yards. Fort St. Phillip stood further up stream, and on the easterly side of the river; but it was within easy range also and its fire would rake the attacking fleet fore and aft. To this raking fire such ships as those in Farragut's fleet could make no reply worthy of mention, because their guns were not mounted for effective service either ahead or astern.

As a part of the Confederate equipment for war, this raft would have been most pleasing to those statesmen who in Jefferson's day wished to build a similar obstacle across New York harbor (at the Narrows), in order to compel the nations of Europe to treat us justly. But in February (1862), the thing began to show signs of weakness. The water in the river rose, as usual, and the effect was, as always, to scour the bottom of the channel below the city, taking with it the anchors sunk in the channel to support the central parts of the raft. Then immense quantities of driftwood piled up on the raft in spite of the flanking boom, and a number of steamboats and skiffs were employed to haul the stuff clear. Eventually, the boom sagged down stream to the limit and then, in the first week of March, the chains snapped and a part of the structure was swept out to sea.

Into the gap thus created eight schooners, each of 200 tons burden, were anchored, and their masts were cut away and allowed to drag astern by their rigging in order to foul the wheels of any steamers that might come to displace them.   These schooners were connected, of course, by the heaviest chains that could be procured.   "This obstruction was, however, far inferior to the other," according to General Lovell, but it was the best that he could then make.   In addition the General "prepared and sent down forty or fifty fire rafts loaded with lightwood and mixed with cotton, rosin and tar oil, which were placed above and below the new obstruction," ready to be sent against Farragut's ships.   He "also sent to Memphis and procured the services of Mr. J. B. Cook, who had much experience with torpedoes, and endeavored to have them placed in the river," but the great depth (130 feet), and the rapid current "rendered such attempts nugatory." [1]

More interesting and more important than the forts and obstructions prepared to check the progress of the National forces were the ships designed for the defense of New Orleans.   The fact is that all the naval work of the Confederacy was a most remarkable combination of strength and weakness. Many officers from the old navy joined their for-

[1] Testimony of General Lovell.

tunes with the Secessionists, and they were in themselves a mighty host. But the rulers at Richmond could find no use afloat for many of these skilled seamen, and gave them commissions in the Confederate army, while those that were employed in service suited to their training usually received no higher rank than they had held in the old navy.

As if to emphasize a prevailing distrust of naval men a river defense fleet was organized by the act of the Confederate Congress of January 9, 1862. "The force intended is a peculiar one," wrote the Confederate Secretary of War Benjamin, on January 19th. "It is not to be a part of the navy . . . and will be composed of the steamboat men of the western waters."

For this fleet, towboats were purchased and were strengthened with timbers and iron stretched around the bows till they could be used as rams, "the mode of attack devised by the enterprising captains" who pushed the scheme through. These captains openly boasted that they were going to show the navy men how to fight. Their valor and dash were to astonish the men trained to war afloat ; and that sort of talk was never discouraged (or resented, so far as I can learn), by any one.

In short, from Jefferson Davis, with his West Point training, down through the Confederate Congressmen and the State authorities, to the backwoods politicians, there was scarcely a man who was not infected with that old-time prejudice against the navy which had roiled John Randolph of Virginia, and D. R. Williams of South Carolina. The

army was to accomplish everything, and the one
characteristic needed in that army was valor.

Nevertheless, some of the Confederates believed
in a navy and a few men found the opportunity to
perform useful service. They turned the frigate
Merrimac into the ironclad Virginia, and made
first-class guns for her. They built the ironclad
Albemarle in a corn-field on the Roanoke, with no
better tools than those afforded by a blacksmith's
shop, and they gathered an engine for her from the
scrap pile at the Tredegar Iron Works. They built
the ironclad Tennessee at Mobile, and the Arkansas
in the backwoods of the Mississippi Valley. Everywhere green timber was used for the hulls, railroad
iron for armor plate and scrap iron for machinery.
In courage, energy and enterprise these men of the
South were unsurpassed by any known to history,
but they were handicapped beyond hope.

At New Orleans the naval work was of particular
interest. A commission of three officers from the
old navy undertook the construction of ten gunboats, by utilizing such hulls as they could find
afloat, and by building others. Two steamers of
the Havana line were purchased, one of which became famous as a commerce destroyer, though commerce destroyers have rarely had any influence
worthy of mention in deciding a war. The other
steamer became the gunboat McRae, and she had a
part in the defense of New Orleans. A little screw
vessel, the Florida, was put in service on the lakes.
A steamer called the Yankee was fitted out as the
Jackson.

By the act of May 21, 1861, the Confederate Congress authorized privateers, offering to pay such boats twenty per cent. of the value of any Union vessel they might destroy. Under this act citizens of New Orleans bought the Boston-built tug Enoch Train (a vessel 128 feet long, 26 feet wide and 12.5 feet deep), which they turned into an iron-clad ram. Her bow was filled in solid with timbers for twenty feet. Her light carpenter work was removed, and a rounding deck of twelve-inch timbers was laid over her. This deck was covered with one and a-half inch bar iron. A port for a single gun pointing forward (a 24-pounder carronade according to her captain), was opened in this deck and there was a tiny hatch through which men and supplies entered. As she floated she looked something like a modern submarine when awash. She was named the Manassas, and was commanded by an officer of the old navy, Lieutenant A. F. Warley.

Then several river boats were purchased, and after placing compressed bales of cotton in them to give some protection to their machinery, they were armed with light guns. These vessels could not be classed even as gunboats. They were of such light construction that they were among the frailest gun platforms ever used in actual war. That they were used at all shows the activity of the naval men, who believed that a gun afloat on a raft was better than no gun at all, and were bound to see that every possible shot would be available when the time of need came.

Two more sea-going steamers were, later, converted into warships. They were high out of water, and had paddle wheels with walking beams that towered still higher. One, named the Governor Moore, and commanded by Beverly Kennon, who had been a lieutenant in the old navy, carried two rifled 32-pounders. The other, called the General Quitman, Captain Grant, carried two 32-pounder smoothbores. The Moore, because it was commanded by a trained naval officer, saw effective service.

This was not all. Because the Federal authorities were building a fleet of ironclads on the upper river with which to descend to the Gulf, the Confederates laid down other vessels of which two must be mentioned here—the ironclad floating batteries, Louisiana and Mississippi.

The foundation, so to speak, of the Louisiana was a floating dry dock that had been used in repairing vessels in the New Orleans trade. This hulk was rebuilt, beginning on October 15, 1861, into a scow, 270 feet long. Amidships a superstructure was erected with its sides and ends inclined at an angle of forty-five degrees. Its walls were heavy timbers and these were covered with two layers of T-shaped railroad iron. The lower layer of iron was bolted to the timbers, and then the other rails were inverted and driven in between the lower rails, thus forming what was almost a solid plate of armor. For motive power there were two paddle wheels placed one before the other in two wells within the hull, and two screws, placed aft, one on each side.

Sixteen guns, of which two were 7-inch rifles, seven were 6-inch rifles, and the others were 8-inch and 9-inch smoothbores, were mounted within the casement.

The Mississippi was the invention of Mr. Nelson Tift, of Florida, who had had no experience in ship building, and the story of this vessel better than any other story of the war, unless it be that of the Louisiana, portrays the innate weakness of the Confederacy. This is shown first by the fact that she originated with a planter who knew nothing about naval affairs. Further than that, she was designed strictly as a river defense craft. There was no thought of building a ship that could steam away to carry on an aggressive war in New York or Boston harbor.[1] But perhaps the most important feature of the weakness of the Confederacy that she exhibited was found in the fact that she was designed to meet an emergency in labor conditions, prevailing not only at New Orleans, but throughout the slave states. Lacking ship carpenters, the plans of the Mississippi called only for straight timbers and planks. There was not a knee or a crooked timber in her. After the work of building was begun in September, 1861, every kind of a carpenter in the region was employed on her, and even then, the contractors failed to get as many mechanics as they needed, being compelled at last to procure between 200 and 300 slaves from the plantations.

[1] Judah P. Benjamin, while serving as the Confederate Secretary of War, wrote a letter in which he showed clearly that he appreciated the value of aggressive warfare.

At the North many a shipshape vessel was built and put in service within ninety days, but at New Orleans the work on the great scow dragged, the work on her machinery dragged still more, and she never was completed. The builders of the Mississippi failed, and the cause for which they fought failed in good part because of a woeful lack of skilled, intelligent laborers. And the South lacked intelligent laborers because of the contempt in which mechanics had always been held by owners of slaves. It was the curse of slavery that weighed down and overcame the splendid energies of the leaders who were striving to defend New Orleans.

This is a memorable matter. The most important benefit we have derived from the creation of our magnificent modern navy is found in the development of men able to design, build and handle such ships. The ships, after a few years, will be out of date and worthless, but the men have been trained ready for the construction of others vastly superior, in quality and force. Moreover, the influence of this trained host has been, and will be, by no means confined to the navy : for the ship, one may say, is nothing ; the development of the man is everything.

The Mississippi was a scow. Her flat bottom was 22 inches thick, " with numerous thick keelsons to brace it," and the walls were two feet thick. Bottom and walls were bolted through and through, in the most substantial manner. There were, as has been said, no frames, crooks or knees. She was simply a great box, 260 feet long, 58 feet broad and

15 feet deep. Above this the plans called for an ironclad casemate with the best guns available. Within the machinery was planned for three screws with sufficient power to drive her eleven knots an hour.

Of the Mississippi, Commander D. D. Porter wrote that if she had been "finished and had succeeded in getting to sea, the whole American navy would have been destroyed." This report was made after hearing the vessel described by those who were not able to give an intelligible account of her. Since she was designed by men ignorant of naval architecture, and built by men who were not trained mechanics, there is no reason for supposing that her machinery would have proved more effective than that of the Louisiana. At best, the two ironclads could have been useful only as floating batteries.

But because good guns had been provided for them, and because they were ironclad, they might have proved powerful enough, even though immovable, when well placed at the forts, to guard the barrier raft. When Farragut arrived at the mouth of the Mississippi with a wooden-walled fleet, these two ironclads were nearing completion—men were working on them day and night—and there was need of prompt action if he were to capture New Orleans.

CHAPTER XIII

PREPARATIONS FOR PASSING THE FORTS

THE work of getting the larger ships of Farragut's fleet into the mouth of the Mississippi had taken two weeks, and more, of precious time. For a fortnight was consumed on the bar, while they were being stripped of every weight that could be spared before they were dragged through the mud and then these weights had to be replaced—a work that required time also. That all this was done without a fight with the Confederates was due to the fact that the authorities at Richmond could see no danger to New Orleans save in the gunboats (called tin-clads because of their thin armor), that were afloat and building on the upper river. Instead of attacking Farragut the Richmond authorities ordered Commodore George N. Hollins to go to Memphis, and take with him nearly every available fighting ship afloat in the lower river. Orders were also issued to send the Louisiana north as soon as she could be made ready. As it appears Hollins went but left a considerable fleet behind him, in spite of the instructions of his superiors.

Hollins had made a dash at the National squadron off the Southwest Pass before Farragut's arrival (it was at 3:45 A. M., October 12, 1861), and had driven the blockading vessels (three good fighting

ships, including the Richmond) helter-skelter from
the head of the Passes down to and across the bar.
The dash on the part of Hollins was as brilliant as
the flight of the Federal ships was disgraceful ; and
if he could have had his way, Farragut would have
been obliged to fight at the bar.   Even after reaching Memphis, Hollins begged for permission to return to New Orleans and attack the National ships
which were then within the river, but he was not
allowed to do so.   Farragut's fleet caused no anxiety
in Richmond during the earlier days of April, 1862.

Accordingly the preparation of his fleet for the
work that lay before it was begun under general orders of which the following extracts ought to be
preserved :

Send down the topgallant masts.   Rig in the flying jib-boom, and land all the spars and rigging except what are necessary for the three topsails, foresail, jib and spanker.   .   .   .   Bring all the rigging into the bowsprit so that there shall be nothing in the range of the direct fire ahead.

Make arrangements, if possible, to mount one or
two guns on the poop and topgallant forecastle ; in
other words be prepared to use as many guns as
possible ahead and astern   .   .   .   bearing in mind
that you will always have to ride head to the current, and only avail yourself of the sheer of the
helm to point a broadside gun more than three
points forward of the beam.

Have a kedge in the mizzen chains (or any convenient place) on the quarter with a hawser bent
and leading through the stern chock, ready for any
emergency ; also grapnels in the boats, ready to
hook on to and tow off fire ships.   Trim your vessel a few inches by the head, so that if she touches

the bottom she will not swing head down the river. Put your boat howitzers in the foremain tops, on the boat carriages, and secure them for firing abeam, etc. Should any injury occur to the machinery, making it necessary to drop down the river, you will back and fill down under sail, or you can drop your anchor and drift down, but in no case attempt to turn the ship's head down stream.

No vessel must withdraw from battle under any circumstances, without the consent of the flag officer. You will see that force and other pumps and engine hose are in good order, and men stationed by them, and your men will be drilled to the extinguishing of fire. Have many tubs of water about the decks, both for the purpose of extinguishing fire and for drinking.

You will be careful to have lanyards on the lever of the screw so as to secure the gun at the proper elevation, and prevent it from running down at each fire. I wish you to understand that the day is at hand when you will be called upon to meet the enemy in the worst form of our profession. . . . Hot and cold shot will, no doubt, be freely dealt to us, and there must be stout hearts and quick hands to extinguish the one and stop the holes of the other.

The ingenuity of all the officers of the fleet was taxed to supplement these orders from the flag officer. Chief Engineer John W. Moore suggested that the chain cables be secured along the sides of each ship to serve as armor to protect the machinery and waterline, and the suggestion was adopted by all of them. He also proposed daubing the vessels over with mud to render them less easily visible at night, and this was done.

Some captains whitewashed the decks and inner

walls of their ships so that the men could better see
to do their work in a night battle.   Bags of coal, of
ashes, of sand, and even the clothes bags and the
hammocks of the crews, were piled around the machinery to stop shot, while nets made of ropes were
stretched where they would catch splinters that the
shot from the forts was sure to knock from the sides
of the ships.   While these preparations were in
hand, Farragut visited every ship to see how the
work was being done and to make sure that his
orders were fully understood.

In the meantime the mortar schooners were put
in place.   Mr. A. F. Gerdes with a party of men
from the coast survey joined the expedition.   He
explored and measured the banks of the river in
order to determine the best location for the mortar
fleet, and the distance from that location to Fort
Jackson.   It was decided to concentrate the mortar
fire on Jackson because it was the stronger, and
what was of more importance, because it directly
guarded the raft that was expected to stop Farragut's ships.

The points chosen for the mortar boats varied
between 2,850 and 3,680 yards from Fort Jackson.
At first one division of them was placed on the east
bank of the river, but the forts soon got the range,
and drove them to the west bank where all were
hidden behind a tall growth of trees, the conceal-
ment being made more effective by lashing tree
limbs to the masts.

At ten o'clock on the morning of April 18, 1862,
the mortar fleet fired the first shot at Fort Jackson.

It had been well aimed and was dropping into the fort when the burning fuse reached the powder, whereupon it exploded in the air. As this shell appeared the crew of the little Confederate ram Manassas (she had been sold to the Confederate navy), that was lying at the Fort Jackson dock, cast off her lines, and at once steamed up and across the river to tie up above St. Phillip. She had barely left her berth at Fort Jackson dock when another shell came, and it fell into the water precisely where she had been lying.

The work of this second shell was in a way like that of the whole mortar flotilla. The mortar fire almost but not quite accomplished something of importance. More than forty shells on the average were thrown at the fort every hour thereafter for a week (nearly 6,000 shells were fired in all), but Lieutenant Godfrey Weitzel, of the United States Engineers, reported on May 5, 1862 :

"To an inexperienced eye it seems as if this work [Fort Jackson] were badly cut up. It is as strong to-day as when the first shell was fired at it."

Because of what he had seen of the French mortar fire at Vera Cruz, years before, Farragut had no confidence in the result of that kind of an attack upon Fort Jackson. The plan having been made before the command of the expedition was offered him, he accepted it without protest. He was so well pleased to be at the head of any squadron that he was not disposed to quarrel about details. But to lie idle in the river while the mortars spouted useless shells at the fort "sorely tried" his patience, as he said afterward.

Porter, in his report of April 30th, admits that "after bombarding the fort for three days I began to despair of taking it, and, indeed, began to lose my confidence in mortars, but a deserter presented himself from Fort Jackson and gave me such an account of the havoc made by our mortar practice that . . . we went to work with renewed vigor."

Farragut, however, made a more accurate esti-mate of the value of the deserter's story. He had already determined to drive his fleet up the river without waiting for the reduction of Fort Jackson and he called his captains to the flagship on the day the deserter came, in order that they might give their opinions "as to the best manner of pass-ing the forts."

His instructions from the Department said, "You will proceed up the Mississippi and *reduce the de-fenses* which guard the approaches to New Orleans," but Farragut was determined to ignore that part of his orders,—a most important fact. He was willing to assume that responsibility *in order to force the fighting*. It is a noteworthy circumstance in the history of our navy that officers have been censured for adhering too closely to orders that kept them out of a battle, but never has one been rebuked for disobeying orders, that he might force the fighting.

All of the captains except Porter attended the council. He was looking after the work of his flo-tilla, as he had been doing, day and night, since his arrival on the river, but Captain Alden, of the Richmond, brought to the council a memorandum written by Porter some time (Soley in his life of Porter says at least a month) before. The captains had assembled, and "the flag officer then proceeded to state the reason why the officers had been summoned, which was to give his plan for passing the forts," says Lieutenant J. M. Wainwright in a letter to Commander Porter, dated June 1, 1862. "The prevailing opinion seemed to be averse to making the attempt to pass the forts at that time ; that it was premature ; that the forts had not yet been sufficiently reduced by the fire of the mortar vessels, and that the risk of the loss of too many vessels was too great to be run." Then Alden read Porter's memorandum which was in part :

"There are two methods of attack : one is for the vessels to run the gauntlet of the batteries by night, or in a fog ; the other to attack the forts by laying the big ships close alongside of them. . . . The large ships should anchor, . . . the smaller vessels to keep under way and be constantly moving about, some to get above, and open a cross fire ; the mortars to keep up a rapid and continuous fire and to move up to shorter range.

"The objections to running by the forts are these : It is not likely that any intelligent enemy would fail to place chain across above forts, and raise such batteries as would protect them against our ships. Did we run the forts we should leave an enemy in our rear, and the mortar vessels would have to be left behind. We could not return to bring them without going through a heavy and destructive fire. If the forts are run, part of the

mortars should be towed along, which would render
the progress of the vessels slow, against the strong
current at that point.   If the forts are first captured, the moral effect would be to close the batteries on the river and open the way to New Orleans;
whereas, if we don't succeed in taking them we will
have to fight our way up the river.   Once having
possession of the forts, New Orleans would be her-
metically sealed, and we can repair damages and go
up on our own terms.

"Nature points out the English Turn as the position to be strongly fortified, and it is there that the
enemy will most likely make his strongest stand.

"If the ships can get by the forts, *and there are
no obstructions above, then* the plan should be to
push on to New Orleans every ship that can get up
there, taking up as many of the mortar fleet as can
be rapidly towed.   An accurate reconnoissance
should be made, and every kind of attainable information provided before any movement is made.

"Nothing has been said about a combined attack
of army and navy.   Such a thing is not only practicable, but if time permitted should be adopted."

It is entirely fair to suppose that this document
was read with Porter's knowledge and consent;
one is almost driven to the belief that it was done
at his request.   And yet Farragut told the captains
(according to Wainwright), that "Captain Porter
had submitted a plan of operations, which em-
braced ideas similar to his own, and with which he
entirely agreed."   To this Farragut added the
further statement, later on during the discussion,
that "Captain Porter urged very strongly the attempt being made [to take the fleet past the forts],
not only on the grounds of its probable success,"

but because the mortar schooner fire must soon slack away for a variety of reasons.

Without trying to solve the mystery of the presence of the Porter memorandum in the hands of Captain Alden the document itself has been given here in part because it certainly represented the views of Alden himself, Captain T. T. Craven and "the prevailing opinion" of those present, and it therefore by contrast brings out clearly the distinguishing merits of Farragut's ideas.[1]

After hearing the opinions of his captains the flag officer delivered his own opinion *in the form of a general order* "immediately after the council." That is to say, he had determined what to do before he called the council and had desired to learn only whether the captains had any ideas that would improve the details of his plan. In writing the general order he gave some consideration to the opposition as it had been embodied in Porter's memorandum. Farragut wrote:

"The flag officer . . . is of the opinion that whatever is to be done will have to be done quickly. . . . He has always entertained the same opinions which are expressed by Commander Porter: that is, that there are three modes of attack, and the question is, which is the one to be adopted? His own opinion is that a combination of two should be made, viz., the forts should be run, and when a force is once above the forts to protect the troops, they [the troops] should be landed at quarantine

[1] See Vol. 18, Official Records, Union and Confederate Navies, p. 131, *et seq.*

from the Gulf side by bringing them through the bayou, and then our forces should *move up the river*, mutually aiding each other.

"When, in the opinion of the flag officer the propitious time has arrived, the signal will be made to weigh, and advance to the conflict. If, in his opinion, at the time of arriving at the respective positions of the different divisions of the fleet, we have the advantage, he will make the signal for close action, and abide the result—conquer or be conquered —drop anchor or keep under way, as in his opinion is best."

To this he added the statement that unless the signal for close action was given, the ships, after passing Fort St. Phillip, were to be formed in "the first order of sailing" and then "proceed up the river in accordance with the original opinion expressed."

It appears, therefore, that while Farragut supposed he might think best to close up and attack the forts with a view of reducing them, he intended to run by them first of all. And then, unless obliged by further obstructions to seek the aid of the troops, he intended to "proceed up the river." The fact that he would be leaving two strong fortifications behind him, as Porter's memorandum had pointed out, was not even mentioned in the general order, except indirectly. When Farragut said that troops from the army transports could be conveyed to the river bank "from the Gulf side by bringing them through the bayou," he answered every objection that had been, or could be, made to the act of leaving "an enemy in our rear." For if troops could come to the ships "through the bayou," sufficient supplies could come to them also by the same route. The forts would become a matter of no pressing importance to the ships. The route to the city of New Orleans would be open, or very easily opened.

But Farragut saw a further and very important reason for making a dash past the forts. As he said to his council of captains, the forts would be cut off from every source of supplies, once the ships were in the river above them. It would then be only a question of time when they would be starved into surrendering, if they did not yield at once from other considerations. The strategy of the case seemed so simple to Farragut that he did not argue the matter, but merely stated it to his captains. And, as said, he did not even mention it directly in his general orders. Further than that, it seemed to him unnecessary to attempt "an accurate reconnoissance" of the river between the forts and the city, as Porter had suggested.

After the ships were prepared for battle one more preliminary bit of work had to be taken in hand, and that was the breaking of the boom across the river. Captain Henry H. Bell, chief of staff, had been sent with the steamers Kennebec and Wissahickon to examine that construction soon after Farragut arrived in the river. He reported that "the obstructions seem formidable," and described the boom as he saw it. The British frigate Mersey, Captain Preedy, and a French warship, had come into the river meantime. The captains of these vessels were representatives of the elements in England and France that were anxious to see the American Union destroyed, and had come there to do everything possible in a neutral way to obstruct the work of Farragut. Both captains had gone up to examine the barrier raft, and on returning, with an assumed air of candor had assured every officer of Farragut's fleet who would listen to them that the raft was perfectly impassable. But Farragut, who remembered how a British captain had deliberately deceived our officers with a similar story when they were before Vera Cruz, during our war with Mexico, was unaffected by their reports, or if influenced at all by them was only the more determined to make the dash.

Lieutenant C. H. B. Caldwell, commanding the Itaska, had previously volunteered to run up to the boom, if supported by another vessel, and break through it. Under the supervision of Fleet Captain Henry H. Bell, Caldwell was now ordered to do the work, and the Pinola, Lieutenant Pierce Crosby commanding, was sent along to assist.

At ten o'clock, on the night of the 20th, the two vessels started on their perilous mission. Foreseeing that they would be discovered, and subjected to the concentrated fire of all the guns in the forts, the mortar fleet was set at work firing shells as rapidly as possible. This fire was of some use, but a brisk cannonade was opened from the forts as the two vessels reached the raft. In spite of that fact both of them attacked it. An effort to break the chain with a torpedo failed because the electric wires

broke. A little later the Itaska, after tearing the
rail from one hulk in a vain effort to drag it from
the raft, boarded the schooner at the east end of the
line of eight dismantled boats.   This hulk was cast
loose from the chain, but as the Itaska was dragging
it from the raft she and her tow were carried hard
aground.   Two hawsers were broken by the Pinola,
in trying to get the Itaska off the mud, but a third
one held and pulled her clear.

As the Itaska floated free, her bow was pointed
up the river and Caldwell saw that by the removal
of the hulk an opening had been made in the raft
wide enough for his little gunboat to pass through.
Thereupon he drove her ahead, and well up above
the raft.   Then he turned around, gave her a full
head of steam, and with the force of the current to
aid him, he struck the chain between the third and
fourth hulks.   The curved stem of the gunboat rose
up over the chain until her bow was more than
three feet out of the water.   Then the chain broke
and the schooner hulks of the raft, with two exceptions—the second and last—were left unsupported.
The third, fourth, fifth and sixth swung around
with the current and drifted down stream, leaving
an ample space for Farragut's fleet to pass through.
It was one of the most brilliant exploits of the war.

Curiously enough, while this work, which required several hours, was in hand, there were no less
than thirteen Confederate vessels at or near Fort St.
Phillip, including the little ironclad ram Manassas,
six of the much-vaunted River Defense Fleet rams,
and the big Louisiana.   But not one of these ves-

sels made the least movement to interfere with the attack on the raft—a fact that has never been explained. Commodore Mitchell commanding the Confederate flotilla had asked the River Defense Fleet to guard the raft, but the captains had declined to do so, and there the matter rested. Nor was any effort made to repair the raft after it was broken.

CHAPTER XIV

WITH the boom broken Farragut was free to put his ships in lines for the passage up the river. He had previously arranged the fleet in two divisions, and at his own earnest request, Captain Theodorus Bailey of the Colorado, had received command of one of them. Under this plan the two were to advance side by side, with Bailey's toward the east bank. Farragut intended to attack Fort Jackson with his own division while the other was to pass on up and engage Fort St. Phillip. But after a further consideration of the width of the opening in the boom, and the probability that the two lines of ships would foul each other in passing the opening, Farragut decided to make three divisions of his fleet.

To Bailey, who was ordered to attack Fort St. Phillip, he gave the Cayuga, Pensacola, Mississippi, Oneida, Varuna, Katahdin, Kineo and Wissahickon. For himself and the attack on Fort Jackson, he added the Brooklyn and the Richmond to the Hartford. Then for a third division to support either of the others as occasion might warrant, he gave to Fleet Captain Bell the Sciota, Iroquois, Kennebec, Pinola, Itaska and Winona. Bailey's division was allowed to lead the others, when the line was formed, because he was to attack the fort

situated higher up the stream, and it was desirable
that his ships should be firing on it at the moment
Farragut opened on Fort Jackson.   And it may be
noted here that the Cayuga, a gunboat, led Bailey's
division because Bailey, at the invitation of her
captain, Lieutenant N. B. Harrison, had hoisted his
flag on her.   Captain Henry W. Morris of the big
Pensacola, the natural leader, did not wish any
divisional officer on board his ship to take from
him the glory that she might earn ; but it seemed
an honor to Captain Harrison to have his little gunboat selected to lead the battle line, and he eagerly
sought it.

The early morning of April 23d was first chosen
for the movement, but the carpenter's crew from
each of two of the big vessels was absent.   The
captains preferred to wait for their return, and the
start, though against Farragut's desire, was postponed one day.   As the moon would not rise until
3:30 o'clock on the morning of the 24th, Farragut
determined to pass the forts—to "conquer or be
conquered "—before that hour.   During the afternoon of the 23d he visited every ship of his fleet,
seeing for himself that each was ready, and that
her commander fully understood the orders.   Porter,
who had come to admit that it was useless to wait
longer for a reduction of the forts, was ordered to
fire with the mortars with the utmost rapidity possible while the fleet was passing, and further than
that, to take his little squadron of mortar-guarding
steamers up within range and do what he could
with their guns to check the fire of Fort Jackson.

The sailing ship Portsmouth, Captain Swartwout, was ordered to this duty also. As night came on, Caldwell, at his own request, was sent up to the boom with the Itaska to see that the way was still open—a task that curiously enough he performed unmolested.

Finally at two o'clock in the morning two red lights, one above the other, were hoisted on the Hartford and a moment later was heard the shrill piping of the boatswains' whistles calling all hands on every ship to get up anchor. The clank of the capstan pawls followed promptly, as the men hove up the anchors, but the mud of the river was tenacious, and a long time—most trying to the commanding officer—passed before all the ships were afloat in their places. At last, however, all were found in order, and the fleet—the mightiest the Nation had ever assembled—steamed with throbbing engines up to the forts. Not a light was displayed, and so little noise was made on the ships that the men, standing at their guns, heard the calls of birds and frogs along the shore.

At 3:30 o'clock (later than was intended) the little Cayuga, a steamer no longer than a harbor lighter, led the way unmolested through the opening in the barrier boom. But as the next ship of the long line behind her, dimly seen in the starlight, passed the barrier a gun on shore was fired. At that signal every cannon in both forts that would bear, began its blazing work, the roar was answered by the boom of the mortars in the flotilla, the air was filled with the curving light of the flying shells, the black walls of the ships began to belch the sheeting flames of their broadside guns, the Porter flotilla of steamers joined in, and then raft after raft, piled high with blazing pine and tar, was cast loose from the river banks above and towed out by the Confederates to meet the fleet. One of the most impressive pictures of fire the world has ever seen was witnessed when Farragut's fleet came to the Confederate forts that guarded the Mississippi.

Peering ahead by the light of the flames around him, Lieutenant George H. Perkins, who was navigating the Cayuga, saw that the guns of Fort St. Phillip were aimed to throw their shot into the middle of the river, whereupon he steered his little ship close under the walls of the fort and passed on. The hull of the vessel "was but little damaged," and because she was low in the water her guns had no noticeable effect upon the fort.

Then came the Pensacola and the Mississippi. Both steamed slowly while their crews, with the energy of men who fight for life, worked their guns, sheeting the air with lurid flames and dusting the walls and ports of the fort with iron hail. So close to the fort were these ships that, at times, crew and garrison saw each other clearly and cursed each other heartily. The fire of the ships proved so deadly that the men in the fort, in spite of their officers, fled to cover. Not until they had been engaged for more than an hour did these ships pass wholly out of range of St. Phillip.

For the ships of the first division the passage up

Order of the Fleet in passing up to the attack of
Forts Jackson and St. Philip, April 24, 1862.

First Division
leading under command
of Capt. Theodorus Bailey.

0 _ Cayuga, Lt. Com'd'r Harrison, Flag Gun Boat.

0 _ Pensacola, Capt. H. W. Morris.

0 _ Mississippi, " M. Smith.

0 _ Oneida, Com'd'r S. P. Lee.

0 _ Varuna, " C. S. Boggs.

0 _ Katahdin, Lt. Com. G. H. Preble.

0 _ Kineo, " " Ransom.

0 _ Wissahickon " A. N. Smith.

Centre Division, Admiral Farragut.

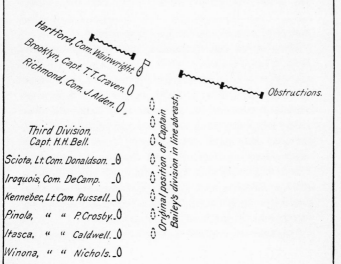

Hartford, Com. Wainwright.
Brooklyn, Capt. T. T. Craven. 0
Richmond, Com. J. Alden. 0

Obstructions.

Original position of Captain
Bailey's division in line abreast.

Third Division,
Capt. H. H. Bell.

Sciota, Lt. Com. Donaldson. _0

Iroquois, Com. De Camp. _0

Kennebec, Lt. Com. Russell. _0

Pinola, " " P. Crosby. 0

Itasca, " " Caldwell. _0

Winona, " " Nichols. _0

to Fort St. Phillip was a simple matter. They were through the barrier raft and away before the Confederates got fairly to work. But for Farragut and the Hartford, the conditions were changed before he reached the raft. The guns of all the fleet and of both forts had been firing for twenty minutes as the bow of the Hartford entered the opening in the boom, and thick clouds of smoke filled the motionless air and settled on the water, blinding the pilots. Worse than all that, time enough had passed to enable the men with the flaming fire rafts to arrive at the barrier; and as the Hartford reached the open water above, the heroic crew of the little Confederate tug Mosher, Captain Sherman, came pushing one of these boats against the side of the flagship.

With wheel hard over, the Hartford strove to dodge the danger, but ran aground instead, and then the raft was held relentlessly to her wooden side. For a moment the fire lapped the planks and then the thick paint with which the hull was covered burst into flames that leaped up almost to her lower yards.

The fierce heat drove the men from the guns on that side of the ship but they returned to their stations as they heard Farragut's voice saying :

"Don't flinch from that fire, boys ; there's a hotter fire than that for those who don't do their duty."

A moment later, however, as the flames spread swiftly over the side of the ship, the case seemed so desperate that even the courageous Farragut "thought it was all up with us." Raising his hands above his head he exclaimed :

"My God, is it to end this way ?"

But while Farragut realized the extent of the danger he by no means lost his head. He instantly "ordered the ship backed with all speed," which was done with such effect that the propeller threw both the ram (tug) and the fire raft forward and on shore, while the ship slid off. In the meantime salvation from the flames on the ship's side was at hand. The Hartford's crew had been well drilled at fire quarters. Master's Mate Allen, of the fire brigade, climbed into the mizzen rigging with a hose in hand, and a moment later he was drowning the flames with a well directed deluge. Incidentally a half dozen shells had been fired into the tug that had done its appointed work so well, and she sank in the black water with all her heroic crew.

The Hartford, in backing off the mud, got her head down stream, presumably because of an eddy, and she was a long time turning about. During this most trying period Farragut stood still, giving such orders as were needed as coolly as if at drill, and "referring occasionally to a little compass that was attached to his watch-chain" to see how near she was pointing to the course up the river.

The next attack on the flagship was quickly repulsed. A vessel, black with men, was seen heading for her as if to board, but a shell from the pivot gun worked by the marine guard was fired into it. The shell exploded and the ship then drifted away. The Hartford was thereafter free.

The Brooklyn which followed the flagship collided with the Kineo, as she reached the opening in the raft, and Captain Craven, being unable to see the little gunboat clearly, supposed and reported that he had struck one of the raft hulks. The Kineo was almost rolled over, but no particular damage was done to either vessel.

The Richmond arrived next in line, and then came the Sciota and the Iroquois. "The gallant Iroquois" was the last of the fleet to pass above the boom, and Commander Porter, while directing his flotilla's fire on Fort Jackson, saw her "provokingly linger and slow her engines opposite the forts to give the rebels a taste of her formidable battery." The remaining vessels of the fleet (all were gunboats), were disabled or stopped by the fire of the forts until too late to pass the raft—a heart-breaking condition of affairs for their commanders.

The ships had come to the barrier as a fleet in orderly line, but once they were above it, the line was broken and each ship became an independent unit that fought as her captain thought best. While the Pensacola and Mississippi overwhelmed the fire of Fort St. Phillip, the smaller vessels of the division slipped past and up the river. But they were then by no means out of danger. As the Cayuga steamed clear of the fire of the fort her crew saw no less than eleven Confederate steamers in the river around her.

The ram Manassas, the Governor Moore and the McRae attacked her at once. Her big 11-inch pivot gun was fired into the Moore with deadly effect.

Captain Kennon, of the Moore, had intended to board the Cayuga, but that shot stopped him. The ram Manassas missed her and went hunting larger ships. The McRae was left astern.

Then came the Oneida and Varuna firing right and left into the Confederate fleet,—"a refreshing fire," according to Captain Bailey. It was manifest to the Confederate crews that the National fleet was succeeding very well in passing the barrier raft, and the opportunity for which the River Defense Fleet had been created had therefore arrived. The National ships were scattered and exposed, as never before and never afterward during the war, to the attacks of rams commanded by resolute men. In fact in the gloom of early morning and the smoke of battle, the confusion was so great that one National ship fired into another. But the River Defense captains with one exception fled.

It was not so with the trained officers of the old navy. When Kennon was driven from his attack on the Cayuga by her big gun and the opportune arrival of the Oneida, he saw that the Varuna was steaming alone up the river in chase of one of the River Defense Fleet. The Varuna carried ten guns and the Governor Moore only two, but Kennon was a man who could "conjugate the verb to do." He therefore went in chase of the over-energetic Boggs of the National ship. His own distinguishing lights had been shot away and he now showed the Federal lights to deceive the Varuna's lookout.

Until the Varuna's steam had been run down by her futile speed Kennon let her go on unmolested.

But when it slackened he opened fire. Having used oil on his coal, Kennon himself had plenty of steam, and he overhauled the ship until his bow gun (it was mounted on a high forecastle) would no longer bear on her. Then he depressed the gun to the full limit, shot a port-hole through the bow of his own ship and raked the Varuna, killing and wounding twelve men.

Captain Boggs now put the Varuna's helm aport to throw her around and give the Moore a broadside. He succeeded in doing this, but Kennon, meantime, put his helm to starboard and drove the Moore into the Varuna's side. The latter's engine was stopped by the shock, and as she lay dead in the water the Moore rammed her again.

The Varuna was a converted merchantman of the usual light framework. The wounds from the ramming were mortal and Boggs was obliged to drive her ashore to keep her from sinking. But her guns were worked until her stern was under water. Many men were killed on the Moore, but no damage was done to her machinery, and Kennon, whose blood was up, turned to face a half dozen National ships that were coming after him. His fight was over. Such a hail of projectiles was fired into his already battered ship that she was wholly disabled. With the aid of a jib she was drifted ashore and burned ; her flag being consumed at the main peak. It was a sad day for the Nation when men like Kennon left the old navy.

In the meantime the River Defense steamer Stonewall Jackson, while striving to flee up the river and

escape the National ships, saw the Varuna ashore
and sinking rapidly. At that her captain shifted
her helm and rammed the wreck. The only stroke
delivered by any of the six River Defense steamers
present at this battle came as an anti-climax.

No less courageous and determined than Kennon
was Lieutenant A. F. Warley, commanding the little ironclad ram Manassas. Having failed in his
dash at the Cayuga, he then headed for the Pensacola, but missed his stroke again, because the
watchful captain of the big ship dodged him. Then
he drove the Manassas at the Mississippi and
reached her, but only succeeded in peeling a heavy
splinter from her hull under water. The Mississippi
fired a useless broadside over the Manassas, as she
approached. As Warley sheered off toward the
barrier raft (for with her speed of six knots, she
could do nothing against the current), he found the
Brooklyn just getting clear, and was able to deliver
a fair blow while steaming directly across the current. The ironclad bow of the ram struck between
two frames and crushed both the outer and the inner
planking. But the chain cable triced to her side at
the water line, thanks to Engineer John W. Moore,
saved the big ship from a mortal wound.

As the Manassas drifted clear of the Brooklyn a
man climbed through her hatch to look at the
wound she had made. For a moment he stood beside her smokestack and then tumbled into the river.
An officer of the Brooklyn afterward asked the
quartermaster who was heaving the lead on that
side of the ship if he had seen the man disappear.

"Yes, sir," replied the quartermaster, "I saw him fall overboard—in fact, I helped him, for I hit him alongside the head with my hand lead."

As the Brooklyn passed up, the Manassas steamed on down stream. Warley had determined to go down through the barrier raft and ram the mortar schooners. But "I no sooner neared the forts," as he wrote afterward, "than both opened fire on me. Fort St. Phillip did not strike me. Captain Squires informed me that he fired seventy-five times at me, but Fort Jackson struck me frequently with her 42-pounder."

As that region was getting pretty hot, the Manassas was turned up stream to look for another opportunity to ram the National fleet, when she was seen by Farragut, who sent the Mississippi to attack her. In Farragut's account of the destruction of the ram, as written to his family, one sees both the feeling of the man and that of the naval officer. He said :

"Loyall [his son] would have been delighted, as I was, to see the contest between the old Mississippi and the Hollins ram Manassas, after we had passed the forts. All saw the ram coming up. I hailed Melancton Smith, and told him to run her down. Smith turned his ship's head down stream, and they ran at each other. We all looked on with intense anxiety. When within fifty yards, the enemy's heart failed him, and he turned to the right and ran on shore. Smith poured in a broadside, which riddled her. Thus ended the Hollins ram. She floated down stream, on fire from her own furnace ;

the officers and men making their escape to the shore. These rams are formidable things, but when there is room to manœuvre, the heavy ships will run over them."

Off Fort St. Phillip, Lieutenant Read, of the McRae, boarded the Manassas, and reported afterward that she was sound save for a cut pipe. But he must have been mistaken, for when she passed Porter's flotilla, she was on fire, and she soon "exploded faintly" and sank.

A curious incident of the battle occurred when the lingering Iroquois was at last beyond the forts. The Confederate steamer McRae fired a broadside of grape shot and copper slugs at her, doing some damage, but the Union ship with her more powerful guns returned a storm of grape and canister. The slaughter on the McRae was great, and among those mortally hurt was Thomas B. Huger, her commander. Huger, but a few months before, had been the executive officer of the Iroquois, and the larger part of her crew at this time were men who had served under him.

To pass the forts, the broken raft, and the Confederate fleet of eighteen vessels, had taken less than two hours. "A more desperate, more magnificent dash was never made," wrote Captain Craven afterward.

The loss of the National fleet was 35 killed, 147 wounded, and the converted merchantman Varuna.

Fort Jackson lost nine killed and thirty-three wounded during the bombardment and the battle; Fort St. Phillip lost two killed and four wounded.

No complete statement of the Confederate loss afloat was ever compiled, but on one of the vessels the destruction was extraordinary. The Governor Moore had 64 killed and wounded out of a crew of ninety-three, and Captain Kennon reported that he thought 57 of these were killed. The McRae lost four killed, including Captain Thomas B. Huger, and 17 wounded. Captain Charles McIntosh, of the Louisiana, who is affectionately mentioned by both Farragut and Craven in their letters as "Charlie McIntosh," was mortally wounded. Of the Confederate fleet, that had numbered thirteen armed vessels, three remained under the guns of Fort St. Phillip—the ironclad Louisiana, the converted merchantman McRae and the guerrilla Defiance. These were destroyed later.

With the exception of the Varuna, the ships that passed the forts were as fit for battle as they were before the fight began. The river lay fair before them and New Orleans was at their mercy.

"I am so agitated that I can scarcely write," said Farragut in a letter to his wife, the day after the battle—a letter that shows the heart of the man —"and I shall only tell you that it has pleased Almighty God to preserve my life through a fire such as the world has scarcely known. I shall return properly my thanks, as well as those of our fleet, for His goodness and mercy. He has permitted me to make a name for my dear boy's inheritance, as well as for my comfort and that of my family."

CHAPTER XV

THAT Farragut was able to pass the forts and fleet of the Confederates with so much ease, and so little loss, is a matter that demands consideration although the cause may be stated in few words—lack of proper preparation on the part of the Confederates. The forts were not armed as they might have been, because the guns that were removed from Pensacola, when the Confederates determined to abandon that place (it was not actually evacuated till May 9th, however), were sent north. Moreover, the soldiers in the garrisons of Fort St. Phillip and Fort Jackson were chiefly foreigners because the fighting men of New Orleans were so active and aggressive that they sought service with the armies at the north; they could by no means endure the stagnation of garrison life. Then, while the commanders of the forts were among the ablest men in the Confederate service, a number of the junior officers were of very inferior fibre. One of those junior officers, "a captain from the back country," had charge of those casemate guns which were firing hot shot. He depressed the muzzles of his guns very considerably, fearing to fire too high, and being desirous of working them vigorously, had them run out with a jerk, the consequence of which was that the balls rolled harmlessly into the moat, while he blazed away powder and hay wads. Some officers on the ramparts, observing this, told him of it. He then commenced operations on one particular vessel, which he kept at until some one informed him that he was devoting himself to one of their own chain hulks.

This story, told in one of the official reports, describes, in a way, the whole Confederate defense. Splendid courage and most praiseworthy activity and devotion were shown by the Confederate army and navy officers; but some of them also showed a woeful lack of training.

The ironclad Mississippi was launched before the forts were passed but her machinery was not installed nor were her guns mounted. The Louisiana was so far completed that her engines had a trial, but they developed so little power, and the wheels were so poorly placed, that she could not stem the current of the river, even when aided by two tugs. She was then (April 20th) ordered down to the forts to serve as a floating battery, and was moored at Fort St. Phillip. Her guns were not all mounted, as yet, but a gang of men went along to finish the work, and they kept at it, night and day, with the result that the riverside guns were soon put in place. It was then found that the ports were so poorly designed that the guns could be elevated only five degrees, and even the excellent 7-inch rifles had an effective range of no more than 2,000 yards, if they really had as much as that. And when the ironclad had dropped her anchor, her crew found that the purchase for getting it up was not strong enough. What might have been a most powerful ship proved defective even as a floating gun carriage because of the lack of skill in those who designed and built her.

When some of the Louisiana's guns were mounted, General Duncan urged Commodore Mitchell, commanding all the Confederate naval ships, to place the Louisiana near the east end of the raft at Fort Jackson. Duncan supposed that the Louisiana, from that point, could drive away the Federal mortar flotilla, and hold Farragut's fleet in check. But Mitchell refused to do this on the ground that if he went there a single shell from one of Porter's mortars could easily sink the Louisiana. For she was unprotected with armor on the flat top of her casemate where a bomb would strike her ; and even if she escaped the bombs her guns, Mitchell said, could not reach the Federal vessels of any kind, while they lay at their anchorage.

Accordingly the Louisiana remained at Fort St. Phillip. Her crew, during the battle, worked their guns bravely and as efficiently as the design of the ship permitted. The Federal ships pounded her at short range, without causing a single shot to enter her casemate, but when her crew tried to depress their guns to reach the waterline of the Federal ships, they were unable to do so. If the guns had been well-mounted on the fort they would have done better service.

Six rams of the River Defense Fleet had been retained to defend the boom. They were under the command, nominally, of General Duncan, but when the general ordered them to guard the barrier by night, the captains refused to go below it. They would neither submit to control nor do any work on their own initiative.

The handling of the fire rafts (with the exception already noted), particularly while Farragut was below the forts, was as badly managed as that of the River Defense Fleet. Rafts were set adrift while Farragut was preparing his fleet, but they were committed to the current, in every case but one, at points whence they drifted ashore, or were towed ashore with ease ; and in the one case there was no more damage done than to cause a collision of no importance between two National ships. Last of all, when Caldwell had broken the raft, no effort was made to reclose the opening or place any ship near the breach to stop the passage of the Federal fleet.

These facts are given in detail because every American ought to see and fully understand the contrast between the opposing forces on that night of battle. On the one hand, Farragut's ships were prepared in every detail that the inventive minds of the officers of the fleet could think of. On the other hand, Mitchell, though of unquestioned courage, was ready in scarcely a single detail. This was through no particular fault of his own, however, for he had labored faithfully.

At bottom the trouble among the Confederates was founded on the unbounded confidence which the people had in valor,—a misplaced confidence not confined to the South, or to that time. Untrained troops, as was supposed, had wrought wonders in the American Revolution. Untrained troops had faced the foreign enemy right there at New Orleans in the War of 1812, with what result was well known and often boasted. For the sake of emphasis, let it be repeated that the War of 1812 had been necessary because Europe thought all Americans were at once afraid of war and too greedy of commercial gain to abandon business in order to resent whatever degrading insult might be offered them. That war proved the courage and spirit of the American people in most striking fashion ; it even taught the British navy the virtue found in caution, betimes ; but unfortunately, the American people did not learn at the same time that the important victories of that war were *in every case* gained because of the superior training of the American soldiers and sailors—particularly the training that had taught them to see, clear-eyed, through the sights of a gun.

There was one other sentiment among Confederates, it appears, that must have hampered thorough preparation and training. I hope that this matter may be mentioned without doing offense anywhere. It is worth while recalling it because the American people, as a whole, now have the same feeling regarding all other nations. The Confederates, except those that had been trained in the old navy, seem to have underestimated the fighting qualities of the Northern men. Confederate periodicals had often said, and the mass of Southern politicians of that time believed, that one Confederate could whip five Yankees. It is the soldier, justly estimating the power of the enemy, and making the most earnest efforts in preparing for the battle that usually wins it.

While some of his officers had overrated the strength of the Confederate defenses, as the proceedings of the council before the battle show, Farragut's estimate was precisely right; and his "genius for war" is as plainly proved by his accurate judgment in this regard as by his careful preparation for the battle, and his brilliant dash past the forts. For the conception of a proper plan was possible only when the strength of the defenses was properly understood.

Having passed the forts Farragut, for the time, wholly ignored them as well as such Confederate vessels as had been left under the guns of Fort St. Phillip. But he did not wholly ignore the existence of batteries on the river above. After the battle with the lower forts he allowed his men to rest for the remainder of that day (April 24), in order that they might be in good condition to meet the fire of the forts that had been erected where Jackson had repelled the British at the end of the War of 1812. He made no further special preparation for the attack on those fortifications because he foresaw that the upper barrier was sure to be less efficient than the lower, and that to pass it would be, as he wrote afterward, "one of the little elegancies of the profession—a dash and a victory." On the morning of the 25th, the National flag appeared before the upper works.

In the meantime a most remarkable condition of

affairs prevailed in New Orleans. As described by
George W. Cable, in the *Century Magazine*, there
had been "a system of espionage, secret, diligent
and fierce . . . the scheme of some of the
worst villains who had ruled New Orleans with the
rod of terror for many years—the Thugs." The
Thugs had created a veritable reign of terror and
when it was learned (April 24th) that Farragut had
passed the forts, they took charge of the streets.

"I went to the riverside," says Cable. "There
until far into the night I saw hundreds of drays
carrying cotton out of the presses and yards to the
wharves where it was fired. The glare of those sin-
uous miles of flame set men and women weeping
and wailing thirty miles away on the farther shore of
Lake Pontchartrain. But the next day was the day
of terrors. During the night fear, wrath and the sense
of betrayal had run through the people as the fire
had run through the cotton. The firemen were out;
but they cast fire on the waters, putting the torch
to the empty ships and cutting them loose to float
down the river.

"Whoever could go was going. The great mass
that had no place to go to, or means to go with, was
beside itself. I saw a crowd catch a poor fellow
whose crime was that he looked like a foreigner
and might be a spy. They swung him to a neigh-
boring lamp-post, but the foreign legion saved the
man. This was one occurrence; there were many
like it. I stood in the rear door of our store soon
after opening it. The junior member of the firm
was within. I called him to look toward the river.

The masts of the cutter Washington were slowly tipping, declining, sinking—down she went. The gunboat moored next to her began to smoke all over and then to blaze. My employers left the city. I closed the doors and ran to the river to see the sights.

"What a gathering! The riffraff of the wharves, the town, the gutters! Such women—such wrecks of women! And all the juvenile ragtag. The lower steamboat landing, well covered with sugar, rice and molasses, was being rifled. The men smashed; the women scooped up the smashings. The river was overflowing the top of the levee. A rain-storm began to threaten.

"'Are the Yankee ships in sight?' I asked an idler. He pointed to the tops of their naked masts as they showed up across the huge bend of the river. They were engaging the batteries at Camp Chalmette—the old field of Jackson's renown. Presently that was over. Ah, me! I see them now as they come slowly round Slaughter House Point into full view, silent, so grim and terrible; black with men; heavy with deadly portent; the long-banished Stars and Stripes flying against the frowning sky. Oh, for the Mississippi! The Mississippi! Just then she came down upon them. But how? Drifting helplessly, a mass of flames.

"The crowds on the levee howled and screamed with rage. The swarming decks answered never a word; but one old tar on the Hartford, standing with lanyard in hand beside a great pivot gun, so plain to view that you could see him smile, silently patted its big black breech and blandly grinned."

And while the Thugs ruled the streets, the "slaves, rushing out, leaving the houses open, disordered, behind them, shouted triumphantly to one another, 'The Yankees are here!' . . . It was their hour of victory—and retribution." [1]

Farragut in describing the scene upon the river says :

"All the morning I had seen abundant evidence of the panic which had seized the people in New Orleans. Cotton-loaded ships on fire came floating down, and working implements of every kind, such as are used in shipyards. The destruction was awful." And again : "The levee of New Orleans was one scene of desolation. Ships, steamers, cotton, coal, etc., were all in one common blaze, and our ingenuity was much taxed to avoid the floating conflagration." [2]

On arriving off the city, Farragut sent ashore Captain Theodorus Bailey and Lieutenant George H. Perkins to see the Mayor. Cable, who was present, says he was drawn to the street by "a roar of shoutings and imprecations and crowding feet down Common Street. 'Hurrah for Jeff Davis! Hurrah for Jeff Davis! Shoot them! Kill them! Hang them!' About every third man there had a weapon out." The two officers on their way to the Mayor's office, were "unguarded and alone, looking not to right or left, never frowning, never flinching, while the mob screamed in their ears, shook cocked pistols in their faces, cursed and crowded and gnashed

[1] Grace King.
[2] Sen. Ex. Doc. 56, 37th Cong., 2d Sess.

upon them. So through the gates of death those two men walked to the City Hall. It was one of the bravest deeds I ever saw done."

Lieutenant Perkins says that when "they began to throw things at us and shout 'Hang them! Hang them!' we both thought we were in a bad fix, but there was nothing for us to do but just to go on."

The Mayor's office was reached at 1:30 o'clock. There Captain Bailey said (to quote the account of Marion A. Baker, the private secretary of Mayor John T. Monroe), "that he came as the bearer of a demand from Flag-officer Farragut for the surrender of the city, the lowering of the state flag on the City Hall, and the hoisting of the United States flag over the post-office, custom-house, and mint."

The Mayor, after consulting with a number of citizens present, said that he had no authority to surrender the city, "and that General Lovell was the proper person to receive and reply to that demand." General Lovell was brought in. He "refused to surrender the city or his forces, but stated that he would retire with his troops and leave the civil authorities to act as they saw fit." Then the Mayor said that he would present the matter to the city council, and the two officers returned to the ships escorted by men furnished by General Lovell, to protect them from the unrestrained Thugs.

The Mayor on his side sent a message to the city council narrating the proceedings in his office, and said that "in reply to the demand to haul down the [Louisiana] flag from the city hall, I returned an unqualified refusal." As to surrendering the city he said : "My own opinion is that as a civil magistrate, possessed of no military power, I am incompetent to perform a military act such as the surrender of the city to a hostile force ; that it would be proper to say that . . . we can offer no obstruction to the occupation of the place by the enemy ; that the custom-house, post-office and mint are the property of the Confederate government, and that we have no control over them ; and that all acts involving a transfer of authority be performed by the invading forces themselves ; that we yield to physical force alone, and that we maintain our allegiance to the government of the Confederate States."

On the morning of the 26th, the common council resolved "That the sentiments expressed in the message of his Honor . . . are in perfect accordance with the sentiments entertained by these councils and by the entire population of this metropolis."

The Mayor wrote a letter to Farragut that expressed these sentiments in simple language, but Pierre Soulé, a citizen of New Orleans, who had been a Senator at Washington and a Minister to Spain, and who (according to Major S. L. James), "seemed to speak for the Mayor and council of the city," wrote a much longer letter to say the same thing, together with many other things that indicated an hysterical state of mind. This letter was also sent to the Hartford.[1]

[1] Private Secretary Baker, in explaining for the *Century Magazine*, Soulé's dominant attitude, in later years, said : "Mr. Mon-

With the streets full of Thugs, and the city authorities dominated by an hysterical politician, Farragut's kindly heart and patience were sorely tried. But he was equal to the occasion. When Private Secretary Baker went off to the flagship, early on the morning of the 26th, to carry a message, he says: "Captain Farragut, who had known me from my boyhood, received me with the utmost kindness, and when my errand was disposed of, readily answered my inquiries about the battle at the forts. He took me over the ship and showed me with almost boyish interest the manner in which the boilers were defended, and the scars upon the ship's sides where the shots had taken effect. Then making me stand beside him upon the very spot where he had stood during the passage of the forts, he described in eloquent terms the conflict, perhaps the most terrific that had ever been withstood.

roe, though a man of much energy and decisive character, was entirely a 'self-made' man and his secretary was very young."

One of Soulé's schemes, as described by General Lovell when courtmartialed for abandoning the city, is also worth recalling here:

"It having been reported to me that a sufficient number of desperately bold men could easily be got together to board the enemy's vessels and carry them by assault, I authorized Major James to seize such steamers as might be necessary for his purpose and to attempt it. He called for 1,000 men by public advertisement, but being able to find but about 100 who would undertake it, he abandoned the project."

Private Secretary Baker also says that this scheme originated with Pierre Soulé. Captain Mahan observes that "the better and stronger element among the men had gone forth to swell the ranks of the Confederate army."

'I seemed to be breathing flame,' said the captain."

Some of the junior officers of the fleet were so incensed at the mob that they urged the flag officer to clear the streets with "a whiff of grape." It is said that Butler favored the same remedy. This Farragut instantly refused to do, saying that the people were in such a state of hysteria as to be not responsible for their acts.

To add to the trial of Farragut's patience, the British frigate Mersey followed the National fleet up the river and anchored near the Hartford where the English seamen, unrestrained by their officers, sang Confederate songs in voices heard on shore as well as on the National ships. On landing these sailors also proclaimed on the street corners their hope that the Confederacy would succeed. Farragut was obliged, at last, to call the attention of the captain of the Mersey to the matter before the ill-mannered outbreaks were stopped.

In the meantime (on the morning of April 26th), the American flag was hoisted over the mint by a boat's crew sent out by Captain Morris of the Pensacola. It was hauled down by a youth named William B. Mumford, and three companions, while the crews of the National ships were attending a thanksgiving service by order of Farragut. The flag was then dragged through the streets, and finally hurled through an open window into the Mayor's office, where two officers from the fleet were negotiating with the city authorities.

The fact that his "officers and men were treated

with insult and rudeness when they landed, even with a flag of truce, to communicate with the authorities," eventually led Farragut to warn the Mayor that "the fire of the vessels might at any moment be drawn upon the city," and on Monday, the 28th, the Mayor was officially notified to get the women and children out of town within forty-eight hours.

These negotiations over the question of who ought to haul down the flag of Louisiana, it seems now were really needless, as well as tedious and annoying. Happily they came to an end on the 28th through the surrender of the forts St. Phillip and Jackson.

General Benjamin F. Butler, commanding the soldiers that had been brought to the Gulf to occupy the city, witnessed Farragut's successful passing of the forts. Hastening to his transports, he took them to Sable Island, east of Fort St. Phillip, and thence carried them in small boats through the bayous to the river bank. At the same time Commander Porter placed six mortar boats in the shoal water behind Fort Jackson. Under the inspiration of battle, the garrisons of the two forts had done well enough, but once the ships were between them and the city of New Orleans, their spirits fell. General Duncan issued a stirring appeal in which he said truthfully that the forts were as well able to resist assault as ever, but the men—particularly those of Fort Jackson—had lost all heart. On the night of the 27th the garrison of this fort rose on the officers, spiked the guns, and informed the commander that they would fight no more. Then 250 of them marched up the levee and surrendered to General Butler. The officers managed to keep the others in some sort of order until the forenoon of the 28th when the forts were formally made over to Commander Porter. The ironclad Louisiana was burned, and soon all the other fortifications were surrendered or abandoned.

The news of the fall of the two forts changed the situation of affairs at New Orleans materially, and Farragut, seeing the futility of discussion with the Mayor's representatives, sent 250 marines ashore under Captain J. L. Broome, with a squad of seamen from the Hartford under Midshipman J. H. Read. The force carried two howitzers, and took possession of the city hall and the custom-house and mint. Lieutenant John Campbell Harris of the marine corps hoisted the old flag over the city hall.

The work of the navy in capturing New Orleans was completed, and in what may be considered "a handsome style," to quote Farragut's words when he passed the forts.

Having taken formal possession of the city, Farragut held it until General Butler came with his command, comprising 13,000 men in all, instead of the force originally intended. He took charge of affairs on May 1st. When he had hanged Mumford for hauling down the flag, and had sent "the doughty but unmannerly mayor," as Grace King calls Monroe, to one of the forts, and it was seen by the citizens that the "two great French lawyers, Soulé and Mazureau, could be sent off like common felons," the Thugs ceased to run through the streets, and order was restored.

In one point of view the capture of New Orleans was but a continuation of the successful work done by the navy elsewhere. In the sounds of North Carolina and on the coast of Georgia, it had already secured a definite foothold for the National forces. At the end of 1862, the inland waters of North Carolina, from Roanoke Island to Newbern, were under National control. So was the coast of Georgia, and so, too, was Pensacola and its navy yard. But even when considered as an incident in the general work of restoring the Nation's navigable waters and ports to Federal control the capture of New Orleans was of vastly more importance than that of all the other places counted together. For New Orleans was not only the metropolis of the Confederacy; its population (168,675), was greater than that of any three of the other Southern cities. In 1860, the exports, imports and domestic receipts of the city amounted to $324,000,000, and the people were looking forward to a time when the business interests of the place would exceed in value and magnitude those of any other port of the United States. When New Orleans was taken an immense territory was at once deprived of those supplies and comforts that the Southern people had been in the habit of obtaining there.

As a feature of the strategy of the war, however, the capture of New Orleans is chiefly notable from the fact that thus was secured a base for further operations on the Mississippi. And one must by no means forget the hope with which the National forces and the Union people were then inspired. It seems certain that without this invigoration the dark days that were to follow would have been fatal to the Federal cause.

But it was in its influence upon our relations with European nations that the capture of New Orleans proved of most importance to the Federals. For there is good reason to believe that Farragut's victory stayed the hand of the French Emperor when he contemplated intervening in behalf of the Confederacy. In May, 1861, "the Duc de Morny, the greatest personage in France, after the Emperor, had told Mr. Rost, the first Confederate agent at Paris, that 'the South would soon be recognized.'" After Mr. Slidell, who was later sent abroad by the Confederates to secure recognition and aid—he who was taken out of the British steamer Trent by Captain Wilkes—arrived in Paris in February, 1862, and had visited M. Thouvénel, Minister of Foreign Affairs, and other men who stood next to Napoleon III, he wrote home to say that "the Emperor has invited the English Government to join with him in recognizing the South."

M. Thouvénel had on two occasions invited Great Britain to join in this recognition—once in June, 1861, and again early in March, 1862. The British Government having declined to do this, the Emperor could not again make the request directly, but he was so anxious to arrange the matter that he began intriguing through W. S. Lindsay, a British ship merchant who was active in his sympathies for the South because of his hatred for Yankee ship-builders. Lindsay had bought a seat in Parliament, and was able to see and talk with members of his Government. On April 11, 1862, the Emperor authorized Lindsay to say to Lord Cowley, that "he [the Emperor], would at once despatch a formidable fleet to the mouth of the Mississippi, if England would send an equal force, and that they would" then raise the blockade.

In a further interview with Mr. Lindsay (on April 18th), the Emperor said "he could not consent that his people should continue to suffer from the acts of the Federal Government. He thought the best course would be to make a friendly appeal to it, either alone or concurrently with England, to open the ports, but to accompany the appeal with a proper demonstration of force; and, should the appeal appear likely to be ineffective, to back it by a declaration of his purpose not to respect the blockade."

It is to be observed that Napoleon's eagerness to intervene was not due to any love for the Southern people. He had seen that he could preserve his throne solely by an aggressive or warlike foreign policy. He had dreamed of recovering the colonial domain which Napoleon the Great had sold. He had already invaded Mexico. He was preparing to make Maximilian emperor of that country. There is some evidence that he was looking to the reëstablishment of the separate nation of Texas. "The French consul [was] exercising, as the French consuls always will in New Orleans, a quasi-paternal authority over the citizens."[1] Napoleon could realize his ambition only through the dismemberment and destruction of the American Nation. But he concluded his conversation with Lindsay by making this important statement:

"The taking of New Orleans, which he did not anticipate, might render it inexpedient to act; that he would not decide at once, but would wait some days for further intelligence."[2]

It was on April 18, 1862, that Napoleon spoke of a "friendly appeal" with "a proper demonstration of force" to back it. While the Emperor talked with the jealous British ship merchant, the mortars of Farragut's fleet were hurling bombs into Fort Jackson, and the crews of the ships were preparing for the mighty struggle on the morning of April 24th. If Farragut had failed, or if he had met with serious delays in the capture of New Orleans, Napoleon would have intervened alone in the hope that Great Britain would come to his support. But the taking of New Orleans rendered it "inexpedient" for Napoleon to act, and a time never came thereafter when it was expedient for him to do so. Farragut's victory at New Orleans was the decisive naval battle of the Civil War.

[1] King.

[2] The quotation is from Slidell's correspondence, as printed in the *North American Review*, October, 1879.

CHAPTER XVI

A FUTILE EXPEDITION UP THE MISSISSIPPI

AFTER General Butler had taken charge of New Orleans (May 1st) Farragut found himself under orders to go up the river to attempt to complete the work of severing the Confederacy. One needs to know the river to understand how great a task was thus contemplated, but some idea of the difficulties in the way may be obtained by considering the fact that a river boat drawing seven feet of water was regarded as a deep ship, while the Hartford drew sixteen feet. Being long as well as of deep draft, the warships were not easy to handle in narrow waters, and this difficulty was all the greater in the Mississippi, because, while the fleet could steam at best but eight knots in slack water, they here had a current of three knots or more to oppose them. Further than that pilots were scarce, and not always trustworthy, because many of the guild were ardent Confederates. Worse yet, even the best and most faithful pilot might go astray because of the constant changing in the river's channel.

At the same time Farragut saw very clearly that his next work ought to be done elsewhere. In a letter to Assistant Secretary of the Navy Fox, dated April 25th, he says, "I will soon be off for Mobile." And in a report to the Secretary of the Navy, dated April 29th, he says, "As soon as I see General

Butler safely in possession of this place I will sail for Mobile with the fleet.''

Nevertheless, he contemplated going up the river first, according to orders, and he did so. Seven of the smaller vessels were sent up in advance. Baton Rouge and Natchez surrendered to them but when Vicksburg was reached (May 18th) the Confederates, in decided terms, refused the summons. The high ground there lay 200 feet above the river. In various fortifications built on the bluffs the Confederates had mounted 8-inch and 10-inch guns. In battle the ships would receive a plunging fire while it would be impossible for them to elevate their guns to reach the Confederate batteries. In addition to these batteries on the bluffs, were several near the water level.

Commander S. P. Lee, the senior officer present, therefore waited for further orders. Farragut arrived, in a day or two, bringing with him a detachment of troops (1,500 men all told) under General Thomas Williams, who had been sent to hold whatever ground Farragut should capture. General Williams made a reconnaissance ashore and found that the Confederates had 30,000 men that could be concentrated in the town within a day. It was therefore impossible for him to land, and it was, as said, impossible for Farragut's ships to reach the forts with an effective fire.

In the meantime the troops under Williams had used up all their rations and Farragut had been obliged to supply them until his own stores were almost exhausted. Moreover his coal was running

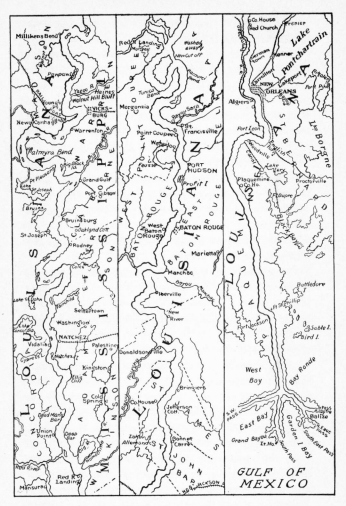

THE MISSISSIPPI RIVER

low, and the ships had come 400 miles, through hostile territory, from New Orleans, the base of supplies.

Farragut saw, as he said afterward, that he could pass the batteries, but running these batteries was a very different matter from running those below New Orleans. Passing these batteries would not cut them off from their source of supplies or in anywise injure them; while the ships, once they were above Vicksburg, would have those heavy hill guns to repass when heading for the sea once more. Moreover, coal and provisions brought up for the ships, would have to run the same gauntlet.

In short, while the original plan for taking New Orleans had been well-conceived and brilliantly executed, the Department's orders requiring Farragut *to open the river* were based on an ignorance of the situation that was most deplorable. Finding it impossible to reach the forts with an effective fire, and discovering further that, even if he could silence the forts, it would not be worth while to do so since there were but 1,500 men to hold them against the assault of 30,000, Farragut returned to New Orleans with the big ships, leaving a number of gunboats to patrol the river, and, as far as possible, prevent communications between the two banks. To his mortification on his arrival at New Orleans, he found letters from the Department ordering him up the river once more. Said Assistant Secretary of the Navy Fox writing on May 12th:

"The only anxiety we feel is to know if you have followed your instructions and pushed a strong force up the river to meet the Western flotilla. We only hear of you at Baton Rouge. The opening of the Mississippi is of more importance than Mobile, and if your ships reach Memphis in the next few days, Beauregard's army is cut off from escape. We listen most anxiously for word that your forces are near there."

"The rebellion" was "caving in all around," if one could believe the optimistic Fox.

Accordingly, Farragut once more took his ships up the river, and without serious mishap. On June 18th, the Brooklyn and the Richmond reached an anchorage just below Vicksburg. The Hartford, after lying aground for a night in the river, followed, bringing Porter's mortar flotilla of steamers, and seventeen mortar schooners.

The Mississippi River, at that time, in its winding course to the sea, flowed up from the southwest to a point just at the northern boundary of Vicksburg. There it made a sharp bend back toward the southwest. There was deep water close to the city, and a sand-bar opposite. To guard this bend the Confederates had two 10-inch guns, one 9-inch, four 8-inch and seven smaller smoothbores, besides 12 rifled guns that ranged from a 32-pounder down to a 12-pounder. The most important battery of all was placed on high ground just opposite the bend where its guns could not only rake the ships as they came up from below but could "put it to them," as Farragut was in the habit of saying, after they had rounded the bend. It was here that the 9-inch gun (a Dahlgren from the Norfolk Navy Yard) was placed, and there were three 8-inch guns and an 18-pounder rifle with it. The distance from the lowest battery to the highest, at this time, was about three miles, and since the National ships could steam against the current at a speed of no more than five knots when passing this point in the river, they would be under fire for at least forty minutes.

On the 26th and 27th, the mortar schooners were put in place ; and at two o'clock on the morning of June 28, 1862, the fleet steamed up the river to run the gauntlet. The Richmond, the Hartford and the Brooklyn were in one column, at wide intervals, near the easterly or city bank, while the Iroquois, the Oneida, the Wissahickon, the Sciota, the Winona, the Pinola, the Kennebec, and the Katahdin, all of relatively lighter draft, formed a column on the westerly side of the big ships. At four o'clock the mortars opened fire, the batteries began to reply immediately, and then the ships of the fleet opened up as their guns would bear. Finally the steamers of the mortar flotilla joined in. The picture drawn by the flaming guns and winking shells was magnificent; the roar was tremendous. It was a grand spectacle—and nothing more. As the fleet drew up opposite the lower batteries the Confederates crouched down behind the earthworks. Their guns seemed to be silenced, but as soon as the weight of the fire of the fleet lessened the batteries opened with undiminished vigor, and continued firing while any ship was in range.

It was noted that in passing the batteries the flag-

ship not only steamed slowly but stopped completely at one time to allow the other vessels to close
up the line. And when she did this, the Iroquois,
Captain James S. Palmer, leading the other column,
came back to draw part of the Confederate fire, and
add to that of the flagship. That is to say, there was
cool fighting afloat and ashore. The entire fleet except the Brooklyn and two gunboats passed the
batteries, but when Farragut had anchored (at 6
A. M.), out of range, he had little more satisfaction
than was due to the knowledge that he had obeyed
orders, and that only a little damage had been done
to the fleet during the nearly two hours it was
under fire.

In the course of the battle Farragut took a stand
in the mizzen rigging, where he would be above the
smoke and could see what the other ships were
doing. After a time the captain of a gun on the
poop deck asked him to get down because the gun
was to be pointed near that point. Accordingly
Farragut did so, and just as he reached the deck a
shot cut away the rigging above the place where
he had been standing. He escaped a bad fall by
a few seconds only.

In his report to the Department, Farragut said
that "the forts can be passed and we have done it,
and can do it again as often as may be required of
us."

Meanwhile Memphis had fallen (June 6, 1862),
and Flag officer Charles H. Davis, who had succeeded Foote, in the upper river, found fairly
clear water below him. Accordingly he started

down the river, having in his fleet six or more iron-clad gunboats, and six mortar boats in tow of transports, while a River Defense ram, called the Queen of the West, one of a number of vessels built by the Union forces that were much like the River Defense Fleet of the Confederates—was picked up on the way down. Davis arrived at the anchorage above Vicksburg early on the morning of July 1st. The union of the two fleets for which the Navy Department had been so urgent was now accomplished. But the junction of forces instead of compelling the Confederates to surrender Vicksburg, only served as a warning to them to make greater exertions to hold the river.

While the National forces had been engaged in the work that brought Farragut and Davis together at the anchorage above Vicksburg the Confederates had been constructing an ironclad ship at Memphis with which they hoped to sweep the river. On a scow hull they had erected a stout timber casemate, with vertical sides and slanting ends, and this had been covered with railway iron to form an armor almost good enough to keep out the projectiles of the National guns, but they furnished the gun crews with additional protection by lining the casemate walls with cotton bales. Twin screws turned by separate engines gave her a moderate speed, and she was thus far an excellent ship ; but for a good draft to the fire in her boilers, they depended on a tall smoke-stack, which was to prove a serious defect.

After Island No. 10 had been passed by the National gunboats under Commander Walke, it was seen that Memphis must fall, and the Arkansas, as this ironclad was called, was taken to Greenwood, on the Yazoo River, while a similar vessel that was yet on the stocks at Memphis was burned. At Greenwood the Arkansas was completed under the eyes of Lieutenant Isaac N. Brown, a competent officer who had held a lieutenant's commission in the old navy. The work was ended a couple of weeks after Farragut's arrival above the batteries of Vicksburg and while he was still lying there.

At this time the Mississippi and Yazoo were both falling so rapidly as to make it appear likely that Farragut would be compelled to remain where he was all summer, and that the Arkansas would also have to lie in her berth for the same time. Farragut was anxious to get away and do something, but must wait for orders from Department officials who did not comprehend the situation. Brown of the Arkansas was equally anxious for action and when he sought the opportunity by applying to General Earl Van Dorn, commanding the Confederate forces at Vicksburg, he was invited (July 14, 1862), to come down the Yazoo and run through the National fleet. That night Brown took the Arkansas down through a raft that had been built across the Yazoo to protect her from Federal assault. It was his intention to steam down the Yazoo on the morning of the 15th, and surprise the National fleet, but on the 14th two deserters carried word to Farragut and Davis that the Arkansas was coming next day.

Accordingly Davis sent the gunboats Carondelet and Tyler, and the River Defense ram Queen of the

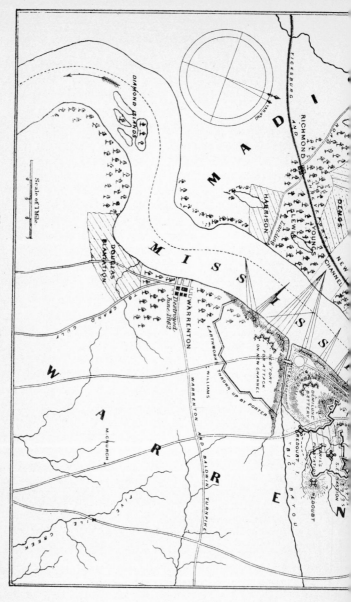

VICKSBURG AND ITS APPROACHES

West, up the Yazoo to hunt for the Confederate ship. They found her. She was very much alive, and her crew so eager for a fight, and so well able to make one, that all three of the National vessels turned back to carry the news of her coming to the anchored ships in the Mississippi. The Queen of the West led the procession, with the Tyler next and the Carondelet last of all, and made as good a fight as possible after the initial error of turning around to expose an unarmed stern to the heavy gun fire of the Arkansas—heavy because the Arkansas carried two 8-inch guns firing solid shot over her bow. In a short time the Carondelet, with her rudder chains cut, ran ashore where the Arkansas, being of deeper draft, could not follow, and she was left there to repair damages while the Confederate boat chased the Tyler out of the Yazoo, both ships firing as rapidly as they could load their guns.

It was at 8.30 o'clock on the morning of July 15th that the crews of the National fleet in the Mississippi saw the Tyler coming from the mouth of the Yazoo with her stern guns spitting fire at an enemy just then unseen. The noise had been heard for some time, but Farragut and his officers "supposed it to be the gunboats firing at the flying artillery," said to be lining the river. Worse yet (to quote Farragut further), "we were lying with low fires; none of us had steam, or could get it up in time to pursue" the Arkansas.

The Confederates had caught the old sea dog napping in fresh water, and "with deep mortification"

Farragut was obliged to report that "notwithstanding my prediction to the contrary, the ironclad ram Arkansas has at length made her appearance and taken us all by surprise."

The National ships were lying, heads up stream, along the easterly or left bank of the river. With her crew working their guns with a good will unsurpassed, the Arkansas passed down the long line, taking the broadsides as they came. Her smokestack was shot so full of holes that the draft from her furnaces was deadened, and she was able to steam but one knot an hour. Heavy projectiles from the big ships crashed through her sides and in two instances a shot wiped out a gun's crew. But undismayed the living took the place of the dead, and with shouts and cheers ("Talk about yelling and cheering—you should have heard it!" [1]) fought on until they were safe under the guns of the Vicksburg batteries. Every National ship was struck by at least one shot from the guns of the Arkansas. Brown was at once promoted for "meritorious conduct." He was the first Confederate naval officer to compel the unappreciative Richmond government to recognize, in this way, the worth of naval work.

It was characteristic of Farragut to acknowledge frankly in his report that he had been mistaken about the strength of the enemy, and that through a "feeling of security" he had been "surprised." He also gave credit for bravery to the Confederate

[1] Report of Lieutenant George W. Gift.

commander by saying in the report that "it was a bold thing" to do.

In the hope of destroying the Arkansas under the batteries of the town, and with the object at any rate of protecting the mortar flotilla below, Farragut ordered his fleet to prepare to pass down the river immediately—that is, on the day the Arkansas succeeded in reaching the shelter of the Vicksburg batteries. But it was six o'clock in the afternoon before the ships were ready to form in line, and dark before they were under fire. When opposite the batteries all of the ships reduced their speed, while several stopped their engines entirely and drifted with the current in order that their guns might be worked more effectively. But the heavy smoke filled the air, and the Arkansas, with her rusty iron sides, was moored under a red bluff. Some of the crews on the National fleet did not see her until her guns lit up the scene, and at best none gave her more than two broadsides. She was, indeed, cut up badly, but she was not sunk, or even silenced.

Then Commander William D. Porter, commanding the ironclad gunboat Essex, of the Davis fleet (this Porter was another son of the old Commodore), offered to run down under the batteries and destroy the Arkansas. The effort (made on July 22d), showed great gallantry, for the Essex remained under fire for more than two hours, and was struck by forty-two heavy shot besides a perfect hail from field guns and musketry aimed at her ports. But she failed to destroy the Arkansas. Meantime the

Queen of the West (Lieutenant Colonel Alfred E. Ellet, commanding), ran down and rammed the much-harried Confederate, but she did no harm, and was badly cut up for her pains. She finally steamed away up stream while the Essex ran below and joined Farragut's fleet.

The Essex was the first ironclad regularly under Farragut's control, for while the vessels of the Davis fleet were his to command while he was present as senior officer, they were regularly a separate fleet. It was natural for Farragut to dislike such ships as the river ironclads, and his first experience with them confirmed his prejudices. Before the Arkansas appeared, and while waiting to learn whether an army corps would be sent to co-operate with the navy before Vicksburg, Farragut went aboard the ironclad Benton—Davis's flagship —and steamed down the river for a look at a new battery lately erected. As the ship arrived within range a heavy solid shot from one of the batteries came crashing through her casemate, armor and all, and killed a man standing beside Farragut. For a moment he looked at the corpse and then said : "Everybody to his taste. I am going on deck ; I feel safer outside." And in a letter dated September 3d, of the same year, when referring to his experiences at Vicksburg, he said : "I would have given my admiral's commission to have gotten up to the Arkansas. I wanted a wooden ship to do it. *The ironclads are cowardly things*, and I don't want them to succeed in the world."

His mention of his "admiral's commission" is

interesting. On May 14, 1862, President Lincoln sent a message to Congress in which he refers to a law, previously enacted, "to promote the efficiency of the navy," and then says :

"Believing that no occasion could arise which would more fully correspond with the intention of the law or be more pregnant with happy influence as an example, I cordially recommend that Captain D. G. Farragut receive a vote of thanks of Congress for his services and gallantry displayed in the capture of Forts Jackson and St. Phillip, city of New Orleans, and the destruction of various gunboats, rams, etc."

Accordingly, Mr. Grimes, of the Senate Naval Committee introduced, on May 21st, a resolution tendering "the thanks of the people and of the Congress of the United States" to "Captain David G. Farragut of the United States Navy, and to the officers and men under his command." The resolution was passed, and on July 11, 1862, it received the President's signature.

Up to this time Farragut had commanded the fleet with the title of flag-officer, which had been established by the act of December 21, 1861. But by "an act to establish and equalize the grade of line officers of the United States navy," that was approved on July 16, 1862, the rank of Rear Admiral was created, with sea pay at $5,000 a year, and Farragut was the first officer to receive a commission in this rank. His commission bore date on the day that the act was signed.

Under orders from Washington, Farragut had

gone up the river a second time. He had passed
the Vicksburg batteries also. But because the Confederates at Vicksburg were well supported in the
country east of the river, and because their more
important batteries were located so high on the
bluffs that the guns on the ships could not reach
them, absolutely nothing had been gained by the
expedition. And to add to Farragut's embarrassments the army had failed to assist him. General
Williams was again with the fleet, but his force
was only 3,000 men, and on July 3d, General Hal-
leck, who, it had been hoped, would furnish an
adequate number, was obliged to telegraph that
"the scattered and weakened condition of my forces
renders it impossible" to coöperate. In short the
expedition, instead of helping the National cause,
aided the Confederates, since Farragut by temporarily shutting off their sources of supplies found
west of the river, had shown them that they needed
to bestir themselves if they were to continue receiving the pork, beef and grain they had been drawing
from the Red River country.

When, therefore, Rear Admiral Farragut, under
orders from Washington, returned to New Orleans
(July 28th), and Davis with his ironclads steamed
up the river for repairs, the Confederates took the
aggressive, and determined to drive the National
forces (5,000 men), out of Baton Rouge. If they
could hold Baton Rouge and Vicksburg, their commerce with the rich Red River Valley would be unimpeded.

General Breckinridge was sent to capture Baton

Rouge, and the Arkansas was ordered to go down and help in the attack. She arrived within sight of the city, on August 5, 1862, but there her engines broke down. They were repaired as far as possible, and next morning an effort was made to attack the National ships that Farragut had sent up from New Orleans to assist in the defense of Baton Rouge. The most important of these National ships, and the one nearest the Arkansas as she headed down the river, was the Essex. A fierce naval duel seemed to be at hand, but soon after the Arkansas got under way one engine broke again. She was then driven ashore, and the Essex, approaching within 400 yards (according to Lieutenant Read of the Arkansas), poured in such a hot fire that the crew of the disabled ship was ordered to leave her, while Lieutenant Henry K. Stevens, who was temporarily in command, set her on fire, and let her go adrift. The Essex kept up a heavy cannonading meantime, and at ten o'clock (August 6, 1862), fire reached the magazine, and the Arkansas was blown to pieces.

"It is one of the happiest moments of my life," said the enthusiastic Farragut in his official report of August 7th, "that I am enabled to inform the Department of the destruction of the ram Arkansas; not because I held the ironclad in such terror, but because the community [Nation] did."

The Arkansas was the last armored vessel of the Confederacy in the Mississippi Valley. After her destruction, the Confederates were never able to put anything afloat that was really dangerous.

But while the National ships were then able to pa-
trol the river almost at will, the Confederates, hav-
ing failed in their attack on Baton Rouge, began
building fortifications well-nigh impassable on the
bluffs at Port Hudson, twenty miles above that city.
As a point for the control of the river by land batteries,
Port Hudson was at least as advantageous as Baton
Rouge; the force soon concentrated there by the
Confederates was so great that the Federal troops at
Baton Rouge were withdrawn on August 16, 1862.

With the fortifications at Port Hudson armed and
manned, the Confederate hold upon the river was
far stronger than when Farragut had first left New
Orleans in May.

CHAPTER XVII

THE STORY OF THE IRONCLAD WARSHIP

So many references have been made already to the ironclad ships of the Civil War, and so much is to be said about them hereafter, that the work of Admiral Farragut will be better appreciated if a concise account of the development of these fighting machines is given in this place.   The idea of building a bullet-proof ship is old, and it was put to practical use in numerous places many years before the Civil War.   For instance, when Pontiac's Indians were besieging the fort where Pittsburg, Pa., now stands, the garrison built and launched a wooden-armored boat that drove the red men from the entrenchments they had constructed in the river banks.

The first contract made by any government for an iron armored ship was that signed in 1843 when the United States ordered a floating battery of Stevens, the Hoboken inventor.

During the Crimean War the French used floating batteries driven by screw propellers, and protected by 4-inch iron plates.   The success of these ironclads at Kinburn (October 17, 1855), led to the use of iron armor on the sides of steam vessels that were of the model then common in all navies, the Gloire, of France, being the first of this class.

The innovation thus made, though widely discussed, did not find much favor among naval men, the bravest of whom felt, as Admiral Farragut did, that armor was a "cowardly thing." After the beginning of our Civil War the Confederates at once saw the need of ironclad ships. In May, 1861, S. R. Mallory, Confederate Secretary of the Navy, wrote, "Inequality of numbers may be compensated by invulnerability. Not only does economy, but naval success, dictate the wisdom and expediency of fighting with iron against wood."

It was in accordance with this belief that the Confederates favored the building of those ironclad floating batteries on the Mississippi which have already been described. It will be remembered that each of these batteries was a floating fort. In designing the Confederate ironclads, casemate ships without masts, and propelled by steam, were alone considered; and when the National government began building armor-clad gunboats on the upper waters of the Mississippi the casemate idea was also adopted. It was on a casemate gunboat, as already said, that Farragut went under fire at Vicksburg.

The most famous Confederate ironclad was the one known to history as the Merrimac, although after she was rebuilt she was named the Virginia. When the National forces supinely abandoned the Norfolk Navy Yard to the Confederates, the steam frigate Merrimac was lying at one of the docks. She was burned and sank at her moorings. During the summer of 1861, when the Confederate naval authorities contemplated building an ironclad with which to gain control of Chesapeake Bay and tribu-

tary waters, they turned to the half-burned hull of
the old frigate because it was already provided with
engines and a screw propeller.

The wreck was raised and placed in the drydock.
Chief-engineer W. P. Williamson overhauled and
improved the machinery, while Naval Constructor
J. L. Porter, after cutting the hull down to where
the old berth-deck had been, built a new deck of
heavy timbers. On this deck he erected a casemate
with sloping timber walls two feet thick, and covered it with a double layer of 2-inch iron plates.
To the bow of the ship was bolted a cast-iron wedge
that projected two feet from the stem. Her guns
included six 9-inch Dahlgrens and four excellent
rifles, two of 7-inch and two of 6-inch calibre.

The Confederates began work on the Merrimac in
June, 1861. In February, 1862, she was ready for
her trial trip. On the 24th of that month, Flag-
officer Franklin Buchanan was ordered to the command of the James River defenses, and he hoisted
his flag on the Merrimac of which he also became
the captain. The letter of Secretary Mallory ordering Buchanan to this command shows great confidence in the vessel. " Her powers as a ram are
regarded as very formidable," he says, and that
was something to " commend itself to " the captain,
"in the present scarcity of ammunition." The
secretary also suggested "a dashing cruise on the
Potomac as far as Washington," and in another
letter dated March 7th, urged an attack upon New
York. "Such an event would eclipse all the glo-
ries of the combats of the sea, would place every

man in it preëminently high, and would strike a blow," said the Secretary, "from which the enemy could never recover."

The next day (March 8) the new Merrimac left the navy yard to begin the career for which the secretary had planned such a dazzling climax. She had not yet had a trial trip, but her engines had been turned over at the dock, her armor plates had been well slushed to make the projectiles slide off easily, and the crew to a man were enthusiastic in their confidence of success.

As the Merrimac left Norfolk the National steam frigates St. Lawrence, Roanoke and Minnesota were lying at wide intervals in a line along Hampton Bar from Fortress Monroe toward Newport News. The sailing frigate Congress lay just east of Newport News Point and the sailing sloop of war Cumberland just around the point to the westward. It was a lovely day, with a gentle breeze blowing, and in the rigging the sailing vessels had put up lines upon which the wash clothes were rapidly drying. In all the National fleet there was not a man who gave serious thought to the ironclad that for months past had been building down at Norfolk; for the naval men of that day were not to be roused from their comfortable trains of thought by any new-fangled notions whatever.

However, at noon exactly, a lookout on the Cumberland saw a heavy trail of smoke in the route to Norfolk, and a little later it was observed that it was coming from a low black hulk that answered the description of the rebuilt Merrimac.

The Cumberland's crew were called to quarters, then, and at the same time the Congress prepared for battle. Slowly but relentlessly, the Merrimac came plowing across the open water. As she arrived within range, the Congress opened fire, but, save for a broadside in reply, the Merrimac gave no heed to this. She was heading for the Cumberland, determined to begin at one end of the Federal line and sink the ships in succession. The men on the Cumberland fired broadside after broadside, but the shot bounded from the iron plates or broke into fragments, until, unharmed and unimpeded, the Merrimac closed in and the iron wedge on her bow went crashing through the wooden wall of the old sloop just under the fore rigging.

As the Cumberland sank into the water the Confederates called on her crew to surrender. But Lieutenant George U. Morris (may his name live forever!) who was in command, replied : "Never! I'll sink alongside!" And the Cumberland went down with her flag flying, and the crew worked their guns till the rising waters wet their feet.

The Congress was attacked next and eventually set on fire with red-hot shot. Then the Merrimac, after seeing that the Federal forces from the shore batteries would be unable to extinguish the flames, headed away for the Norfolk Channel. The ebb tide was running and the Merrimac drew more than twenty-two feet of water. If she had remained to attack the three steam frigates mentioned she would have run a great and needless risk of getting aground. She was apparently unhurt by the day's battle, but she had lost the iron wedge from her bow when ramming the Cumberland, and several of her crew had been hurt by projectiles that had entered her port, among whom was Captain Buchanan, who had to relinquish the command to the executive officer, Lieutenant Thomas ap C. R. Jones.

No ship of war built before or since has had such a trial trip as that of the rebuilt Merrimac. And no ship has ever created a greater local panic than she did. When the news was telegraphed to Washington, a cabinet meeting was called and the opinion was there expressed that the new ironclad would "destroy, *seriatim*, every naval ship ; she will lay all the cities on the seaboard under contribution . . . not unlikely we shall have a shell or cannon ball from one of her guns in the White House before we leave this room." Worse yet, Assistant Secretary of War, John Tucker, wrote to Cornelius Vanderbilt of New York to ask : "For what sum will you contract to destroy the Merrimac ? . . . answer by telegraph, as there is no time to be lost."

March 8, 1862, was the darkest day known in the naval history of the Civil War, but the next day was to be the most memorable, all things considered, in the history of fighting ships. While naval men as a class had been opposed to the use of armored ships, a few had been found willing to try experiments with them. The National government had plenty of old wooden hulls that might have been converted into abler ironclads than the Merrimac, but nothing of the kind was done. On August 3, 1861, however, Congress made an appropriation for building ships of this kind. Designs were called for, and from those submitted, three were selected. One proved a failure, and need not be considered here. Another was a hull much like the old frigate hulls, and when covered with 4½-inch iron plates proved a good ship under the name of the New Ironsides. The third design selected for trial was that of the epoch-making Monitor submitted by John Ericsson, who had previously gained a reputation by introducing the screw propeller. Ericsson's plan was something no sailor could have invented. He began by designing a hull 124 feet long by 34 wide and 6 deep that was in shape like an elongated saucer—rounded at the ends and rounding in cross section. Above and across this he laid a superstructure like a great box or scow, 172 feet long, 41 wide and 5 deep. This superstructure projected 3 feet 8 inches beyond each side of the lower hull, and 24 feet beyond each end. The whole hull was like a flatboat riding a canoe, and one may say now that a worse sea-going hull it would be hard to design, even though it did ride the waves easily.

Nevertheless, because of one other feature this vessel was to work a tremendous revolution in the world. The hull of the Monitor floated but a few inches above water, and there was no good place in or on it for mounting guns. To arm this ship it was necessary to erect a superstructure, but instead of building a casemate, as had been previously done in Europe as well as in the South, Ericsson made a revolving turret, 9 feet high and 20 feet in diameter (inside dimensions), which he located on the centre of the deck. The turret was composed of eight layers of one-inch thick iron plates, and it revolved on a spindle turned by steam engines. Two 11-inch Dahlgrens were mounted in the turret and fired through ports cut in the iron walls.

It should be remembered here that the revolving turret was invented by Theodore R. Timby, of Syracuse, N. Y., in 1843, and Ericsson paid him a royalty for the use of it; but it was first brought into use on the ill-shaped hull which was built and launched under the name of the Monitor.

The government contract with Ericsson was signed on October 4, 1861—about four months after the Confederates began rebuilding the Merrimac. But the work was driven with such speed that the hull was launched on January 30, 1862, and on the night of March 8th, while yet the flames of the old frigate Congress were illuminating the waters of Hampton Roads, the Monitor under Captain J. L. Worden appeared upon the scene.

At 7:30 o'clock on the morning of March 9th, the great casemated ironclad Merrimac left her anchorage at Sewell's Point and steamed across toward Hampton Bar to continue the work of destroying the National steamers, before making the "dashing cruise on the Potomac" which had been planned by the Confederate secretary of the navy. The little Monitor got under way at the same time, and with a tired but eager crew at the guns in the turret (they had been at work all night), she steamed into deep water and waited. An hour passed in idleness, for the Merrimac was slow, but at 8:30 o'clock the Confederates opened fire on the Minnesota at a range of a mile. At that Captain Worden drove the Monitor out to meet the Merrimac, and ranging up within pistol shot gave the order : "Commence firing."

Each gun had been loaded with a solid shot, and when Lieutenant S. D. Greene, commanding in the turret, after careful aim, pulled the lock string of a gun, the iron plates of the Merrimac broke and rattled under the impact of the projectile, but the casemate was not penetrated. To the Monitor's fire the Merrimac replied with a broadside, every shot of which struck the Monitor's turret, but not one entered it.

Thereafter the crews of both ships, having perfect confidence in the protection of their armor, worked their guns with unsurpassed deliberation, and for two hours with an unheard of lack of success. As one lieutenant on the Merrimac said, "I find I can do her [the Monitor] about as much damage by snapping my thumb at her" as by firing the gun. The Merrimac tried to ram the Monitor but failed because the latter was able to dodge the blow. The Monitor fired a shot while her side touched the Merrimac. It broke the plates and bulged the wood backing but it did not enter, and when the Monitor tried to ram the Merrimac she failed to do any damage.

It is easy now to see that if the Monitor's guns had been aimed at the Merrimac's water line, or at any one spot on the Merrimac's casemate for several shots in succession, they would have penetrated

and won a decisive victory. But Greene did neither.
Eventually Lieutenant C. A. R. Jones of the Merrimac began firing at the Monitor's conning tower, a
superstructure made of iron logs. A shell exploded
against a slit in the wall through which Captain
Worden was looking, and the flaming powder
blinded him. While waiting to learn the extent of
Worden's injury Greene took the Monitor out of
the fight. The Merrimac's crew supposed the
enemy was retreating, and as their boat was leak-
ing rather badly, and the tide was falling so that
she was likely to go aground if manœuvred further
on the battle-ground, she was taken over to the
channel leading to Norfolk.

Lieutenant John Taylor Wood, of the Merrimac,
writing after the war, said truly that "the battle
was a drawn one, so far as the two vessels were con-
cerned. But in its general results the advantage
was with the Monitor." She saved the Federal
ships from destruction, and she kept the Merrimac
from every kind of a "dashing cruise" until the
National land forces encompassed Norfolk and compelled the Confederates to destroy her.

By her achievement, the Monitor conquered the
prejudices of the naval world. Farragut, though
he believed that armor was "cowardly," soon acknowledged the value of monitors, and a time came
when he delayed a battle in order to add one of
them to his fleet.

The Confederates clung to the casemate plan per-
force. They had no shops fit for the construction
of revolving turrets, and but few mechanics able to

do the class of work that would have been needed in building them. It was clearly seen, however, that the casemate plan had some serious defects which were emphasized, for instance, in the Louisiana. The inability of her crew to train the guns through any considerable arc, or even to elevate or depress them, was manifest. Other Confederate casemate ships had better ports, but the handling of the guns was restricted nevertheless. The single revolving turret, on the other hand, had an all-around fire, and even with two turrets the guns of both could be easily trained on an enemy, no matter what his bearing. The turret, therefore, became a permanent feature of armored ships in Europe as well as in America. In time, when it was desirable to carry more guns than could be placed in two turrets, they were mounted between the turrets and a casemate was then built from turret to turret to protect them. That is to say, the twentieth century battleships of the world have been developed from the two classes of ironclads used in our Civil War.

Yet, when Farragut declared that armor clads were "cowardly things," and that the best defense against an enemy's fire was an accurate fire of our own guns, he was entirely right, and the present trend of naval opinion is in support of those sentiments. We have built ships with the idea that they must carry thick armor in order that they may *stay in* the battle line, but the memory of the Essex with her short guns and lack of power to reach the Phœbe is not lost. The aggressive men of the navy see that a ship must be able first of all *to get into* the battle line, and that when there the next requisite is "a well-directed fire from our own guns." Acting according to the theory of our first admiral our naval constructors in time will develop a battleship that with thinner armor will have far greater speed and a far more efficient battery than any now in hand.

CHAPTER XVIII

AT PENSACOLA AND BEFORE PORT HUDSON

AFTER returning from the unfortunate expedition up the Mississippi River, Farragut proceeded from New Orleans to Pensacola, where he arrived on August 20, 1862. Having been abandoned by the Confederates for lack of men to hold it, Pensacola had become a base of supplies for the Gulf blockading fleet, and Farragut went there to direct the work.

It is to be noted that while Farragut was in the river the ships had done nothing but blockade the ports off which they were stationed. On October 15th, however, he wrote to the Secretary of the Navy: "I am happy to inform you that Galveston, Corpus Christi and Sabine City and the adjacent waters are now in our possession. . . . All we want is a few soldiers to hold the places, and we will soon have the whole coast. It is a much better mode and a more effectual blockade to have the vessels inside instead of outside." And on December 4th he said: "I have all the coast except Mobile Bay, and I am ready to take that the moment I can get troops to hold the forts, etc." He was constantly strengthening his grip on the coast, and extending the sphere of his influence.

Nevertheless the later days of 1862 and the earlier of 1863 together made up a period that was disas-

trous to the National forces afloat as well as ashore,
and Farragut's command suffered its share of re-
verses. Galveston and Sabine City were retaken.
The Confederate cruiser Florida, commanded by
Captain John N. Maffitt, ran the blockade (September 4th) and entered Mobile.   There she was refitted
and on the night of January 15, 1863, she ran out
again to make a most destructive raid on the commerce of the United States. In a private letter
mentioning the escape of the Florida, we get an
interesting glimpse of Farragut's spirit. In speaking of the fact that the gunboat Cuyler chased the
Florida off shore, he said : "If the Cuyler runs
her down, as I think she will, in a gale, as it was
blowing, both vessels will go down. I would not
hesitate a moment, and I don't think Emmons will."
The admiral would have rammed an enemy on the
high seas in a gale of wind.

The National cruiser Hatteras, a converted merchantman, while blockading Galveston, was attacked and sunk by the famous Alabama, under
Raphael Semmes.

To understand how the appearance of these two
Confederate cruisers within his jurisdiction, affected Farragut, we may very well digress a moment
to consider the career of the warships which were
afloat upon the high seas, first and last, under the
Confederate flag. The fleet comprised more than
twenty all told, which number included several
merchantmen captured by other cruisers and fitted
out while at sea to aid in the work begun by their
captors.

The object for which these cruisers were commissioned was the destruction of the high-seas commerce of the Northern States. That such destruction was then, and is yet, entirely within legal bounds is not to be questioned, and it is to be observed that the swift cruisers in modern navies, commonly called commerce-destroyers, are very good peace preservers. On the other hand, history shows very clearly that commerce destruction never ended a war.

The Sumter, commanded by Raphael Semmes, was the first Confederate cruiser to raid northern merchant ships. Originally a screw merchantman called the Habana, she was fitted out at New Orleans with five light guns. She steamed out of the Mississippi River on June 30, 1861, and after cruising with much success through the West Indies, during which time Semmes eluded the Federal cruiser Iroquois, he took the Sumter to Europe, where he was finally blockaded at Gibraltar (January, 1862), by the Federal cruisers Kearsarge, Tuscarora and Chippewa. Being unable to escape, Semmes laid up his ship and eventually sold her to a Liverpool merchant who made a blockade-runner of her. She had captured 18 vessels, of which eight were burned.

The Florida, of which Farragut wrote as quoted above, was the first Confederate cruiser built for war purposes. She was from the yard of William C. Miller & Sons, Liverpool. Under the name of Oreto, the Florida sailed from that port on March 22, 1862, bound for Nassau in the Bahamas. Her

guns and stores were sent in another steamer to the
same port.   The two ships then went to an unin-
habited island of the group where the Florida
was fitted out and her flag hoisted under the
orders of John Newland Maffitt, lieutenant commanding.

The Florida had but eighteen men on board all
told, and within five days yellow fever prostrated
all but Maffitt and five others.   At Cardenas Bay,
Cuba, to which the Florida steamed to recruit,
Maffitt was stricken with the fever, and then while
yet in bed he was ordered by the Spanish to take
his ship to Havana.   Knowing that he should find
trouble at that port, Maffitt put to sea and headed
for Mobile instead.   He arrived off the bar on September 4, 1862.   Three blockaders were lying where
they commanded the channel, but hoisting British
colors Maffitt steamed boldly in, and arrived between two of them before he was ordered to stop.
Then he hoisted his own flag and ran for the fort
with success.   It was a dash that Farragut might
have described as "one of the elegancies of the
profession."

After refitting at Mobile the Florida escaped on
January 15, 1863, and went on a cruise across the
Atlantic to Brest, France, and back to the West
Indies.   She finally anchored in Bahia, Brazil, on
October 4, 1863, having captured, meantime,
37 merchantmen.   The United States steamer
Wachusett, Commander Napoleon Collins, was in
port at the time, and Collins, like Hillyar of the
Phœbe, would not respect the port of a neutral

government that was unable to compel respect.
While Maffitt and some of his men were on shore,
Collins captured the Florida and took her to
Hampton Roads. The Washington authorities
disavowed the act and ordered her returned
to Bahia. But while she was lying near Newport News in charge of three men she sank at
her moorings. One of the men probably opened
the seacocks.

The most famous of all the Confederate cruisers
was the Alabama, to which Semmes was transferred
from the Sumter. She was built by the Laird
Brothers, near Liverpool, and sent to sea on July
29, 1862. Steaming to the Azores, she met two
other British vessels bringing arms, stores and
crew. The Alabama was able to make ten knots
under sail alone, and eleven and one half under
steam and sail. Having large fore and aft sails she
could lie closer to the wind than ordinary merchantmen, and being commanded by an able sailor,
she proved a most efficient cruiser. Her career
lasted until June, 1864, and the losses she inflicted,
as estimated by the owners of the ships and cargoes
destroyed, amounted to $6,547,609. Semmes's story
of his "Service Afloat" is one of the most interesting of the books relating to the Civil War, because he wrote as he felt.

On June 11, 1864, the Alabama reached Cherbourg, France, where she was blockaded by the
Kearsarge, Captain John A. Winslow. On June
19th, the Alabama steamed out, and a most interesting naval duel followed. For while the Kear-

sarge carried heavier guns, and a few more men the
two ships were as nearly matched as two opposing
naval ships are ever likely to be.

The Kearsarge headed off shore in order that the
fight might take place so far from port that the
Alabama could not escape when beaten, and then
she turned suddenly and headed back under a full
head of steam. The firing began at a range of a
mile, but the Kearsarge rapidly closed in and the
two ships were soon steaming in a circle that was
in time reduced to a diameter of half a mile.

The Alabama for pivot guns carried a 100-pounder
British rifle, and an 8-inch shell gun; the Kearsarge
two 11-inch Dahlgrens, and it was chiefly on these
guns that the result of the battle depended. But
all guns were worked with the full powers of their
crews, and at the end of an hour and ten minutes,
according to the report of Semmes, the Alabama
was in a sinking condition.

Finding that she was going down, he headed the
Alabama for the beach, but the Kearsarge ranged
up within 400 yards and continued the fire. The
rising water soon drowned the fires in the Alabama's
stoke hole, and the Confederate flag was hauled
down. The wounded and some who could not swim
were sent off in two boats. Semmes threw his
sword into the sea, and then, with the remainder of
his crew, jumped overboard, where he and a number of his men were picked up by the steam yacht
Deerhound, belonging to Mr. John Lancaster, an
Englishman. They were carried to Southampton.
Said Farragut, after hearing the story of this bat-

tle : "I would sooner have fought that fight than any ever fought on the ocean."

The Georgiana was also built by the Lairds and she was a much more powerful cruiser than the Alabama. But on March 20, 1863, while striving to get into Charleston, S. C., where she was to fit out, she was driven ashore by the blockaders and destroyed.

More important still were two double turreted ironclads built by the Lairds in 1862–63. The armor was from $4\frac{1}{2}$ to $5\frac{1}{2}$ inches thick, and two 9-inch rifles were mounted in each turret. Confederate officers (notably, Captain Hollins) expressed the belief that these ships were powerful enough to lift the blockade and lay Northern ports under contribution. Their power was never tested, however, for when they were ready for sea, and Lord Russell had declared that "her Majesty's government cannot interfere in any way with the vessels," the American Minister, Charles Francis Adams, wrote a note to say that allowing these ironclads to escape was "practically opening to the insurgents free liberty in this kingdom to execute a policy of attacking all the seaboard cities of the North." And to this he added, "It would be superfluous in me to point out to your Lordship that this is war." And it was seen, as Farragut said at the time, that, in spite of the Civil War, any European government would find the United States "a hard nut to crack." Her Majesty's government therefore found a way to stop the ships.

Another ironclad called "the Ram Stonewall"

was built in France, but it was not until January 6, 1865, that she got to sea under a Confederate commander (Captain T. J. Page). After she was in battle trim she appeared off Coruna, Spain, within sight of the Federal frigate Niagara and the sloop Sacramento, that were under the command of Commodore Thomas T. Craven. Craven was under orders to capture the Stonewall, but now that the opportunity was come he refused to fight her. However, the war ended before Page could do anything more with his ship.

Passing over other cruisers because their services were of less significance, the last to be considered is the Shenandoah, Captain James Iredell Waddell. She was a British merchant ship, originally, and was fitted for steam and sail power. She left London on October 18, 1864, and went to the north Pacific where she wiped out the American whaling fleet. In all she captured 38 ships, and destroyed 34. Some of these vessels were retaken after the end of the war. On learning definitely of the peace, the Shenandoah was headed for Liverpool, where she was eventually surrendered to the United States authorities.

After the war the United States Government pressed a claim against Great Britain for damages arising out of the work of the British built Confederate cruisers, but Lord Russell, "with some impatience," [1] declined to listen to the claim. Persistence, however, led to the Treaty of Washington (May 8, 1871), which expressed " the regret felt by

[1] Foster.

her Majesty's government for the escape . . .
of the Alabama and other vessels," and formulated
an agreement to submit the claim for damages to
arbitration.   The actual damage done to individual
ships and cargoes by 11 different cruisers, according to claims submitted, amounted to $17,900,633.
The matter went before what is known as the
Geneva Tribunal—a commission that included one
American, one British and three neutral members.

The upshot of the arbitration was the payment
to us of $15,500,000 for the damages adjudged actu-
ally to have been done to ships and cargoes.   For
that sum Great Britain was able to sweep her only
rival from the ocean, and during the forty years
that have elapsed since their ships were destroyed,
the American people have made no serious effort to
recover their old place upon the high seas.

After remaining at Pensacola for some weeks
Farragut was obliged to return to New Orleans by
the action of unfriendly foreigners.   "I deemed
that my presence here would be well, as the French
Admiral is here with two vessels at the city, and a
frigate at the bar.   There is also an English corvette
off the city, and we sailors understand each other
better in many cases than landsmen," the Admiral
wrote on November 14th.   The British ship was the
Rinaldo, Captain Hewitt, and her crew not only
learned to sing Confederate songs, such as the
"Bonnie Blue Flag" [1] but cheered for Jefferson

[1] The most popular song of the war on the Confederate side.
The people sang it, and the bands played it.   It began :

Davis on all possible occasions. Farragut eventually heard the singing, and said : "We must stop that. If it isn't stopped we shall have to drop down and blow him out of water." When Captain Hewitt learned how the Admiral felt about the matter, he quickly put an end to the singing.

As an additional reason for returning to New Orleans, Farragut noted that General Butler was operating in the Opelousas, and coöperation by the naval forces was advisable. More important still, both Butler and Farragut were now looking toward Port Hudson.

That Farragut should contemplate an attack on a river town when but a few months before he had deprecated taking his fleet up the Mississippi is a matter readily explained. He had objected to the expedition at the previous time because there were not enough soldiers available to make the move-

> " We are a band of brothers
>   And native to the soil,
> Fighting for the property
>   We gained by honest toil;
> And when our rights were threatened,
>   The cry rose near and far —
> ' Hurrah for the Bonnie Blue Flag
>   That bears the single star ! ' "

> CHORUS

> " Hurrah ! hurrah !
>   For Southern rights hurrah !
> Hurrah for the Bonnie Blue Flag
>   That bears the single star."

The first flag of the South was of solid blue bearing one white star.

ment successful. But now, with 5,000 men on shore, he thought Port Hudson might be taken and held. At the same time, however, he kept one eye on Mobile, as already noted. "If they will only let me *do something*," he said in a private letter, he would be contented.

On December 16th, General N. P. Banks came to New Orleans and relieved Butler. He brought "troops to open the Mississippi and occupy Texas," and in the first conference with him, Farragut "recommended the occupation of Baton Rouge," as a "base of operations" in an attack on Port Hudson. Baton Rouge was therefore occupied by the troops, supported by the naval forces, before the end of December, 1862, and then, early in 1863, Farragut determined to make a dash past Port Hudson, although he foresaw, of course, that doing so would by no means compel the Confederates to evacuate their forts.

The chief reason for undertaking this dash was that an attempt had been made by vessels from the upper river National fleet to take charge of the river between Vicksburg and Port Hudson, and it had failed, while the necessity for the control of that part of the Mississippi by the Federals was imperative.

The National army under Grant was at that time before Vicksburg, and the upper river flotilla, under Acting Rear Admiral D. D. Porter, was rendering efficient aid. Grant had taken command on January 30th. It was his purpose to lead his troops across the peninsula opposite Vicksburg, and on reaching the river south of the city to cross over to the easterly bank, and march up to attack the town from below.   To further this plan, and at the same time shut off the flow of supplies sent by the Confederates to Vicksburg from the Red River country, Admiral Porter ordered the river ram Queen of the West, commanded by Colonel Charles R. Ellet (a youth of twenty, by the way), to run past the batteries of Vicksburg.   Ellet succeeded on February 2d, and promptly destroyed several steamer loads of Confederate provisions.   The ironclad gunboat Indianola—a vessel that carried two 11-inch and two 9-inch guns besides several smaller ones—was sent down to support the swifter Queen. On the night of February 12th, the Indianola passed the batteries without any loss whatever.   A vessel captured from the Confederates below Vicksburg was then armed and Admiral Porter reported with justifiable pride that "this gives us complete control of the Mississippi except at Vicksburg and Port Hudson."

But Ellet, who was a youth of extraordinary enterprise and courage, in making a dash up the Red River to destroy three well-loaded Confederate transports, ran his boat aground under a Confederate battery where she had to be abandoned.   The Confederates got her afloat and after making repairs, sent her with three other armed river steamers, to hunt the ironclad Indianola.   They found her on the night of February 24th, and by a well-managed and courageous attack rammed her until she sank, later capturing her consort.

This victory again gave the Confederates the command of the Mississippi from Vicksburg to Port Hudson, and to render their triumph more complete, it appeared that Porter could not spare another detachment from his flotilla to go down to retrieve the lost ground.

The situation on the Mississippi, therefore, at the end of February, 1863, was as follows : General Grant was investing Vicksburg and was supported by Porter's flotilla, every vessel of which, however, lay in the river above the city.   At Baton Rouge General Banks was concentrating 12,000 men for an attack on Port Hudson, and Farragut's fleet was ready to support him.   But the river from Vicksburg to Port Hudson was under Confederate control, and the armies defending both of the towns named had free communication with the Confederate sources of supplies in the Red River watershed and beyond. It was obvious to Farragut that the first important service he could render the National cause was to deprive the Confederates of food and thus aid Grant and Banks in their attacks on Vicksburg and Port Hudson.   He saw, too, that such a service was then so important as to be worth even the risk of placing himself between the two heavily fortified towns where his own line of communications with a base of supplies would be cut off.

That is to say, in order to cut off the Confederate source of supplies, Farragut determined not only to take the risk of running past the heavy batteries at Port Hudson, with their plunging fire from bluffs eighty and one hundred feet high, but he was going to depend for his coal supply on the chance of floating barges by night past the batteries at Vicksburg, or on the more hazardous chance of another dash up past those batteries.

The general order which Farragut issued to his captains after determining to pass Port Hudson is the document which, perhaps, is remembered better among naval men than any other the Admiral ever wrote. It said:

The ships will each take a gunboat on her port side, and secure her as well aft as possible, so as to leave the port battery clear for the enemy's battery on the port side of the river, going up, after we round the point opposite Port Hudson.

Each ship will keep a little on the starboard quarter of her next ship ahead, so as to give free range to her chase guns, without risk of damage from premature explosion of shrapnel or shell.

The captains will bear in mind that the object is, to run the batteries at the least possible damage to our ships, and thereby secure an efficient force above for the purpose of rendering such assistance as may be required of us to the army at Vicksburg, or, if not required there, to our army at Baton Rouge.

If they succeed in getting past the batteries, the gunboats will proceed up to the mouth of Red River, and keep up police of the river batteries between that river and Port Hudson, capturing everything they can.

Should any vessel be disabled so that she is unable to pass Port Hudson, she will use the gunboat to the best advantage. If the captain thinks he can get by, try it; if he thinks not, let the gunboat drop her down below the range of the batteries. If both are disabled, then club down with a light

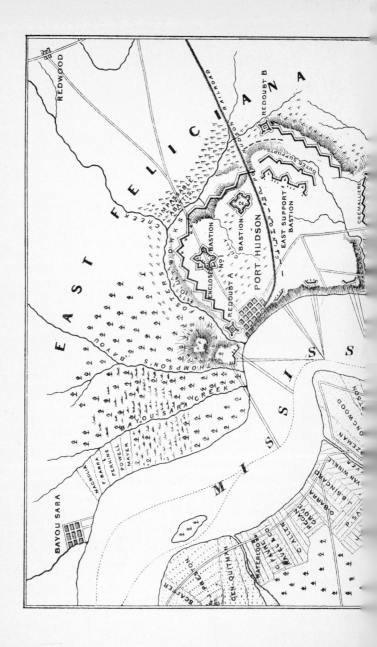

PORT HUDSON

anchor, or use the sails, as in his judgment may seem best.   But I expect all to go by who are able ; and *I think the best protection against the enemy's fire is a well-directed fire from our own guns*, shell and shrapnel at a distance, and grape when within four hundred or five hundred yards.

It is a most interesting fact in the history of our navy that several of our greatest sea fighters have used expressions that will serve to inspire the American sailor until warfare ends.   When John Paul Jones in the fight with the Serapis, was asked if he had surrendered, he replied, though his ship was sinking :   "*I have not yet begun to fight.*"   In the battle of Lake Erie, when the sailing master of the Lawrence called attention to the fact that, as the wind was blowing, the British fleet would have the weather gauge, the heroic Perry replied :   "*To windward or to leeward, they shall fight to-day.*"   And Farragut, with his wooden ships (he who had called ironclads "cowardly things"), when preparing to run the bluff-top batteries of Port Hudson, told his captains that "*the best protection against the enemy's fire is a well directed fire from our own guns.*"   This is the only instance on record where the whole art of battle has been described in a single sentence.

Lieutenant John C. Parker, who was then executive officer of the ironclad Essex, has left a description of the Admiral, as he appeared when preparing to pass Port Hudson :

"He was at this time in the full pride of his manhood, and presented a perfect picture of an ideal sailor.   Rather undersized, his figure was faultless, and, dressed with the neatness and care customary in the navy, he appeared much younger than he was. His smooth face with its prominent features was as clearly cut as a cameo, in which was blended firmness with gentleness. He always wore the regulation service cap, and his face as it lighted with a smile made an indelible impression, a mental photograph, which time has never effaced."

Parker also describes the Admiral as seen in action at this time. The Hartford had steamed up the river to draw the Confederate fire and give the Admiral a chance to see the location of the shore batteries:

"Steaming ahead with the ship's company at quarters, the Hartford soon began to draw the enemy's fire, and the shot from the lower battery began to reach her. At this moment the Admiral was standing under the mizzen boom and a shot having struck the boom further aft, threw a quantity of splinters over the younger officers standing near. The Admiral, who was intently observing the range of the guns as they opened upon the flagship, hastily turned his head as the shot struck, and noticing the slight muscular movement which is the result of a close call from a solid shot, exclaimed with a smile, 'What! Are you youngsters dodging?' The words were scarcely spoken when a round shot struck the boom square over his head. Dropping his left shoulder a mere trifle, and without moving an inch from his position, he turned his head toward the young officers and said:

" 'Gentlemen, bravery is a mere question of pride, but it is some comfort to dodge even as much as that,' illustrating his remark by raising his left hand and with the first finger of his right, measuring perhaps the width of his finger nail."

As for the other features of the general order to his captains when preparing to pass Port Hudson, one must note that, having ships with single propellers, Farragut secured some of the advantages of twin screws by lashing the ships together, two and two, and it is remembered that the most powerful gunboat was lashed to the slowest ship. Moreover, by putting the gunboat on the port side of the big ship, he sheltered the small boat from the fire of the batteries, all of which were on the easterly side of the river. In short, in the order of the procession and the location of the various ships the Admiral showed a strong desire, first of all, to secure the greatest efficiency of gun fire, and then as much protection as possible for the weaker vessels.

Port Hudson, as Private James K. Hosmer saw it somewhat later, was "a little cluster of perhaps forty or fifty houses on the edge of the bluff." It was enclosed on the landward side by a line of entrenchments seven miles long. Along the edge of the bluff were seven batteries mounting 19 guns, of which two were of 10-inch and two of 8-inch calibre, eight were rifles — 80-pounders and 50-pounders, while the remainder were smaller smoothbores. Furnaces were provided to heat the shot of the smoothbores, and all the guns were fitted "with delicate sights," by means of which "hot shot and shell could be thrown, almost with the precision of rifle balls, at objects passing below." Thirty-five field pieces to sweep the decks of the ships with shrapnel were also in place.

To pass these batteries, Farragut took the leading place with the Hartford, Captain James S. Palmer, the gunboat Albatross, Lieutenant Commander J. C. Hart, being lashed alongside. The Richmond, Captain James Alden, with the gunboat Genesee, Commander W. H. Macomb, came next. She was followed by the Monongahela (a 10-gun ship), Captain J. P. McKinstry, with the Kineo, Lieutenant Commander John Watters. Last of all came the Mississippi, Captain Melancton Smith, a side wheeler without a consort. The ironclad Essex was not included, but was placed with the gunboat Sachem near five mortar schooners that anchored within easy range of the batteries.

Of the details of preparing the ships only one item need be mentioned. The Hartford was provided with a speaking tube from the mizzen top to the wheel, and the pilot was placed in the mizzen top.

The night of March 14, 1863, was chosen for the dash past the batteries. At five o'clock in the afternoon of that day, Farragut visited all the ships of the squadron and talked over the situation and his general orders for the work until he saw that each captain was fully informed in the matter, and that each vessel was thoroughly prepared. As the night, still and damp, came on, a red light was hung over the stern of the Hartford, to serve as a preparatory signal, and just before ten o'clock, the squadron got under way. At eleven o'clock, as the flagship was abreast of the lower batteries, some pickets saw her through the gloom, and fired a rocket into the air. A minute later a number of locomotive head-lights were turned on the river—the first use of search-lights in war, perhaps—and then great fires of light wood flamed up on the westerly bank of the river, and threw a glare over the water by which the shore gunners were able to aim almost as well as if it were day. A storm of shot and shell soon burst upon the fleet and the thunder of the guns was heard by men working with cotton on the banks of the Courtableau, forty miles away.

"The Hartford," as Parker saw her, "being in the lead soon had the Citadel battery on her star-board quarter, and as she steamed ahead was thrown in bold relief by the huge signal fire on the west bank of the river. She stood out with the bright background of firelight as clear as a silhouette. On her poop deck stood a group of officers while the Admiral was mounted in the mizzen rigging, his pilot being above him in the mizzen top. At this time there was no smoke to obstruct the vision and every particle of her spars and rigging were visible. A moment later, when she commenced to fire her broadside guns, clouds of smoke enveloped her and she was lost to sight."

The other ships then opened in turn on the shore batteries. The smoke spread over the water and swelling up, fogged in the fleet until nothing was visible from the shore but a flame-riven cloud that drifted slowly up the stream.

The critical moment of the expedition had come. Blinded by the smoke, the faithful pilot of the Hartford, Thomas R. Carroll, called through the tube that he could no longer guide the ship aright. The firing was stopped and as she slowly emerged from the smoke it was seen that she was headed for the eastern shore with the current driving her on ; and the bluffs were already so close that her crew could distinguish the words of the Confederates when they called to each other. But by backing the engines of the Albatross at full speed while driving ahead those on the Hartford, Farragut cleared the bank and rounded the point, safe at last.

Several men who were in this fight remember now that when the danger of disaster to the Hartford seemed greatest, the Admiral showed his ability to grasp instantly the meaning of everything that was done or said around him. He saw when a gunner made a good shot, and said, "That's your sort," or "Well done, you! Give them another." He noted the position of the wheel. He hailed the mizzen top occasionally, to learn whether the pilot were yet alive. He conversed with and gave orders to his aides in a way that infused them with his own serene spirit. But when the forts were passed and he turned to look for the others of his fleet he could only exclaim :

"My God, what has stopped them ?"

A moment later as he gazed at the cloud of smoke he had left he saw it illuminated by a light that grew until he discerned the outlines of a ship in flames. The Mississippi, the last of the fleet, while driving at full speed past the batteries, was headed by her pilot too far to the westward, and getting into the eddy under the lee of the long bar opposite Port Hudson, she ran ashore so hard that no possible exertion could free her, though the Essex steamed up to help. For more than half an hour her crew labored, while the Confederates fairly ballasted her with the shot that they hurled into her hull. Then she was set afire and abandoned. It is a matter of record that Captain Melancton Smith was the last to leave the ship, and that her executive officer, Lieutenant George Dewey,—he who is Admiral of the navy at this writing—remained with him, and showed great heroism in rescuing her crew.

As the fire spread the flames "caused her sides to warp which threw her head off the reef where she was grounded, and being caught by the current she turned her head down stream, straightened herself up and with her entire lower rigging a blaze of fire passed down with the current." [1] Then the flames having reached the vents of her guns, she fired shot after shot until she reached the foot of Profit Island where the fuse that had been laid to her magazine did its work and she was blown to pieces.

In the meantime the Richmond had almost rounded the turn when a plunging shot released her safety valves and thus exhausted the steam in her boilers. Her captain then turned her around by the aid of her consort and ran below out of range, while her executive officer, Lieutenant Commander A. B. Cummings, who had just had a leg shot off,—

[1] Parker.

a mortal wound—said to his shipmates, "I would rather lose the other leg than go back."

The Monongahela, too, was unfortunate, for she was aground for twenty-five minutes, and, while making a heroic effort to continue on her way, her crank pin heated and the engines stopped. She was then obliged to drift down out of range.

Partly because of the excellent marksmanship of the Confederate gunners, and partly through misfortune that could not have been foreseen, Admiral Farragut was able to carry but two of his squadron past the batteries.

Loyall Farragut, a youth in his teens, the Admiral's only child, was on the quarterdeck of the Hartford, acting as aide while the batteries were passed. Fleet Surgeon J. M. Foltz said afterward that before reaching the batteries he went to the Admiral and asked for the assistance of the lad below with the wounded in the safest part of the ship. He explained that the boy was not in the service, and therefore had nothing to gain but everything to lose through exposure on the quarterdeck. To this the Admiral replied:

"No, that will not do. It is true our only child is on board by chance, and he is not in the service; but, being here, he will act as one of my aides, to assist in conveying my orders during the battle, and we will trust in Providence and *la fortune de la guerre.*"

The surgeon then appealed to the lad but he "wanted to be stationed on deck and see the fight." That ended the discussion.

As the batteries loomed up through the night, the Admiral took "from his pocket a simple piece of hempen rope, about a yard in length, to which was securely fastened at one end a cross-piece of wood," and showed his son how to pass the rope around a wounded limb and with the piece of wood set it tightly enough to stop the flow of blood from an artery.

Another view of Farragut's character was obtained when a lookout reported that a steamer was bearing down on the Hartford from above. In an instant the Admiral ordered the port battery manned. Then he called another division of the crew to repel boarders, drew his sword, and saying under his breath, "Let them come," prepared to lead his men in the hand-to-hand fight that was expected at the rail. He could have made a mark with his sword in such a fight, for though he was nearly sixty-two years old, he was an athlete in person, and those who saw him in attack have testified that he was most resolute in spirit.

By the reports of Major-General Franklin Gardner, commanding Port Hudson, there were five steamboats unloading supplies for the Confederate garrison when Farragut's fleet advanced. The work of discharging cargo was continued to the last moment possible, showing that the supplies were badly needed, but the steamers finally fled to Red River. Gardner in two different reports thereafter said that he had on hand only "ten days' subsistence" and a report from his commissary, on March 23d, proves that only 15,724 rations of flour then re-

mained.   On April 15th, there were 3,644 rations
of flour and 3,760 of bulk pork, while bacon and
corn were so scarce that the soldiers had to live on
reduced quantities of these articles.   The garrison
at this time numbered twenty thousand men.   Private Hosmer, previously quoted, says that the Confederates told him, after the surrender, that they
were reduced to a point when mule meat was eaten
by many of them after Farragut had closed the river.

Farragut in his letter to General Grant, when he
had passed Port Hudson, said : "Having learned
that the enemy had the Red River trade open to
Vicksburg and Port Hudson, and that two of the
gunboats of the upper fleet had been captured, I
determined to pass up, and if possible recapture the
boats and stop the Red River trade."

He stopped the Red River trade, and as a letter
to the Confederate Secretary of War, Seddon,
pointed out, "The enemy [National forces] having
command of the river, and innumerable transports
in their service, can move nearly 200 miles in
twenty-four hours, and thus have it in their power
to land an attacking force in large numbers without
timely notice of their approach."

General Grant in a letter written toward the end
of the month said, "I see by Southern papers that
Vicksburg must depend upon Louisiana or west of
the Mississippi for supplies.   Holding Red River
from them is a great step in the direction of pre-
venting this."

With Grant and an adequate force before Vicksburg, and Banks with another force at Port Hudson,

the taking of even a part of Farragut's fleet up past the latter's guns was worth the cost, even though the steamer Mississippi was lost. It was a movement conducted on Farragut's own initiative, when circumstances warranted it, and it was, as already said, a very different movement from the passage that had been made the previous year on orders from officials who were ignorant of the conditions prevailing in the Mississippi. Farragut now steamed up the river by easy stages to Vicksburg, where he communicated with General Grant and obtained coal from a barge load which the latter floated down past the Vicksburg batteries at night.

Acting Rear Admiral Porter was then in the bayou country on the east side of the river, north of Vicksburg, on an abortive expedition, and Farragut, who was anxious for more vessels, had an interview with General Alfred W. Ellet, commanding the River Defense Ram Fleet of the National forces, who at once offered to bring down his ram flotilla. It is worth noting here that this ram flotilla did effective work, while the Confederate flotilla failed utterly, and for a very good reason. The Confederate flotilla officials not only refused to work with the Confederate naval forces, but they would not work together, while Ellet's rams operated steadily and faithfully with and under the National naval officers. At the same time the Ellet family was most remarkable for reckless courage, and when sending two rams to Farragut disaster overtook them. Early in the morning of March 25th, the Lancaster and Switzerland sailed down to pass the Vicksburg batteries. Fearing no danger they started late and broad daylight was upon them before they arrived under the guns ashore. The Lancaster was shot to pieces and the Switzerland was disabled but passed down with flag flying, and was repaired.

While before Vicksburg Farragut sent his son Loyall home, saying that " the anxieties of a father should not be added to those of the commander," and then on the 27th, he steamed down with his two vessels and the ram Lancaster to blockade the Red River, where he arrived on April 2d. There he remained until April 30th. Remembering the fate of the Indianola, Farragut surrounded the Hartford with big logs, through which the Confederate rams would not be able to cut their way, and he lowered the yards of the ship down to the rail, connecting their ends with chain cables to keep at a distance ships bringing boarders. The blockade of the Mississippi was not absolutely complete ; but it was efficient enough severely to restrict the Confederate food supply, and to show the Southern leaders how badly they were handicapped by their lack of ships.

While lying at the mouth of the Red River with the Hartford, Albatross and Switzerland, early in May, a reinforcement from the fleet below Port Hudson joined the Admiral. General Banks had temporarily abandoned the siege of that place for a swift dash into the country west of the Mississippi. Four gunboats from the lower fleet worked their way through the bayous to support this movement. It was a dash at the Confederate source of food, and according to Private Hosmer, who was on the expedition, the movement was a feint that led the Confederates to reduce the garrison of Port Hudson materially. At any rate, the expedition was successful in capturing supplies, while two of the gunboats worked their way through to the Red River and Farragut.

At the end of April the Admiral went down to Port Hudson to communicate with the part of his squadron below ; for of course he was still in command of the whole Gulf blockading fleet, as well as of the squadron at the mouth of Red River. He also wished to communicate with General Banks. To get letters through to him, Farragut's private secretary, Edward C. Gabaudan, at his own request, was set adrift in a dugout, covered with dead brush in such fashion that it looked like a drift log. The Confederates came afloat once, to look at the strange thing, but it passed clear.

In the meantime, Grant was carrying out the plans that placed his army on the south and east sides of Vicksburg. Porter with a powerful squadron passed the Vicksburg river defenses (there were guns for eight miles along the Mississippi at that time), and reached New Carthage, which was then fifteen miles below Warrentown, the site of the southernmost of the Vicksburg batteries. Transports were brought down later. Then various feints were made to deceive the Confederates, and on April 29th a serious attack was directed by Porter's fleet on Grand Gulf, a point that had been

recently fortified to strengthen Vicksburg. This
attack failed, but on April 30th, the advance corps
of Grant's army crossed the Mississippi at Bruins-
burg, nine miles below Grand Gulf. On May 1st,
this advance corps met the Confederate General
Bowen and defeated him, and when two days later
Porter moved up to renew his attack on Grand
Gulf he found it had been evacuated. He at once
took possession, and then leaving the captured forts
in charge of Lieutenant-Commander Elias K. Owen,
he started that same day down the river to relieve
Farragut's blockaders at the mouth of Red River.
Thereupon Farragut, on May 6th, turned over the
Hartford and the minor vessels to the command of
Captain James S. Palmer, and went down the west
bank of the river (overland), to New Orleans,
arriving on May 1st. There he took charge of the
fleet in the river, and with it started up to Port
Hudson to aid in the campaign against that place.
These operations were, at last, pushed effectively,
though the siege proved rather monotonous. Four
Dahlgren guns were landed, under Lieutenant-
Commander Edward Terry, and did good service in
worrying the Confederates, who were already in
straits for lack of food. From time to time the
ships moved up in range and battered the forts
with the result that the Confederates, after a time,
having used up their ammunition, had to reply with
pieces of railroad iron in place of regular projectiles. With a less heroic commander than
General Franklin Gardner, the place would have
surrendered early in the season.

Rear Admiral Schley, who was serving on the Monongahela under Farragut, while before Port Hudson, has in his "Forty-five Years under the Flag" several stories of the Admiral.

Schley, at one time temporarily in command of the Monongahela, was sent up to bombard one of the forts, and through being unable to read a recall signal, continued firing longer than was intended by Farragut. Accordingly, when Schley reported on board the flagship, the Commander-in-Chief reprimanded him. The story is told as follows:

"'Captain, you begin early in your life to disobey orders. Did you not see the signal flying for near an hour to withdraw from action?'

"The decided manner and tone in which Admiral Farragut asked this question, taken with the surprising inquiry itself, confused and embarrassed the writer, who felt that the ship's work was creditable rather than censurable. An attempt to explain, somewhat stammeringly made, and to the effect that we could not read the signals, which were seen only with difficulty through the smoke, elicited the quick reply from the Admiral that he 'wanted none of this Nelson business in his squadron about not seeing signals.'

"The writer succeeded, however, in stating to him that the lack of wind and the smoke of battle enveloping the ship made it impossible to interpret the signal, which, from the nature of his orders to destroy the citadel, could hardly have been supposed to refer to the writer, whose duty in the premises seemed clear—to retire only when the duty was done.

"The Admiral then invited the writer into his cabin. The moment the door was closed behind him there was an entire change in his tone and manner as he said smilingly, 'I have censured you, sir, on the quarterdeck for what appeared to be a disregard of my orders. I desire now to commend you and your officers and men for doing what you believed right under the circumstances. Do it again whenever in your judgment it is necessary to carry out your conception of duty.'"

"The Admiral," says Schley, writing of this period, "was a man of perhaps five feet seven inches in height. His gait and step were those of a very young man, and in conversation he was an animated and interesting talker. His information and experience were general, and upon almost all subjects—professional, scientific or political—he was interesting and attractive. Like all great men he was affable and accessible. His manner was one of great mildness and self-poise. His ideas were clear and his methods of doing things were always decided. When he had made up his mind to give battle in a certain way, it was realized that his way was the best. In any of the emergencies of battle, his towering genius was readiest and his cool self-possession was an inspiration to everybody. The wide difference that was apparent between this sprightly, kind, mild and pleasing gentleman, even when under a heavy load of responsibility, and his lion-like character and presence when battle was going on, was the contrast between sunshine and storm.   His judgment of men was excellent, as the choice of officers with whom he surrounded himself indicated.   The unvarying and complete success he met in everything he undertook in that great war was due largely to his strong personality, unerring purpose and dashing example."

After a paragraph to show wherein Farragut and Nelson were alike, Schley adds: "Farragut's private life and high ideals, however, gave him preeminence over his great English compeer."

On July 4, 1863, Vicksburg surrendered to Grant; Port Hudson capitulated on the 9th.   "I am growing old fast and need rest," said Farragut at this time; and with the surrender of Port Hudson he was able to enjoy it.   The command of the Mississippi was turned over to Porter, who arrived at New Orleans on August 1st, and Farragut, taking the Brooklyn and Richmond with the Hartford, at once headed for New York where he arrived on August 10th.

CHAPTER XIX

IN WAITING BEFORE HIS LAST BATTLE

IN December, 1861, on his way to Washington to consult with the Secretary of the Navy and other government officials, Farragut passed through New York unnoted by the people, who knew so little of his talents and character that they even expressed doubts about his loyalty to the flag under which he had served for more than fifty years. Under date of August 13, 1863, a committee of eighty-one influential men of the city wrote to him to say that "the citizens of New York are too familiar with your brilliant career in the public service not to feel earnestly desirous of showing, in some appropriate manner, their high appreciation of your personal and professional character. The whole country, but especially this commercial metropolis, owes you a large debt of gratitude for the skill and dauntless bravery with which . . . you have sustained the authority of the government and recovered and defended the national territory." Therefore they extended to him "a cordial welcome" and asked him to name a convenient time when he would allow them in person to assure him of their high respect and regard.

The Chamber of Commerce sent an engraved set of resolutions in which it was declared that Farragut at New Orleans had "achieved one of the most celebrated victories of any time;" that "in the progress of the war for the unity and life of this great Nation, no services have been more eminent than those of Admiral Farragut;" and that "in the daily increasing commerce of the port of New Orleans," was to be found "a pleasing omen of the renewed happiness and prosperity" that would accrue to all the Southern cities once they were brought under the old flag.

It was characteristic of the man to say in reply to these resolutions "that we did our duty to the best of our ability, I believe; that a kind Providence smiled upon us and enabled us to overcome obstacles before which the stoutest of our hearts would have otherwise quailed, I am certain."

In the meantime the Admiral must see that his ships were thoroughly overhauled and repaired. And there was yet the capture of Mobile Bay to engage his thoughts.

From the beginning of the war the effective work of the Federal navy—the work that had tended to restore and preserve the unity of the Nation—had consisted, as already set forth, in maintaining and strengthening the blockade of the Confederate ports, and in opening and holding the Mississippi for the use of Federal warships and merchant boats. In one point of view the National control of the Mississippi was an extension of the blockade. Scores of blockade runners had taken supplies to Matamoras, Mexico. From that place they were conveyed across the Rio Grande into Texas, whence the Confederates carried them by whatever conveyance

was possible—bull team, dugout, or steamer—to
Vicksburg and Port Hudson. When a port like
New Orleans was occupied, and a line of communication like the Mississippi was wholly secured, the
Confederate trade was effectually stopped, and successful work for the ending of the war accomplished.

As already noted, Farragut had wished to capture Mobile Bay immediately after the fall of New
Orleans. It might have been done then with comparative ease, for the forts guarding the main entrance to the bay were not fully manned, and were
not well supplied with ammunition or guns ; indeed
the fort guarding the western pass had not yet been
built. The opening of the Mississippi on which
the Navy Department was then bent was a matter
of much greater importance—no one doubts that
fact, but the Department was in error in supposing that any naval force could do the work single
handed. When Farragut had shown that it was
not possible to control the Mississippi with sea-going ships alone the Department might well have allowed him to go to Mobile while awaiting the co-
operation of the army in occupying the river. The
navy, with a small force of soldiers at that time
might have occupied Mobile Bay, and compelled
the forts there to surrender as they had done on the
Mississippi. For with the National fleet in the bay
and a force of soldiers on Mobile Point neither Fort
Morgan nor Fort Gaines could have obtained supplies, and surrender through starvation would have
been inevitable. The failure to allow Farragut to

make the attack gave the Confederates the opportunity to prepare for a vigorous defense.

Mobile Bay is now a fine harbor with a deep water channel to the city docks, where business is increasing, and is to increase, by marvelous strides. At the beginning of 1864, it was but a harbor of refuge. A bar at the upper end with only nine feet of water on it, shut off the city from the sea and the ships that might have come there for the great white staple of the South had a channel been provided.

A glance at a good chart of war-time date shows that Mobile Bay was about thirty miles long, north and south, by fifteen miles wide at the lower end and six at the upper. From the shores the water gradually increased until a depth of from twelve to seventeen feet was found, and maintained throughout the whole bay, save at the lower end where there was a pocket six miles long by two and a half miles wide, in which the water was from twenty to twenty-four feet deep.

On the easterly side, the bay was protected from the off shore seas by a long peninsula called Mobile Point ; on the westerly side by Dauphin Island, one of a chain alongshore. The open water between Mobile Point and Dauphin Island was more than three land miles wide. This open water, however, was at best but ten or eleven feet deep, except on the easterly or Mobile Point side, where a channel that averaged about half a mile in width ran nearly north and south into the bay. The shoals on each side of this channel extended off shore for more than three miles from Mobile Point, and two islands, Sand Island and West Sand Island, were found at the outer limits. A lighthouse on Sand Island was two and one-fourth nautical miles from a lighthouse on Mobile Point. The shoalest water in the channel, even on the outer bar was three and one-half fathoms ; it was therefore deep enough everywhere for all the ships of Farragut's fleet.

On Mobile Point stood Fort Morgan, " on the site of old Fort Bowyer." It was "a pentagonal, bastioned work, built of brick whose full scarp wall was four feet eight inches thick." Alabama troops had taken possession of it on January 5, 1861, the garrison numbering at that time only two hundred men. Slowly, as men and means could be spared, the strength of this fort was increased until the time came for the Federal attack, when it mounted eighty-six guns, in all, of which some were small smoothbores scarcely worth counting, and the most important were seven 10-inch and three 8-inch smoothbores, with two 8-inch, two 6.5-inch and four 5.82-inch rifles. In a separate battery near by, built to command the channel, were one 8-inch and four 10-inch smoothbores, with two 6.5-inch rifles. There were sixteen 32-pounder smoothbores bearing on the channel, and that was a calibre sufficient to penetrate Farragut's wooden ships. Fort Morgan was commanded by R. L. Page, a commander in the old navy whom the authorities transferred to the army, with rank as Brigadier-General.

Fort Gaines stood on Dauphin Island. It mounted three 10-inch and five 32-pounder smoothbores, be-

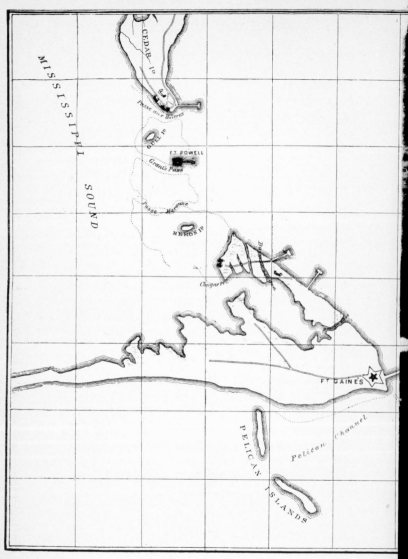

MISSISSIPPI SOUND

CEDAR IP

Passe aux Huitres

Gull IP

FT POWELL

Grants Pass

Passe Marianne

HERON IP

Oniga Pt

FT GAINES

PELICAN ISLANDS

Pelican Channel

MOBIL

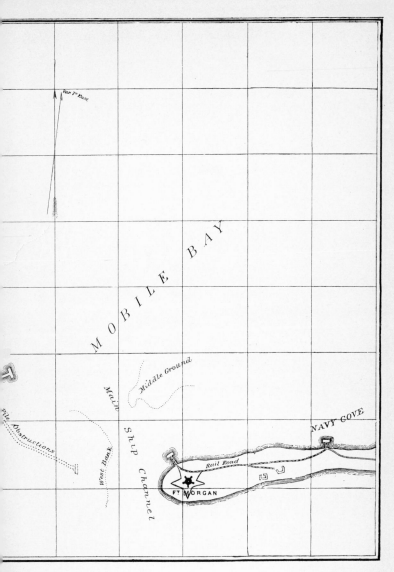

MOBILE BAY

Var 7º E. Mag.

Middle Ground

Main Ship Channel

West Bank

Pile Obstructions

Rail Road

NAVY COVE

FT. MORGAN

sides smaller guns; but it was of no particular consequence in the battle because it was too far from the
channel.   On a little sand bar called Tower Island,
at the extreme westerly side of the bay, and adjoin-
ing a channel leading to New Orleans by way of
Mississippi Sound, was another fort that was of
some importance, however, because this channel
(called Grant's), might become very useful to the
National fleet after passing into the bay.   For
while the Confederates should hold Fort Morgan,
Grant's Channel, if under the National flag, could
be used for carrying supplies to Farragut.   A structure called Fort Powell had been erected on Tower
Island.   It was not completed when the attack on
the bay was ordered, but it mounted one 32-pounder,
one 10-inch, and two 8-inch smoothbores, besides
two of the excellent Brooke 7-inch rifles.   All
of these guns but one commanded the approaches
from the westward; the fort on the side of Mobile
Bay was not completed and was practically defense-
less.

To supplement their fortifications on land the
Confederates had obstructed the water between
Dauphin Island and the channel under Mobile
Point, by driving rows of piles that would stop
any light draft vessel striving to cross the flats.
Then in the westerly part of the main or real channel three rows of torpedoes were anchored, with a
red buoy at the easterly end of the line.   This buoy
was but a little more than three hundred feet from
the easterly edge of the channel, and the water thus
left free was, of course, directly under the guns of

Fort Morgan. This open channel was for the accommodation of blockade runners.

It is to be noted that torpedoes were first generally employed in our Civil War, and it was the Confederate, or the physically weaker side, naturally, that made the greater use of them. Beer kegs filled with powder and supplied with fuses that might be exploded on contact with a ship, were favored by the torpedo makers. Tin cans of various shapes were also utilized. Whatever the device it was generally buoyant enough to float on the water's surface when unrestrained, and it was secured by a flexible mooring—chain or rope—to an anchor of some kind resting on the bottom of the channel. Fixed torpedoes attached to sunken frames were also used, though not in the channel Farragut was to follow.

To show the effectiveness of these devices in the hands of the Confederates it may be recalled that the ironclad Cairo was sunk in the Yazoo River by a torpedo on December 12, 1862. On February 28, 1863, the monitor Montauk was seriously injured by a torpedo in the Ogeechee River, and in the course of that year two other Federal ships were injured or destroyed in the same manner. A new and most fearsome peril had thus been added to war, and there was no escaping it when aggressive movements were undertaken.

In addition to their fixed defenses the Confederates had provided a small squadron of armed ships to defend Mobile Bay. An open-deck river steamer called the Selma, had been converted into a gunboat by so placing bales of cotton as partially to protect her machinery and by arming her with one 8-inch and two 9-inch smoothbores and one 6-inch rifle. Two gunboats had been built—poorly built because of a lack of mechanics and materials. One, the Morgan, carried two 7-inch rifles and four 32-pounders. The other, the Gaines, carried one 8-inch smoothbore and five 32-pounders. In short, here were three poor steamers, splendidly armed, and that they were well-manned scarcely need be said.

In addition to these, however, two or three iron-clads were in hand, one of which just missed being among the most formidable ships of the war. This ironclad was named the Tennessee. Her keel was laid at Selma, on the Alabama River, where the Confederates had established a naval station which was under the charge of Commander Ebenezer Ferrand. The timber was cut in the forest and the ore for making the iron for her armor was dug from the ground as the work on her frames progressed. She was 209 feet long over all, and 48 feet wide. In the middle of the hull a casemate was erected that was 79 feet long by 29 feet wide, inside measurements. The walls of the casemate were inclined at an angle of forty-five degrees and were twenty-five inches thick. The forward end of the casemate was covered with three layers of 2-inch iron plates—six inches in all—while the sides and after walls were covered five inches thick. Plating and wooden walls were bolted through and through.

For the battle that was impending a still more

important feature of the armor remains to be described. The walls of the casemate were carried out and down beyond the hull proper as the eaves of a country house project beyond its walls. This projection extended two feet below the level of the water, and therefore two feet from the side of the hull. Then it turned in at a right angle and came back to the hull which it reached four feet below the water line. The knuckle thus formed was filled in solid with timber, as a protection against ramming. The flat parts of the deck were covered with two inches of iron.

As the ship, when completed drew but fourteen feet of water, it is plain that her design for the intended purpose—defending Mobile Bay—was the best then extant. But in carrying out details, one serious mistake and one remarkable blunder, were made. To close the ports when the guns were run in for loading, she was provided with five-inch iron shutters revolving on pivots in such fashion that the shot of an opponent could hammer the surrounding armor in upon them, rivet the pivots, and thus prevent the crew from moving them. This was the mistake. The blunder was made when the steering chains were laid on top of the armored flat deck, abaft the casemate where they were exposed to every shot coming that way. It was foreseen, too, that the chains might be shot away, for deck tackles were put on board for use in that emergency.

The guns of the Tennessee were few in number but superior in quality. She carried a 7-inch rifle at each end of the casemate, and two 6-inch rifles on each side.   The ship was driven by a screw, and she was able to make six knots an hour, or about the speed of the monitors in the National service.

Admiral Franklin Buchanan (formerly of the Merrimac), the first officer to attain that rank in the Confederate service, was placed in command of the Mobile squadron, and Commander J. D. Johnson of the formidable Tennessee, on which Buchanan hoisted his flag.   It was not until March, 1864, that this ship was ready for commission, and even then she was still at Selma on the Alabama River.   While she was to draw fourteen feet of water, loaded, the bar between her and the bay, called Dog River Bar, had but nine feet of water on it.   Accordingly, she had to be lightened to the last ounce (no guns or ammunition were put upon her), and as a helpless hulk she was towed to the bar.   There large floats, called camels, were fitted on each side, and by these she was lifted and carried over into deep water, on May 18, 1864, while the National fleet lay in the offing—within view of the work, possibly, if the air were clear—but wholly incapable of interfering.

In short, the Confederates were able to give the last stroke of the hammer in completing their defenses long before the attack was begun on Mobile Bay.   The disadvantages which the National forces were thus compelled to face were serious ; but because their opponents were fully prepared the opportunity of a lifetime came to Admiral Farragut.

Leaving New York in the Hartford, early in January, 1864, Farragut arrived off Mobile, and once more took command of his squadron. He was anxious to lead his fleet inside the bay at once; for he learned from refugees that the Tennessee was yet uncompleted, and that once he was able to pass Fort Morgan he should find no force within to molest him seriously.

Moreover, Mobile had developed rapidly as a centre of commerce in the Confederacy. Blockade runners had passed in and out frequently, and because of the facilities for inland transportation offered by the river system and the railroads of the back country, the manufacturing interests of the town had increased steadily.

The problem for Farragut here was slightly different from that which confronted him in passing the forts on the Mississippi. Once he was above these forts they were, as repeatedly noted, wholly cut off from their sources of supplies; but Fort Morgan was on a point of the mainland, and a mainland route for supplies could be followed by the Confederates in spite of anything that could be done by the deep-water ships under Farragut. Accordingly it was absolutely necessary that troops should be provided to invest the landward side of Fort Morgan, and thus isolate it from the mainland while the ships were holding the bay. In no other way, it appeared, could the fort be secured.

But just then troops were not to be had. Banks, who still commanded in the Mississippi country had gone away on an expedition into the Red River valley which accomplished and could accomplish nothing; in fact it very nearly led to the destruction of a large part of Porter's Mississippi squadron. Therefore no troops could be spared from New Orleans, and none could be had from any other point to assist the navy at Mobile.

On January 20th (two days after his arrival), Farragut went with a couple of gunboats to a point within three miles of Fort Morgan for an examination of the defenses. It was a clear day and he was able distinctly to see the forts and such vessels as were within the bay. As a result of his examination, he wrote to the Department saying :

" I am satisfied that if I had one ironclad at this time I could destroy their whole force in the bay and reduce the forts at my leisure, by coöperation with our land forces—say 5,000 men."

The work of the ironclads had compelled all the old marlin-spike sailors to acknowledge the efficiency of armor. Having seen the Arkansas shed 9-inch shot like hail stones, at Vicksburg, Farragut was compelled to believe that the ironclads building above Mobile for the defense of the bay would prove effective fighting machines. His information regarding these vessels was fragmentary —he had heard no more than that one called the Nashville would be ready in March, and that the Tennessee would have to be lifted over the Dog River Bar by camels. He said that if he could have one shoal draft ironclad, he would be willing to go in ; "but without ironclads we should not be able to fight the enemy's vessels of that class with much prospect of success, *as the latter would lie on the flats, where our vessels could not go to destroy them.*

Wooden vessels can do nothing with them unless by getting within one hundred or two hundred yards, so as to ram them or pour in a broadside."

Admiral Buchanan in a speech to his men promised to raise the blockade with the Tennessee. Farragut heard of this threat though he cared nothing for it. But to take deep-draft wooden ships into the bay, where the room for turning was at best restricted, to meet a shoal-draft ironclad, was a serious matter. It is a notable fact, too, that Farragut at this time understood and was willing to consider the power of public opinion. In the letter quoted he says :

"It is depressing to see how easily false reports circulate, and in what a state of alarm the community [Nation] is kept by the most absurd rumors. If the Department could get one or two of the ironclads here, it would put an end to this state of things, and restore confidence to the people of the ports now in our possession."

The ironclads he desired were monitors. We have learned by sad experience that the monitor type of ship is worthless as a deep water fighting machine ; and that it is by no means desirable even for coast patrol service. But for use in enclosed waters like Mobile Bay—if we were to adopt the porcupine policy in foreign affairs, and invite the enemy to fight us in our own harbors, as the Confederates were doing—the monitors were, and would be, fairly good warships.

For more than six months Farragut was unable to get either monitors or troops, and the greater part of that time was passed in rocking to the waves of the Gulf, off the Bay of Mobile. It is therefore manifest that one element of the man's greatness was his ability to wait—to stand by, as a sailor would say—during heart-breaking delays, and then, when the time did come, to take hold with a masterful will.

During this most tedious season, his Diary, as edited by his son Loyall, gives several little stories and letters that well show the bent of the man's mind under varying circumstances. Thus, the captain of a captured blockade runner, when brought before the Admiral, proved to be one of his old personal friends. The ship had cleared for Matamoras, Mexico, but was caught trying to enter Mobile—300 miles north and east of the course to Matamoras. Farragut asked how that had happened and the captain went into a detailed statement of the effect a northeast gale had on his ship. Farragut listened without interruption till the flow of explanations ran dry and then, putting his hand on the captain's shoulder, said :

"How could you be blown to the north'ard and east'ard by a northeast gale? I'm sorry for you, but we shall have to hold you for your thundering bad navigation."

On April 4th he wrote home : "If any one asks what I am doing, answer,—nothing but waiting for the world to turn round till it comes my turn to do something, and then I will 'pitch in' ; but I am like cold sauce—always ready."

On May 13th he wrote : "The rebels had a jubilee yesterday at Fort Morgan, in honor of the capture of Steele by Price. I expect Porter to save Banks. I am very much afraid the army will be captured. I get right sick, every now and then, at the bad news. . . . I am at work on the old Hartford, to make her ready for any work I may have to do.''

A week or so later, while off Mobile he wrote to his son : ''I am lying off here, looking at Buchannan and waiting his coming out. He has a force of four ironclads and three wooden vessels. I have eight or nine wooden vessels. We'll try to amuse him if he comes. . . . We started with few good officers of experience, but shall end with some of the best in the world. Our fellows are beginning to understand that war means fighting. It is the duty of an officer to save his men as much as possible, but in almost all cases there has to be a certain amount of sacrifice of life.''

To Admiral Theodorus Bailey, at Key West, he wrote, saying among other things, that he could see the Confederates ''very industriously laying down torpedoes'' in the channel at Fort Morgan. Bailey replied : ''Nothing will please me more than to hoist once more the square red flag, and lead the van of your squadron into Mobile Bay, to the capture of Forts Morgan and Gaines, as well as the city. Put me down for two chances, as the Jackass said to the Monkey at the Lion's ball.''

Concerning the crew of the Hartford, Farragut said :

''I have never seen a crew come up like ours.

They are ahead of the old set in small arms, and fully equal to them at the great guns. They arrived here a mere lot of boys and young men, and have now fattened up and knock the 9-inch guns about like 24-pounders, to the astonishment of everybody.''

Blockade work was dreary, but not wholly devoid of humor. The most cheering incident of the long wait was the receipt of a sword sent by the Union League Club of New York—a beautiful weapon with brilliants in the hilt and a scabbard of silver ornamented with gold. As his son says, no one could appreciate such a compliment more deeply than Admiral Farragut, whose letter of acknowledgment was dated June 24, 1864.

The time of waiting was not yet over but finally on July 31st, he was able to write that '' the monitors have all arrived, except the Tecumseh, and she is at Pensacola and I hope will be here in two days.''

A day for which Farragut had been preparing during fifty-three years of service in the navy, was now at hand.

CHAPTER XX

THE BATTLE OF MOBILE BAY

THE fleet that was gathered under Farragut for the attack upon Mobile Bay was, for that time, notably formidable. Two single turret monitors, each carrying two 15-inch guns, had been ordered from the Atlantic squadron—the Tecumseh, Commander Tunis A. M. Craven, and the Manhattan, Commander J. W. A. Nicholson. The 15-inch gun, it should be observed, was then the most powerful weapon afloat. The projectiles weighed 440 pounds, and the powder charge about sixty pounds. The iron turrets of these monitors were ten inches thick. Two double-turret monitors, the Winnebago, Commander Thomas H. Stevens, and the Chickasaw, Lieutenant Commander George H. Perkins, had been drawn from the Mississippi. The reader will remember that Perkins was the executive officer of the Cayuga when Farragut passed the Mississippi forts. The turrets on the Mississippi monitors, which were nine and one-half inches thick, carried two 11-inch guns each, and it is a curious fact that these vessels, being of very shoal draft, were driven by four screws each. But all the monitors were slow boats, the best speed that could be made by those at Mobile being no more than seven knots.

The best of the wooden fleet was the Brooklyn, Captain James Alden. She now carried twenty-four guns of which twenty were 9-inch smoothbores throwing solid shot weighing ninety pounds, and four were Parrott rifles. Two of these, so-called 100-pounders, threw projectiles weighing seventy pounds, and two were 60-pounders, properly so called. The Hartford carried eighteen 9-inch guns and three Parrotts. The Richmond, Captain Thornton A. Jenkins, carried eighteen 9-inch guns and two Parrotts. The remainder of the wooden fleet included the Lackawanna, Captain John B. Marchand; the Monongahela, Commander James H. Strong; the Ossipee, Commander William E. Le-Roy; the Oneida, Commander J. R. M. Mullany; the Octorara, Lieutenant Commander Charles A. Greene; the Metacomet, Lieutenant Commander James E. Jouett; the Port Royal, Lieutenant Commander Bancroft Gherardi; the Seminole, Commander Edward Donaldson; the Kennebec, Lieutenant Commander William P. McCann; the Itasca, Lieutenant Commander George Brown; and the Galena, Lieutenant Commander Clark H. Wells.

These latter vessels had mixed batteries—badly mixed, in fact. Thus the Lackawanna carried one 150-pounder Parrott rifle (which fired a projectile of 135 pounds), one 50-pounder rifle, two 11-inch smoothbores, four 9-inch smoothbores, two 24-pounders and four 12-pounders. The others carried from four to five different calibres of guns, the distinctive feature of the armament of the fleet being, however, the great power of the guns even on the smaller vessels. In all, there were eighteen ships carrying 159 guns of considerable size, besides howitzers.

In the meantime General E. R. S. Canby, who had relieved the defeated Banks in the Mississippi Valley, notified Farragut that enough troops could be spared to invest one of the forts at Mobile, and on August 3d, 1,500 men under General Gordon Granger, were landed on Dauphin Island to begin the advance on the bay by attacking Fort Gaines. It had been agreed by Farragut that the fleet should attempt to pass within the bay the next morning (August 4th), but the Tecumseh had not yet arrived from Pensacola, and the Richmond was also at that place preparing for the battle ; therefore the attack was postponed.

The preparations for the battle have been discussed by the best informed tacticians of the world, since that day, with the result, to use Mahan's words after reviewing the facts, that they find "much to praise and very little to criticise." The individual captains were left to their own devices in preparing their ships for action, and the work done was much like that when the forts on the Mississippi were to be passed, the chief difference being on the Richmond. Captain Jenkins built a wall of sand bags on the starboard side, from the berth deck up, to stop shot and splinters.

For the order of the battle, the Brooklyn was put at the head of the wooden-ship line, followed by the Hartford, the Richmond, the Lackawanna, the Monongahela, the Ossipee and the Oneida in the order named. Farragut at first determined to lead the line with the Hartford, but he yielded when the captains unanimously remonstrated against his taking what they supposed to be the post of greatest danger—a yielding which he afterward regretted, though it gave him the opportunity for making one of the greatest displays of courage and resourcefulness known to naval history. Another reason for giving the Brooklyn first place was the fact that she carried four chase guns, and had a device on her bow that was intended for use in catching up and removing torpedoes from her path.

Alongside each of the seven larger ships of the fleet just named was lashed a smaller one—a gunboat—as had been done in the dash past Port Hudson. The Brooklyn had the Octorara, the Hartford had the Metacomet, and the others in the order already named, had the Port Royal, the Seminole, the Kennebec, the Itasca and the Galena. Because Fort Morgan was the point of danger, and the ships would expose their starboard sides to its fire, the gunboats were lashed to port, where they would be as well protected as possible. For the guns of Fort Gaines were, as has been said, so far away that they could do no damage.

The four monitors were ordered to form just to the right and ahead of the Admiral's line, so as to interpose their fire between the fort and the wooden ships. The Tecumseh, Commander T. A. M. Craven, had the honor of leading the monitors. The Mississippi monitors followed the big ones, the Chickasaw, Lieutenant Commander George H. Perkins, being the last in the line, though by no means of least importance.

Having arranged the order of his ships, the Admiral looked to the conditions of tide and weather. The start was to be made, as the general order said, with the flood tide; for *Farragut had determined that every ship must go through and pass the forts.*

"If one or more of the ships be disabled, their partners must carry them through if possible; but if they cannot then *the next astern must render the required assistance.*"

The direction of the wind was considered—one from the southwest was desired, to blow the smoke of the fleet into the eyes of the gunners in the fort. A subsequent general order called attention to the "black buoys placed across the channel, from the piles on the west side of the channel toward Fort Morgan." Because these buoys marked the sites of the torpedoes the ships were ordered to pass to eastward of the red buoy, "which is clear of all obstructions."

It is worth while recalling, too, that the first general order said, "It will be the object of the Admiral to get as close to the fort as possible before opening fire." This was not uttered in any spirit of bravado; it simply meant that by getting close in with the ships their fire would be more effective and the lives of the crews therefore in less danger.

Six other small steamers not hitherto mentioned— the Genesee, Pinola, Pembina, Sebago, Tennessee and Bienville, all under the command of Lieutenant-

Commander Edward C. Grafton, were ordered to take a station at a point southeast of Fort Morgan, whence they could shell it and thus help beat down its fire. But Grafton kept them at so long a range that they were unable to reach the fort, and thus he lost the one opportunity for distinction that ever came to him.

This fact is, perhaps, worth emphasizing for the admonition of the officers of the navy now, and in time to come. Two classes of officers have been found afloat. In one class are included men like George Upham Morris, of the old Cumberland, and Raphael Semmes, of the Confederate Alabama— men who fought till their ships sank from under them. The other class always kept well in mind all orders that had been received from the Department, or other superior authority, cautioning them not to risk their ships. The cautious class never accomplished anything for peace by their caution, but fighting men have achieved immortality even when, through their eagerness, they have disobeyed orders as did one captain—Craven—in Farragut's fleet at Mobile.

Because the Tecumseh did not come upon the scene in time, the agreement to go in on the morning of August 4th was not kept. But during the 4th the Tecumseh steamed up. When Craven had received his orders from Farragut at Pensacola he had not an ounce of coal on board, but aided by Jenkins, of the Richmond, he managed to put everything in order and to arrive off Mobile not too late. During the night of the 4th, the monitors

anchored behind Sand Island. The remainder of
the fleet anchored farther out. There was then
nothing more to do but wait for morning and the
battle.

With a full appreciation of the character of the
contest before him, when he had done all that
he could do, Farragut's thoughts turned, as the
thoughts of every good man in the navy always
turn on the eve of battle, to his home, and sitting
down in his cabin he wrote this letter :

"MY DEAREST WIFE :—I write and leave this
letter for you. I am going into Mobile Bay in the
morning, if God is my leader, as I hope He is and
in Him I place my trust. If He thinks it is the
proper place for me to die, I am ready to submit to
His will, in that as all other things. My great
mortification is, that my vessels, the ironclads,
were not ready to have gone in yesterday. The
army landed last night, and are in full view of us
this morning, and the Tecumseh has not yet arrived
from Pensacola.

"God bless and preserve you, my darling, and
my dear boy, if anything should happen to me,
and may His blessing also rest upon your dear
mother, and all your sisters and their children.

"Your devoted and affectionate husband, who
never for one moment forgot his love, duty or fi-
delity to you, his devoted and best of wives."

Save for the work of the engineer forces in keeping up steam, and of the watches on deck with
their sharp lookout for a dash of the ironclad Tennessee, the night was absolutely quiet. The weather
proved lowering with a strong threat of rain from

the Gulf. But as daylight approached the clouds vanished, and a gentle southwest wind came in with the tide beneath a clear sky.

At four o'clock the shrill piping of the boatswains' whistles, with the call of "all hands up hammocks," was heard from ship to ship, and the crews turned out to find ready for them their pannikins of refreshing coffee. A little later the gunboats got under way, and steaming over to their consorts, were made well fast with hawsers.

At 5:30 the Admiral was sitting at the table in the cabin of the Hartford, with Captain Drayton and Dr. James C. Palmer, a volunteer from the naval hospital at Pensacola. Seeing that daylight was at hand the Admiral said:

"Well, Drayton, we might as well get under way."

The signal was promptly displayed, and at 6:10 o'clock the flagship was crossing the outer bar, bound in. At 6:30 the column of wooden ships was formed in the channel, and then, to the inspiration of every man who could see, the old flag was flung to the breeze from each mast head and flag-staff in the fleet.

Next came the monitors to take their positions in line in the channel and wait for the wooden ships to overtake them; and finally at 6:55, the whole battle line moved forward toward the fort, the eager captain of the Tecumseh firing her two guns as she started ahead.

Ten minutes later—at 7:05, the fort opened fire on the fleet; the Brooklyn replied instantly, and the crews of the guns that would bear from the other ships joined in. Then the Confederate squadron within the bay steamed out from behind the shelter of the fort and took its station across the channel just within the line of torpedoes. It was an awe-inspiring scene as the long line of National ships moved slowly in, with clouds of smoke bursting from their sides as they hurled storms of shell and shrapnel upon forts and beach, while the guns of the fort thundered back with shot that knocked sprays of smoking splinters from the wooden vessels.

As the smoke began to cover the water and fog in the monitors, Farragut left the poop deck of the Hartford, and going to the port main rigging climbed up where he could get a full view of his fleet. From this place he could see all the ships : Captain Drayton, on the poop deck, was within reach of his voice ; Lieutenant Commander Jouett of the Metacomet was standing on her wheel house just below him ; above him in the top was Captain Martin Freeman, the faithful pilot, while a quarter-master, not far away, was leaning out from the ship's side, swinging the lead and calling in a voice plainly heard, the depth of water—"By the mark three !" and "A quarter less four !"

It was a most advantageous position for a fleet commander, and as the smoke thickened Farragut climbed higher and higher until he reached the fut-tock shrouds, just under the maintop. There he stopped. Then Captain Drayton, fearing that the Admiral might be thrown to the deck by a wound, sent up Quartermaster Knowles with a piece of lead line, which he passed around the Admiral's body, making the ends fast in the shrouds. It was a simple incident, but the people of the Nation were thrilled as rarely before when the newspapers told how the Admiral went into battle "lashed to the mast."

After the wooden ships overhauled the monitors, Captain Stevens of the Winnebago was seen walking to and fro on deck between the turrets, wholly regardless of the fire of the fort that was directed at her, while Perkins of the Chickasaw, showing the uplift of a daring soul going into battle, was on top of his forward turret.

Craven, in the Tecumseh, having once fired his guns at the fort, ceased firing. Both guns were then loaded with full charges of powder and in each was placed a solid steel projectile. The Tecumseh was leading all, and the captain had determined to reserve his fire for an attack upon the Confederate ironclad Tennessee.

In perfect silence, thereafter, but with every man ready, the Tecumseh led the way in until so near the line of torpedoes at the slight bend in the channel that the Brooklyn and Hartford, though well in the rear of the monitors, were both able to fire full broadsides at the fort, driving the men of the water battery and the barbette guns hastily to shelter. Inspired by the spectacle thus afforded, and impatient to get at the ironclad ram, which was then seen steaming just to westward of the line of torpedoes, Craven said to his pilot :

"It is impossible that the Admiral means us to go inside that buoy ; I cannot turn my ship."

He was arguing with himself, rather than with the pilot—seeking an excuse for a dash at the Tennessee, and finding it, too ; for the next instant, he said firmly : "Hard a-starboard," and then headed the ship across the torpedo line.

Over on the Tennessee Captain Johnson saw the Tecumseh change her course, and said to Lieutenant Arthur D. Wharton, commanding the forward division :

"Do not fire until the vessels are in actual contact."

"Aye, aye, sir," replied Wharton, taking in the slack of the firing lanyard of the bow gun. Both of these officers, indeed all the officers of the fleet that could see the two ships, were looking for "a deadly fight at close quarters," but as the Tecumseh's bow touched the black buoys of the torpedo line she lurched from side to side. An instant later she pitched down by the bow ; her stern rose until her wheel was seen whirling in air, and then with a score of men leaping from deck and turret, down she went.

And while she reeled during that moment on the surface, Pilot John Collins and Captain Craven met at the foot of the ladder that led up through the turret to possible safety. The Captain came first, but he stepped back and said :

"After you, pilot."

The pilot reached the top of the ladder, but when there the "vessel seemed to drop from under him.

He alone was saved to tell the story of the captain's heroism." [1]

It was a frightful disaster, and over on the Brooklyn the captain ordered the engines stopped. At once the rest of the line began closing in on her rapidly.

"What is the matter with the Brooklyn?" said Farragut to his pilot. "She must have plenty of water there?"

"Plenty of water and to spare, Admiral," said the pilot, "but her screw is moving—I think she is going ahead, sir."

Unhappily she began to back, instead, and with her bow turning toward the fort she drifted, broadside to, athwart the channel, blocking the way. Glancing hastily around, the Admiral saw his whole fleet becoming disordered. The fire of all the ships died away, while the Confederates, seeing their advantage, worked their guns till the fort seemed to be sheeted with flames. The gladiator was staggering under the blows of the enemy: the supreme moment of the battle and of the Admiral's life had come. Instinctively he breathed a prayer —"Shall I go on?" A voice seemed to whisper in his ear, "Go on!"

---

[1] "When the divers went down to examine the wreck of the Tecumseh they found nearly all the crew at their posts as they sank. The chief engineer, who had been married in New York only two weeks before, and who had received from the flagship's mail his letters while the line was forming, stood with one hand upon the revolving bar of the turret engine, and in the other an open letter from his bride, which his dead eyes still seemed to be reading" (Scharf).

Turning to the Brooklyn, now close aboard, he hailed :

"What is the trouble?"

"Torpedoes," replied her captain.

"Damn the torpedoes! Full speed, Jouett! Four bells, Captain Drayton," shouted Farragut.

And when the crew of the Hartford heard those orders they leaped as one man to the starboard rail, facing the fort, and gave three yells of defiance.

When, in the battle on Lake Champlain, Macdonough invoked the aid of God, his act undoubtedly gave resolution to the hearts of his crew ; but it was the spectacle of a rooster crowing in the rigging that roused them to the shouting pitch. And (such is the heart of the fighting man) while the crew of the Hartford loved and trusted their Admiral for the sincerity of his religious convictions it was when they heard his good, vigorous "damn the torpedoes" that they were inspired with the full joy of battle.

The channel was blocked by the Brooklyn, but the helm of the Hartford was put to starboard, and aided by the Metacomet she was pointed clear. Then, regardless of the lurking danger that had destroyed the Tecumseh, Farragut drove his ship straight at the torpedo line. In a few moments the torpedoes were heard knocking against her bottom, and several of the percussion primers exploded as she crossed, but none was fired, and victory was close at hand. When the Hartford passed the three monitors her crew saw Perkins of the Chickasaw dancing about on top of her forward turret, and waving his hat for joy at the sight of the Admiral's ship saving the day by leading the fleet into battle.

But while the scales of fortune yet hung quivering Farragut's thoughts turned to the unfortunate men who had leaped from the Tecumseh into the water, and hailing Lieutenant-Commander Jouett, of the Metacomet, he ordered a boat sent to their aid. The thoughtful Jouett had already done so. Acting Ensign Henry C. Nields, a mere boy, had been put in charge of the boat. Pulling through the storm of shot Nields headed for the men in the water. A little later he remembered a small flag that should have been floating from his boat, and dropping the tiller ropes, he drew it from its case and shaking its folds to the breeze, stepped it above the stern. The Tennessee at that moment had a gun pointed directly at the boat, but the officer in command, thrilled by "this most gallant act," elevated the muzzle and the shot "flew harmlessly over the heads of that glorious boat's crew."

The fort was passed but the Confederates might have said, as John Paul Jones said, that they had not yet begun to fight. In fact, General Page, commanding Fort Morgan, did say that, while the ships had forced their way in, the door was closed behind them and he held the key.

As the Hartford cleared the torpedo line the Tennessee made a dash at her, but missed her because the Hartford was moving more swiftly than the Confederate. "Farragut took no further notice of her than to return her fire." The three gunboats being of far inferior strength, retreated, but they

fought as they went. Their huge guns were worked
with vigor and skill, and because the Hartford was
chasing them bow on, their shot raked her fore and
aft, making a slaughter pen of her forward gun deck.

In the meantime the Tennessee had been following the Hartford, but seeing, after a time, that he
could not catch her, Admiral Buchanan turned his
vessel back to meet the other National ships; for
the flagship had gained a lead of nearly a mile
over the others.

Then the Hartford reached the pocket of deep
water in the bay and was able to yaw around and
bring her broadside guns to bear on the three gunboats, with the result that the Gaines was struck a
number of times, seeing which Farragut turned to
Jouett, of the Metacomet, and ordered him to cast
loose and go in chase of the gunboats. "Aye, aye,
sir," said Jouett, with enthusiasm, and at the same
moment two sailors, who had been stationed with
axes beside the fastening hawsers awaiting such an
order, chopped the Metacomet clear, and away she
went. Just as she got fairly headed for the Confederates, a heavy rain squall came across the bay,
shutting in the ships so that it was impossible to
distinguish one from another. While it lasted the
Confederate gunboats Morgan and Gaines turned
back toward Fort Morgan. The Selma, however,
kept off to eastward, and when the squall cleared
away the Metacomet was found to be in chase of
and overhauling her. But after a time the leadmen
on the Metacomet announced that the water was
growing shoaler, and finally it was seen that her

keel was actually plowing through a foot of mud
on the bottom.

"Call in the men from the chains," said Jouett,
when the executive officer reported this fact to him.
"Call in the men; they are only intimidating me."

Hearing these words the crew shouted with laugh-
ter. The pursuit was continued until a shot killed
the executive officer of the Selma with six of her
crew, when her flag was hauled down.

The Gaines and Morgan reached the shelter of
Fort Morgan, but the Gaines had been so badly cut
up that she was beached and burned. The Morgan
made a good retreat up to Mobile that night.

After failing to catch the Hartford, the Tennessee
tried to ram several of the other National ships,
in turn, but the fatal defect of inferior power prevented success, and the whole National fleet joined
Farragut at the upper end of the deep water pocket.
In spite of the disorder and the delay of the fleet in-
ident to the Brooklyn's flinch at the torpedo line,
the ships had in no case been so seriously damaged
as to put them out of commission. The Oneida had
suffered most of all because, being the last ship in
the line, she had been obliged to pass the fort un-
aided by the fire of the other ships. One shot
entered her starboard boiler, another cut her wheel
ropes, and a third set her on fire. But Captain Mullany (a fighting Irishman) led his crew in quench-
ing the fire, and in making the needed repairs;
when she joined the Admiral her crew could boast
that her guns had never for a moment ceased firing
on the fort while she was within range.

At 8:30 o'clock—an hour and a half after the battle with the fort began—the Hartford anchored four miles above Fort Morgan and sent her crew to breakfast.

"The Admiral," says Mahan, "had come down from his post in the main rigging and was standing on the poop, when Captain Drayton came up to him and said : ' What we have done has been well done, sir ; but it all counts for nothing so long as the Tennessee is there under the guns of Morgan.' "

One of the officers on the Tennessee made a similar remark to Admiral Buchanan. The Confederates believed that they had the Federal squadron bottled up, and Farragut appears to have felt that he was not yet the victor, for he replied to Drayton :

" As soon as the people have had their breakfasts I am going for her."

But this he did not have to do. The Tennessee came to him. The tacticians unite in condemning Buchanan for taking the offensive. The Tennessee had been well hammered by the broadsides of every ship that entered the bay. Every sort of projectile, including the solid round shot of 11-inch and 15-inch smoothbores, and the long 136-pound bolts of the big rifles, struck her as the fleet passed, but when her armor was examined it was found that not even a rivet had been started. At long range she was invulnerable to all the guns of the National fleet.

Further than that the projectiles from the Tennessee's rifles—the bow and stern guns threw bolts of 140 pounds—had been able to pierce the wooden walls of the Union fleet. The fact is to be considered too that the Tennessee drew but fourteen feet of water. She might have taken a position on the shoals where Farragut's big wooden ships could not get near her, and at long range it would have been possible for her to shoot them to pieces while lying secure from their fire. The tacticians say that the Tennessee should have done as the British Phœbe did at Valparaiso, when fighting the ill-armed Essex.

But in defense of Buchanan, it may be said that *the monitors could follow him wherever he might take the Tennessee,* and there were three of these, all practically invulnerable to his guns. They could gather like bloodhounds around a bull, *to compass his destruction.* Farragut saw that they were the ships to send against the Tennessee, for he wrote, some time later, that he had intended to attack her with them if she had remained under the fort. Buchanan was right in fighting it out at once.

Whether it was due to what Mahan calls "inconsiderate bravery," or to a feeling that if he could conquer at all he could do it better while the National crews were tired and his crew fresh, cannot now be told definitely. The fact is, when he saw that the last of Farragut's ships had passed up the bay, he turned to the captain and said :

"Follow them up, Johnson. We can't let them off that way."

While Captain Drayton talked with Admiral Farragut on the poop deck of the Hartford, the Tennessee was seen under motion. She seemed to be heading out to sea, as if to attack the vessels outside, and when this was reported to Farragut, he said :

"Then we must follow him out."

To get alongside the Tennessee Farragut would have taken his ships once more through the fire of the forts.   But the Confederate was merely turning in a wide circle to "follow them up."   By the time this fact was ascertained Farragut had gone below and was eating his breakfast in the cabin.

"What!   Is that so?" he said, as an officer told him the Tennessee was coming.   "Just like Buchanan's audacity.   Signal to all frigates to get immediately under way and run the ram under, and to the monitors to attack at once."

Fleet Surgeon Palmer who had started in the Admiral's launch, Loyall, to make a round of inspection among the wounded of the fleet was recalled and ordered to go to each of the monitors with individual orders to attack the Tennessee.   And in his diary (quoted by Mahan), Palmer wrote of the Chickasaw's captain :

"Happy as my friend Perkins habitually is, I thought he would turn a somersault overboard with joy when I told him, 'the Admiral wants you to go at once and fight the Tennessee.'"

Clearing away their messkits, the men of the Federal fleet hurried to their work, and with anchors at the hawse pipes, in some cases, the whole fleet flocked down to meet the lone ironclad.   The Monongahela had the lead, and at full speed she charged the Tennessee.   But the Tennessee's helm was put over so that her opponent struck her a glancing harmless blow ; and yet the impact made the Confederate whirl as if on a pivot, and Lieutenant Wharton, commanding the forward division, felt as if he " were going through the air."

The Tennessee responded by firing two shots that passed clear through the Monongahela and dropped in the water beyond.   Then the Monongahela fired a broadside at the ram, but the solid shot literally rolled down her inclined armor like marbles on a plank.

As the Monongahela swung clear " a hideous looking monster whose slowly revolving turret revealed the cavernous depths of a mammoth gun"— the monitor Manhattan—appeared to the crew of the Tennessee.   Lieutenant Wharton had time only to shout, "Stand clear of the port side !" when the great gun was fired, and the 440-pound shot struck the casemate, crushing in the plates and solid mass of wood till daylight showed through. Then it rebounded into the water.

The Lackawanna came next, plowing up the water at a ten-knot gait, and striking the Tennessee at right angles on the port side near the after end of the casemate.   The bow of the Lackawanna was crushed in both above and below the water line, but she did the Tennessee no damage, while the hammering broadside that she delivered as she swung around had no more effect than the guns of the Monongahela had had.   But both the Monongahela and the Lackawanna at once headed off to circle around and return for another attack at full speed.

Then came the Hartford, her anchor dragging on

the surface of the water because the eager crew had found no time to get it higher. The Tennessee turned slightly and the two met, port bow to port bow. The Hartford's anchor was doubled up, but the blow did no other damage, and the two ships scraped along, side against side. Seven guns of the Hartford's battery were fired at that short range, but without effect.

There was even hand to hand fighting, in spite of the thickness and inclination of the walls of the Tennessee's casemate. As ship after ship rubbed along the walls of the Tennessee, the men on each side could see and reach each other through the port-holes.

Engineer Rodgers of the Tennessee "was off watch and had nothing to do but sit on a hatch-comb and note incidents." While there he said later, "A Yankee cursed me through a port-hole, and I jabbed him with my bayonet in the body and his comrade shot me with his revolver." The story is related by Surgeon D. B. Conrad of the Tennessee, who had curious wounds to dress. The shot from the National ships could not penetrate the Tennessee's armor but flaming cubes of powder were hurled through her port-holes, there to pierce the skins of her guns' crews, for the men were stripped to the waist. And no more painful wounds were ever endured than these.

As the Hartford turned to ram again she got across the bows of the Lackawanna, from which she received a crushing blow near the port mizzen rigging. Admiral Farragut had long before that time climbed into the mizzen rigging, and had been "lashed" there again by Lieutenant J. C. Watson. As the ships came together every man on deck turned to look at the Admiral, while the sailors, believing that the collision would sink the Hartford, wholly forgot their own danger, and began to shout:

"Save the Admiral!" "Get the Admiral on board the Lackawanna!"

Happily the Admiral was unhurt. Clearing away his lashing he climbed down to the rail, where he found that the injury to the Hartford did not extend to the water line, and then he ordered the ship headed once more for the Tennessee.

By this time the Confederate was, as Farragut wrote, "sore beset." She was fairly surrounded —mobbed—by the ships that were headed in to ram her. Worse yet, the Chickasaw had taken a position under her port quarter, and remained there, firing her four 11-inch guns at one small area on the casemate—firing them so rapidly, indeed, that no less than fifty-two solid shot struck the stern end of the casemate within half an hour. The Tennessee's armor had resisted the blow from a single 15-inch shot, but it could not withstand the prolonged hammering of the smaller guns. Three shutters over the port-holes of stern and port-side guns were riveted fast in place at times when they were covering the port holes, and the guns were thereby silenced. Then, while four mechanics were trying to release the shutter over the stern port, and Admiral Buchanan was personally directing the work, another shot struck the weakened casemate, bulging it in, and splitting two of the mechanics into shreds that were gathered up with a shovel, besides hurling a splinter that broke Buchanan's leg.

"I saw their limbs and chests, severed and mangled, scattered about the deck, their hearts lying near their bodies," wrote Surgeon Conrad, when speaking of the horrors of the battle. The shots that followed this one set the plates jingling and bolts flying—Death was swiftly finding a way through the armor.

In the meantime the Tennessee's smoke-stack had been broken off below the deck of the casemate. The furnaces lost their draft. The hot smoke and gases from them filled the space where the guns were worked, and overpowered the crew. The steering chains had also been shot away, and when tackles were hooked on instead, they were quickly destroyed.

The Tennessee had become a helpless hulk, unable either to steer or to work her guns. Her officers had fought with unsurpassed gallantry and endurance, but now they could do no more. Going down to the berth deck, Captain Johnson found Admiral Buchanan under the hands of Surgeon Conrad, who, alone, had carried him below for treatment. Buchanan had said to Johnson, "They have got me again. You'll have to look out for her now; it is your fight." But Johnson had now come to report the helpless condition of his ship, and the further fact that all three monitors were in position to hammer the casemate to pieces as the Chickasaw had been doing.

"Well, Johnson, fight to the last," said Buchanan. "Then to save these brave men, when there is no longer any hope, surrender."

The flagstaff of the Tennessee had been shot away long since, but her banner was flying bravely from a boat hook. Going on deck, regardless of the storm of shot that the monitors were hurling at him, Captain Johnson took down the flag. "It had been raised in triumph, it was lowered without dishonor." And then when he saw that the absence of the flag was not observed, or was misunderstood, he attached a handkerchief to the boat hook, and standing alone on deck, waved it in the air.

In an instant the order "cease firing" was heard ringing from ship to ship, and then the little Ossipee that, with two or three larger ships had been heading full speed to ram the Tennessee, sheered alongside of her. Captain William E. LeRoy, of the Ossipee, and Captain Johnson, of the Tennessee, had been close friends in the old navy, and going to the Ossipee's topgallant forecastle, as he neared the Tennessee, LeRoy shouted:

"Hello, Johnson, old fellow! How are you? This is the United States steamer Ossipee. I'll send a boat alongside for you. I'm LeRoy; don't you know me?"

A few minutes later LeRoy took charge of the surrendered Tennessee and raised above her the Stars and Stripes. The battle of Mobile Bay was won.

"It was one of the hardest victories of my life," wrote Admiral Farragut, "and the most desperate battle I ever fought since the days of the old Essex."

CHAPTER XXI

STORIES TOLD AFTER THE BATTLE

It was exactly ten o'clock when the Tennessee surrendered. The guns at Fort Morgan had opened on the National ships at 7:05—the battle had raged for just under three hours. The losses in the Federal fleet were : On the Hartford, 25 killed and 28 wounded; on the Brooklyn, 11 killed and 43 wounded; on the Lackawanna, 4 killed and 35 wounded; on the Oneida, 8 killed and 30 wounded, while the other vessels of the fleet suffered enough to bring the total losses up to 52 killed and 170 wounded, besides 113 who went down in the Tecumseh—a total loss of 335 men and one good ship. But the Confederate fleet was overwhelmed, and, unlike the event below New Orleans, the guns of the one formidable Confederate ship were secured in good condition to be turned upon the Confederate forts. The Confederate ships lost 12 killed and 19 wounded all told.

Immediately after the surrender of the Tennessee she was boarded by Farragut's fleet surgeon, Dr. Palmer, who hastened to the side of Admiral Buchanan. Finding his wound serious, Dr. Palmer returned to Farragut, who arranged with General Page, commanding Fort Morgan, to send the Metacomet, with Buchanan and others that were seriously wounded, under a flag of truce, to Pensacola, where better care could be given them. Surgeon Conrad, of the Tennessee, went along and afterward published Buchanan's plan of battle and anticipations of the result, as Buchanan discussed the matter while lying in the hospital at Pensacola. Buchanan said :

" I did not expect to do the passing vessels any serious injury ; the guns of Fort Morgan were thought capable of doing that. I expected that the monitors would then and there surround me and pound the ' shell ' in ; but when the Federal vessels had passed up and anchored four miles away, then I saw that a long siege was intended by the army and navy, which, with its numerous transports at anchor under Pelican Island, were debarking nearly 10,000 infantry. I determined, then, having the example before me of the blowing up of the Merrimac in the James River by our own officers without a fight, by being caught in such a trap—I determined by an unexpected dash into the fleet, to attack and do it all the damage in my power ; to expend all my ammunition and what little coal I had on board—only six hours steaming ; and then having done all I could with what resources I had, to retire under the guns of the fort, and being without motive power, there to lay and assist in repelling the attack and assaults of the fleet."

Dr. Conrad gives us also a glimpse of Farragut and the Hartford in the flush of victory, for he went to the flagship to arrange for the transfer of Admiral Buchanan from the Tennessee. He says :

" Ascending by the man rope I mounted the hammock netting, as the whole starboard side amidship and the gangway had been carried away. From the hammock netting the scene was one of carnage and devastation. The spar deck was covered and littered with broken gun carriages, shattered boats, disabled guns and a long line of grim corpses, dressed in blue, lying side by side. The officer accompanying me told me that these men—two whole guns' crews—were all killed by splinters, and, pointing with his hand to a piece of weatherboarding ten feet long and four inches wide, I received my first vivid idea of what was meant by a splinter.

" Ascending the poop, where all the officers were standing, I was introduced to Admiral Farragut, whom I found a very quiet, unassuming man, and not in the least flurried by his great victory. In the kindest manner he inquired regarding the severity of the Admiral's wound, and then gave the necessary orders to carry out Admiral Buchanan's request."

Farragut had gazed upon that " long line of grim corpses dressed in blue," of which Conrad speaks, and the sight brought tears from his eyes. " It was the only time I ever saw the old gentleman cry," said Quartermaster Knowles, afterward, " but the tears came to his eyes like a little child."

In his report of the battle Farragut made some statements showing his feelings as a man in time of battle; and they are well worth repeating here. He said :

"Notwithstanding the loss of life, particularly on this ship, and the terrible disaster to the Tecumseh, the result of the fight was a glorious victory and I have reason to feel proud of the officers, seamen and marines of the squadron under my command, for it has never fallen to the lot of an officer to be thus situated and thus sustained.

"Regular discipline will bring men to any amount of endurance, but there is a natural fear of hidden dangers, particularly when so awfully destructive on human life as the torpedo, which requires more than discipline to overcome. . . . After I saw the Tecumseh, struck by a torpedo, disappear almost instantly, beneath the waves, . . . I determined at once, as I had originally intended, to take the lead; and . . . I dashed ahead with the Hartford and the ships followed on, their officers believing they were going to a noble death with their commander-in-chief.

"As I had an elevated position in the main rigging near the top, I was able to overlook not only the deck of the Hartford, but the vessels of the fleet. I witnessed the terrible effects of the enemy's shot and the good conduct of the men at their guns, and although no doubt their hearts sickened, as mine did, when their shipmates were struck down beside them yet there was not a moment's hesitation to lay their comrades aside and spring again to their deadly work."

For Craven the Admiral had nothing but praise; and this is a significant fact that should be treasured by young naval officers. For the sake of em-

phasis let it be said here again that in the history of
our navy it has been observed that officers have had
their reputations tarnished by too strictly adhering
to orders that kept them far from the enemy, while
honors have always been accorded to every one
who, for the sake of getting his ship alongside the
enemy, or *for the sake of making a better fight*, has
disobeyed his orders.

A paragraph from Admiral Buchanan's report is
especially memorable because it is, indirectly, a
severe arraignment of the policy of the Confederate
authorities toward their navy.   He said :

" I seriously felt the want of experienced officers ;
all were young and inexperienced, and many had
but little familiarity with naval duties, having been
appointed from civil life within a year."

A grouty, able, far-seeing old sailor was he, and
given to telling the truth even when it was unpleas-
ant.   Officers of the old navy who gave their
swords to the Confederacy were shifted into the
army, or set at tasks that could never, in any degree worth mention, aid the cause for which they
worked, and boys were " appointed from civil life "
to take the places that might have been filled by
experienced sailors on such battleships as were got
afloat.

A private journal, as quoted by Loyall Farragut,
says that, as the fleet headed in for the fort " the
calmness of the scene was sublime.   No impatience,
no irritation, no anxiety, except for the fort to
open ; and after it did open, full five minutes
elapsed before we answered.   In the meantime the

guns were trained as if at a target, and all the sounds I could hear were, 'Steady, boys, steady! Left tackle a little. So! so!' then the roar of a broadside, and an eager cheer as the enemy were driven from their water battery. Don't imagine they [the Confederates] were frightened; no man could stand under that iron shower; and the brave fellows returned to their guns as soon as it lulled, only to be driven away again."

While the Ossipee and Itasca were passing the fort a splinter struck Lieutenant-Commander George Brown, commanding the Itasca, and caused him intense pain.

"What is the matter, Brown?" asked Lieutenant J. A. Howell of the Ossipee, "have you been struck by a splinter?"

"You may call it a splinter on your big vessel," replied Brown, "but aboard this little craft it ranks as a log of wood."

In all eighty-three men before the mast received medals of honor for showing coolness and bravery in the battle of Mobile Bay—a sufficient proof that the gallantry of Admiral Farragut inspired his men throughout the fleet. Though unnamed in history the men at the oars were as heroic as was young Nields when he went to save the crew of the Tecumseh.

Of the many letters of congratulation that Farragut received, after entering Mobile Bay, there was none that described the effect of the victory upon the Nation as well as that of General Benjamin F. Butler. The letter also shows by what route the news reached the North.   Writing on August 11th, he said :

"I had the exquisite gratification of telegraphing from the Richmond papers the first account of your most glorious success, and the noble exploit of your fleet.   I need not use the language of compliment where none is needed.   It is all said in one word. *It was like you.*   Reminding me so much of the passage of the Mississippi forts, was it wonderful that, boy-like, in my tent all alone, when the rebel journal was brought and the official telegram read that you and seventeen of your vessels had passed Fort Morgan, I called out, 'Three cheers for Farragut' ?   They were given with a will that brought in my staff and orderlies, who thought their general had gone crazy, perhaps with sunstroke, whereas it was only a stroke of good luck, of high daring and noble enterprise, quite as brilliant as anything the sun could do.

"Let me assure you, admiral, that those cheers, the first given on the occasion in the loyal North, are not done ringing yet; but every hilltop is resounding with them as they are caught up from hamlet to hamlet and city to city, of a grateful Nation.   I speak no language of hyperbole, and only the words of sincere admiration when I say I envy you alone of all men, for the place you have in the hearts of your countrymen—a feeling, however, which will not prevent me from, at all times, adding my mite to the tribute."

However, there was more work for Farragut to do even after the Tennessee had been captured.   It makes one proud of the old navy to recall the fact that General R. L. Page, who had been a commander in it, now "looked upon Farragut's fleet as practically prisoners in a port whose keys he held." General Page was mistaken; he was soon to be cut off from every source of supplies, but he had the John Paul Jones spirit, and would fight to the last gasp, looking for some turn in affairs that would save the day.

Moreover, Fort Gaines was yet in the possession of the Confederates, and because Farragut had been unable to enter the port on the 4th, they had thrown a large quantity of supplies and an additional force of men into it to strengthen it against the assaults that had been commenced by General Granger's command. Further than that, Fort Powell, commanding Grant's Pass westward from the bay, was in position to sink any vessels trying to bring supplies from New Orleans to Farragut's fleet.

While General Granger was landing on Dauphin Island (Aug. 3d), to attack Fort Gaines, Lieutenant-Commander J. C. P. DeKraft was sent with the Conemaugh and a number of other light-draft gunboats to cover the landing. This was accomplished without trouble, and then DeKraft, on the 5th, went around to the westward and attacked Fort Powell. The fort was struck several times during the forenoon, but nothing was accomplished toward its capture. In the afternoon of the 5th, however, the bay being wholly under the command of Farragut, the Chickasaw was sent to attack Fort Powell in the rear. Steaming up within 700 yards of the fort Perkins opened on it with his four 11-inch guns. Lieutenant-Colonel J. M. Williams, commanding the fort, had but one gun mounted and able to reply to the Chickasaw. It was a 7-inch Brooke rifle, and he managed it as well as circumstances permitted, but the earth work before the gun was not high enough to protect the men, and at the same time too high to permit a sufficient depression of the weapon for a ricochet fire at the Chickasaw. Moreover, there was no platform for the men to stand on when loading the gun, and they therefore handled the ammunition slowly. Worse than all else was the fact that, because the fort had not been completed, the bomb proof could be and was pierced by a shell. The shell did not explode, but it was manifest that the magazine might be blown up at any moment ; and the projectiles that reached the face wall of the fort from time to time knocked it down so rapidly that its destruction was plainly a matter of time only.

Being wholly unable to hold the fort longer, Colonel Williams, after consultation by wire with Colonel Charles D. Anderson, commanding Fort Gaines, abandoned Fort Powell on the night of the 5th, and when his men were well clear of it, he fired the magazine, destroying the whole work.

The case of Fort Gaines was somewhat different. On the 4th, in anticipation of a siege, the Confederates, as has been said, added to the garrison until there were 864 officers and men in it. They had carried in supplies to last six months. It was a brick fort, well-planned, and it mounted twenty-seven guns of which three were 10-inch Columbiads and four 32-pounder rifles. There was a chance here for a long fight.

On the 6th, preparations were made in Farragut's fleet for bombarding this fort, and late in the afternoon the Chickasaw was sent to drop a few shells into it and get the range. Then, being anxious to save life where possible, Farragut forwarded a flag of truce and invited Colonel Anderson and his staff to consider the matter of surrender in a conference. Colonel Anderson accepted the invitation. On arriving in the cabin of the Hartford Admiral Farragut said to him : "Surrounded on three sides by my vessels, and on the fourth by the army you cannot possibly hold it. Submit, then, like a man to this hard necessity, and prevent further loss of life." A major who accompanied the Colonel wanted "to fight it out," but Farragut continued :

"Gentlemen, if hard fighting could save that fort, I would advise you to fight to the death ; but by all the laws of war, you have not even a chance of saving it."

The Admiral was a sincere man and his sincerity was manifest to the Confederate officers. It was true that they could not save the fort and by agreement it was surrendered to officers representing the navy and army at nine o'clock on the morning of the 7th. The garrison was sent to New Orleans, and the flag of the Nation was once more hoisted above the walls.

Until the surrender of Fort Gaines the unfriendly British authorities had professed to see nothing striking in the work of Farragut in Mobile Bay. But on learning that Fort Gaines had surrendered and Fort Powell had been abandoned, the *British Army and Navy Gazette* said :

"There can now be no doubt of the signal character of his victory and of the serious blow given to the Confederates in that quarter. It was argued that he had done nothing more than run past Fort Gaines and Fort Morgan, and sink and destroy a certain number of the enemy's fleet ; that his position was precarious, and his transports could not pass the batteries and he would have to run back for supplies ; that he could not get up to the town, in consequence of shoal water and of formidable works on land ; and that he could not hope to hold his own ; as he had not troops to make an impression on the east side of the bay and prevent the transmission of supplies to the forts at the entrance.

"Yesterday's news blew all these speculations, arguments and assertions into the air without exception. By the surrender of Fort Gaines on the west side of the entrance and by the voluntary destruction of Fort Powell, the position of Farragut is rendered secure. The middle channel is left open, and stores can be landed under the guns of Fort Gaines ; and the channel to New Orleans, which was closed by Fort Powell, must now fall into the hands of the victor.

"Next to New Orleans, the city of Mobile was the greatest cotton port in the States. It was lately driving a considerable trade in blockade-running, and gave abundant supplies to the Confederacy. Now neither can cotton go out nor goods run in, and Mobile, its inhabitants and garrison are thrown on the resources of the impoverished and hard-pressed Confederacy.

" Already a fleet of transports, laden with fresh provisions and ice, has sailed from New York to supply the doughty Admiral, whose feats of arms place him at the head of his profession, and certainly constitute him the first naval officer of the day, as far as actual reputation, won by skill, courage and hard fighting, goes."

This quotation is specially memorable, for it was not until this time—after Farragut's victory at Mobile—that the army and navy authorities in England would admit that the Union forces were likely to win. Moreover, the quotation shows how *" skill, courage and hard fighting" make friends for a Nation* as well as for a man. Beginning with the naval victories of the Civil War, the old time prejudices of the British against the " Yankee" nation wore slowly away until our victories in the war with Spain almost entirely dissipated them. Indeed, near the end of 1904, when an American squadron visited London the King of England at a luncheon given to the officers of the squadron proposed the toast :

"The American navy—may its power never grow less !"

After the surrender of Fort Gaines, Flag Lieutenant John Crittenden Watson and Major James E. Montgomery, were sent to Fort Morgan to demand its surrender, but "General Page replied that he would defend his post to the last extremity." Accordingly on the 9th increased forces and a train of heavy artillery landed at Navy Cove, on the bay side of the Peninsula, four miles from Fort Morgan.

From this point a steady advance was made by throwing up earthworks until there were sixteen mortars and twenty-five heavy cannon (including four 9-inch navy guns under Lieutenant H. B. Tyson), mounted within 500 yards of the fort. On August 22d the fleet, including the Tennessee, closed in and "began one of the most furious bombardments that sailor or soldier has ever witnessed." [1] Without break the storm of shells was hurled at the fort until sunset. Thereafter the fire became irregular until nine o'clock when it was seen that the fort's citadel was burning, whereupon the National forces renewed their fire and maintained it all night.

"Yet, amid all the horrors of this disastrous night, with their walls breached, almost every piece of ordnance disabled, and the magazine endangered by the conflagration which raged fiercely for several hours, the garrison of Fort Morgan was not dismayed. Some of the soldiers applied themselves to throwing their powder into the cistern, others to spiking or destroying dismounted guns, while others again contended successfully with the devouring flames." [2]

At daylight of the 23d, all the powder in the fort had been destroyed. The citadel was again set on fire. The walls had been breached until there was "no bomb-proof in the fort." All means of defense were gone. In short "crumbling walls, broken guns and water-soaked powder were all that remained of Fort Morgan, and at two o'clock on August 23d the white flag was displayed."

[1] F. A. Parker.   [2] Ibid.

The work of Admiral Farragut in the Civil War was done. He remained in the bay until November, but beyond clearing out the torpedoes, and examining the shores, nothing worth while could be effected. The Confederates had obstructed the channel above Dog River Bar by sinking in it a hulk that had been planned for an ironclad. Piles were also driven so that the vessels that might otherwise have crossed the Bar were unable to go up to the city. Admiral Farragut advised that no attack be made on Mobile at that time, but it was not because of these obstructions. His reason, as he gave it, is memorable. "It would be an elephant," he said, "and take an army to hold it. And besides, all the traitors and rascally speculators would flock to that city and pour into the Confederacy the wealth of New York."

Meantime the Admiral's health was failing. What with the anxiety he had had to endure, and the effects of the hot climate, his system was breaking down. On the day after Fort Morgan surrendered he fainted away while talking to Perkins of the Chickasaw.

Late in August he wrote to the Department saying : "As long as I am able I am willing to do the bidding of the Department to the best of my abilities. I fear, however, my health is giving way. I have now been down in the Gulf and the Caribbean Sea nearly five years out of six, with the exception of the short time at home last fall, and the last six months have been a severe drag upon me, and I want rest if it is to be had."

The Department had already made out orders assigning him to the command of the Atlantic squadron in order that he might direct the operations against Fort Fisher at Wilmington, N. C., a port that was then doing a thriving business with blockade-runners. But the order was revoked. Having seen Fort Morgan surrender, and having put his fleet in order for his successor (Commodore James S. Palmer), Admiral Farragut sailed from Pensacola on November 30, 1864, and arrived at New York on December 12th.

CHAPTER XXII

THE LAST DAYS

ACCORDING to Captain Loyall Farragut the best existing description of the Admiral as he appeared at the time of the battle of Mobile, is that written in "The Southerners," by Cyrus Townsend Brady who says, "He was a rather small man who still preserved his waist and figure although he had already entered upon his sixty-third year." While he was "rather small" he yet had "broad shoulders and a well-knit frame" that showed unusual vigor for one of his age. In reading he wore eye-glasses, and "when he removed them a slight contraction of his brows was noticeable, which turned the upper curves of the eyelids into straight lines, giving a singular eagle-like directness to his glance ;—if an eagle's eye could be kindly and filled with humor which is the completing quality of greatness. His face, which was rather long, was smooth-shaven. His forehead was round and high. His nose was aquiline, and his upper lip long ; the curves of his mouth bespoke an indomitable resolution which the firm, bold chin and resolute jaw confirmed. He was bald on the top of his head, but his black hair, already turning white about the temples, which was allowed to grow long on the left side, was carefully brushed over the denuded spot ; in seaman's parlance, 'the after guard was made to do fok's'l duty.'

"His natural very dark complexion was intensified by an exposure of many years to wind and weather, largely in tropic seas," and a whitish line across his forehead showed where his cap had protected it from the sun's rays.   "In spite of his dark skin his color came and went like a boy's, especially when he laughed or grew excited. His manners were simple, genial and unaffected, his address easy and pleasant.

"Fifty years of naval service had given the Admiral the authoritative appearance of long command. There was about him that indefinable stamp of power and its habitual use, or enjoyment, which held the most presumptuous at a proper distance. At the same time he was easily approachable, too. In his bearing there was dignity without stiffness. When he knitted his brows, as he frequently did on account of slightly impaired vision, and his mind turned to action, his hazel eyes fairly flashed with fire and spirit. In repose there was a twinkle of humor, and good humor, in them, which yet neither invited presumption nor allowed familiarity. The predominate impression that an observer accustomed to reading men would have gathered from his appearance was one of absolute fearlessness. . . . You could see that he was a sailor beyond peradventure, a thousand things indicated it to the observing or experienced eye. He could no more disguise it than he could disguise his character. Yet there were none of the popular accepted signs of his profession about him; nothing of the 'roll, like-a-seventy-four-in-a-gale-of-wind' in his manner; nothing of the bluff, burly, bull-like, blow-hardness of the so-called Benbow school of sailors in his appearance. Nor was he of the red-faced, irascible type, which so many ancient seamen affect —especially in novels. He was not full of strange oaths and uncouth phrases more or less technical. There were about him none of the common affectations of the sea—indeed no affectations of any sort. Here was a cultivated gentleman of the very highest type, an accomplished officer, a lion in his bravery, almost a woman in gentleness.''

To do honor to this man a committee representing the officials and people of New York met the Hartford as she entered the Narrows in the harbor on her return North from Mobile. This committee invited the Admiral to attend a public reception to be given him at the custom house that afternoon, and he consented to do so. The Battery was covered with a cheering host when he landed a little later, and the leading men of the city were in the custom house when he arrived there. The collector, Mr. S. Draper, welcomed the Admiral to the city, and then read a series of resolutions that had been adopted by the New York merchants, wherein it was said that the people recognized "the illustrious service, heroic bravery, and tried loyalty which have distinguished the life of Rear Admiral D. G. Farragut in the cause of his country—especially the lofty spirit of devotion by which he has been animated during all the period of the present war, and the signal victories achieved by him.''

To mark this recognition it was resolved ''That the city of New York, following the example of the great free cities of the world, in doing honor to their illustrious countrymen, honors itself by tendering Admiral Farragut an invitation to become a resident thereof.'' It was further resolved '' That we see with the highest satisfaction that the President, in his annual message, and the Secretary of the Navy, recommend the creation of a higher grade of naval rank with the designation of Admiral Farragut as the recipient, as a national recognition of distinguished service and exalted patriotism.''

Farragut's greatest words had been, theretofore, uttered in the smoke of battle, when he said : ''The best protection against the enemy's fire is a well directed fire from our own guns,'' and '' Damn the torpedoes ! Go ahead.''   Standing now before the most prominent gentlemen of New York he spoke as appropriately as he had done in his accustomed sphere.   He said :

'' My friends, I can only reply to you as I did before, by saying that I receive these compliments with great thankfulness and deep emotions.   I am entirely unaccustomed to make such an address as I would desire to do upon this occasion ; but if I do not express what I think of the honor you do me, trust me, I feel it most deeply.   I don't think, however, that I particularly deserve anything at your hands.   I can merely say that I have done my duty to the best of my abilities. I have been devoted to the service of my country since I was eight years of age, and my father was devoted to it before me. I have not specially deserved these demonstrations of your regard. I owe everything, perhaps, to chance, and to the praiseworthy exertions of my brother officers serving with me. That I have been fortunate is most true, and I am deeply thankful for it for my country's sake. I return my thanks to the committee for their resolutions, especially for the one in regard to the creation of an additional grade."

The invitation to the Admiral to make his home in New York was accompanied, a few days later, by a gift of $50,000 donated by men of means to enable him to do so. The presentation took place at the custom house on December 31, 1864, and it was accompanied by an address engrossed on parchment which was directed to "Vice Admiral Farragut."

In his message of December 6, 1864, President Lincoln wrote : "I cordially concur in the recommendation of the Secretary [of the Navy] as to the propriety of creating the new rank of Vice Admiral in our naval service."

In furtherance of this recommendation a bill to create the grade of Vice Admiral was introduced in Congress on December 22d. It passed both houses the same day and was signed by Lincoln the next. Farragut was, of course, immediately nominated for the rank and his commission bore the date of December 23, 1864.

At this time the Civil War was drawing rapidly
to an end. Porter was in command of the fleet
that a little later captured Fort Fisher at the entrance to the harbor of Wilmington, N. C.
(January 15, 1865). The arrival of Sherman at
Columbia, S. C., compelled the evacuation of
Charleston, February 17th. Richmond, Va., was
surrendered on April 3, 1865. But toward the end
of January, 1865, a number of Confederate vessels
in the James River tried to " cut off both the army
of the James and that of the Potomac from their
base of supplies at City Point," by a descent of the
river. The Federal naval force in the waters around
and above City Point had been depleted to give
strength to Porter's fleet, and the Confederates at
that time had three relatively good ironclads and a
number of wooden gunboats in the James. To meet
what seemed to be an emergency, Farragut was
ordered to the command of the National ships in
the James. But when he arrived he found that the
Confederates had been repulsed and were again
wholly on the defensive. He was therefore at
once relieved, and this was his last service in the
Civil War.

On April 4th, Farragut entered Richmond,
having passed up the James by steamer after hearing that the Confederates had evacuated their capital. Charles C. Coffin, correspondent of the *Boston
Journal* (quoted by Loyall Farragut), described the
appearance of the Admiral when entering the Confederate Senate chamber :

"General Weitzel was in the Senate chamber,

issuing his orders. General Shopley, Military-Governor, was also there. The door opened, and a smooth-faced man with a keen eye, and a firm, quick, resolute step, entered. He wore a plain blue blouse with three stars on the collar. He was the old hero who opened the way to New Orleans, and who fought the battle of the Mobile forts from the masthead of his ship—Admiral Farragut. He was accompanied by General Gordon of Massachusetts. They heard the news yesterday noon, and made all haste up the James, landing at Varina, and taking horses to the city. It was a pleasure to take the brave Admiral's hand and answer his eager questions as to what Grant had done : 'Thank God, it is about over,' said he, meaning the rebellion.''

On June 14, 1866, Senator Grimes, of Iowa, introduced a bill from the Naval Committee ''to define the number and regulate the appointment of officers in the navy.'' As immediately amended and passed by the Senate, this act provided '' that the number allowed in each grade of line officers on the active list of the navy shall be one admiral, one vice admiral, ten rear admirals,'' etc. In this way the rank of admiral was established in our navy, and the reason for establishing the grade was, as senators explained, the desire to place Farragut on a level with Grant, for whom the rank of general was to be provided. Congress and the people appreciated Farragut's work afloat as they did that of their greatest general ashore. It was agreed, too, that it would be unjust to the navy, after its splendid part in the work of preserving the Nation, to leave its most conspicuous leader with a lower rank than that of the first general.

The act further provided that the Admiral's salary should be $10,000 a year (as Vice Admiral, while on leave of absence, his pay was but $5,000), and that a secretary should be provided for him at a salary equal to the sea pay of a lieutenant of the navy. This act was approved July 25, 1866, and Farragut was commissioned as admiral next day.

It was afterward provided "That vacancies occurring in the grades of admiral and vice admiral shall not be filled by promotion." Porter was made vice admiral and afterwards admiral, but at his death the grades ceased to exist in the navy. It was the judgment of the people that since the ranks of admiral and vice admiral had been created to reward extraordinary services to the Nation, they should not be filled except by men who had in like manner earned such a reward. And there was no American admiral after Porter until Commodore Dewey, by his services in Manila Bay, showed himself worthy of the honor.

In the summer of 1867, Farragut was assigned to the command of the European station, and on June 17th his flag was hoisted on the steam frigate Franklin, one of the stately, full-rigged ships with auxiliary steam power that were especially favored by the Department in those days. Then, very unexpectedly, the President sent orders that Mrs. Farragut and a kinswoman should be allowed to accompany the Admiral on the cruise. It was a permit that greatly pleased him.

The Franklin sailed from New York on June 28th, and anchored behind the breakwater in Cherbourg Harbor on July 14th. A great fleet of French and American ships gathered in the harbor, and among the latter were the vessels from Annapolis with the naval cadets on their practice cruise.

Farragut was promptly invited to dine with Napoleon III. The Emperor had not forgotten that Farragut's work at New Orleans had prevented French recognition of the Confederacy, and he had no love for the government which had thwarted his designs upon Mexico. But because the Americans had proven their ability in war, afloat and ashore, he had determined to cultivate the old friendship that had existed between the French people and those of the United States. This is a point of sufficient importance to bear emphasis. When our Nation was staggering under the first burden of the Civil War, French rulers talked only of intervention and the sending of a squadron to the American coast to support their plan for ending the war by the division of the Nation. In our weakness the French Government (and it was not alone) became aggressive. In 1867 as a nation we were far weaker than in 1862, for we had an enormous debt to pay, broken industries to rebuild, the flower of the country's manhood, destroyed in battle, to replace. But in the meantime we had built and armed a fleet of ships so powerful that there was no other in the world to equal them; and what was of still more importance, we had manned them with veterans whose ability, skill and courage were then preëminent. It was not because Napoleon loved the American Republic that he invited Farragut to dinner. He did it because good policy demanded that he make friends with the people having for the moment the most powerful navy in the world. The changed attitude of the French monarch is a very good proof of the assertions often made by naval men, that in a powerful navy lies the Nation's strongest hope of peace.

In England, the attentions bestowed upon the Admiral were of a similar significance. It by no means detracts from the honor done to him personally, to say that the receptions given him had a political significance. For it was his work that had, most of all, impressed the nations of Europe with the idea that peace with America was desirable. No American army was likely to land on a coast of Europe ; but it was now plainly evident that the thunder of American guns might be heard in the ports of any European nation which should force a war upon the United States.

While our civil contest was yet undecided the British sailors sang Confederate songs at New Orleans, at Norfolk—and in fact wherever there were Confederate ears to hear them. But when Farragut reached Malta, in 1867, the sailors sang :

" ' God save the Queen ' delights you still,
    And ' British Grenadiers ' ;
  The good old strains your heart strings thrill,
    And catch you by the ears;

And we, oh, hate us if you can,
    For we are proud of you —
We like you, Brother Jonathan,
    And ' Yankee Doodle ' too !

*   *   *   *   *   *

" As friend with friend and man with man,
    Oh, let our hearts be thus —
As David's love to Jonathan
    Be Jonathan's to us ! "

The ports of the north of Europe were visited after the sojourn in France. Russia showed the Admiral particular honor and when he visited the Czar's officers at Cronstadt the orders of the day issued by the Russian Admiral contained these words :

"Let us remember the glorious example of Farragut and his followers at New Orleans and Mobile."

From the point of view of a naval officer the most interesting feature of the Admiral's diary while cruising around the coasts of Europe is the attention he gave to matters that might be of use to his government in time of war. He was well advanced in years but the position and strength of forts, the novel features of ships, the relative power of a 15-inch Dahlgren and a 9-inch rifle which he saw tested in England, were of as much interest to him as if he had been a young lieutenant. It was the persistence of the habit of a lifetime ; and the opportunity to make such studies gave him much more pleasure than any entertainment offered him by any person of any degree however high.

Nevertheless one reception in his honor was particularly pleasing—that which he received at Ciudadela on the island of Minorca, one of the Balearic group. It must be remembered that Farragut's blood was half Spanish. A Spanish troubadour had written in the thirteenth century about Pedro Ferragut, an ancestor of the Admiral, as follows:[1]

PEDRO FERRAGUT

Troba 237.

Sobre camp bermell una ferradura
De finisim or, ab un clau durat,
Pere Ferragut pinta, é en tal figura
Esplicà lo agnom. La historia asegura
Ser aragones, de Jaca baixat.
Apres que en Mallorca servi de sargent,
Venint á Valencia, hon gran renom guanya
De expert capitá per lo dilitgent;
Los anys, é sucesos lo feren prudent
Té en lo pelear gran cordura é manya,
Pergue á totes armes fácilment se apanya.

This is translated as follows :

"Peter Ferragut, in order that all might know his agnomen, painted upon the vermilion of his shield a golden nail and horseshoe. History informs us that he was born in Jaca, in Aragon. After serving as a sergeant in Mallorca, he went to Valencia where he gained great renown as a captain whose age and experience had made him at once adventurous and prudent. *He was famous for his*

[1] Quoted by Loyall Farragut, also by Parker in " The Battle of Mobile Bay."

skill in the use of arms and for his great amiability in battle."

The visit to the town of Ciudadela, the original home of the Admiral's father, was made on the day after Christmas. Landing at Port Mahon the Admiral found the people of the island assembled in great throngs along the route of his journey. The Alcalde and other officials of Ciudadela, met him four miles from the city's limits to bid him welcome and escort him to the town, and when he entered the streets he found not only the way but the house-tops covered with people "filling the air with cheers and exclamations." A committee escorted him to the places of interest about the city. He was lodged at the house of one of the distinguished citizens. He was visited by the Alcalde and Auyuntamiento (town council), "in a body, and by them presented with a book containing the register of the baptism of his father ; and also with a copy of a law passed that day making him a citizen of Ciudadela." That night a grand banquet was held in his honor, the principal ornament of the table being "a large centre piece representing the castle of Ciudadela, on the four walls of which was written 'Homenage de Respeco y Patriotismo, Ciudadela.' From the centre of this castle rose a column of victory marked 'El Gran Almirante Farragut.' The whole was decorated with ribbons representing the American colors. It was presented to Mrs. Farragut after the banquet. The roads were once more thronged with an enthusiastic populace when the Admiral returned to his ship."

"This unexpected reception by the people of Ciudadela was to our naval commander one of the most gratifying incidents of his cruise," says James E. Montgomery, who wrote a book to describe "The Cruise of Admiral Farragut," and the ovation that was extended to him on the coasts of Europe by men who were best able, of all the Old World, to appreciate the work that he had done.

In 1869 the Admiral went to California, and only those who have enjoyed the comforting hospitality of the Californians can fully understand how he was received there. Perhaps of all the journeys of his life this was the most satisfactory, for it showed him, as he had never been able to see it before, the development and extent of the Republic he had done so much to preserve.

In the meantime (1868), prominent politicians had asked Farragut to allow them to place his name as a candidate for President before the National Democratic Convention, to be held that year. In reply to a letter urging him to accept this offer Farragut wrote:

"My entire life has been spent in the navy; by a steady perseverance and devotion to it I have been favored with success in my profession, and to risk that reputation by entering a new career at my advanced age, and that career one of which I have little or no knowledge, is more than any one has a right to expect of me."

On his way East from California, Farragut was taken seriously ill at Chicago, and it was found that his heart was affected. He was, after a time, able to reach home, but when there he suffered from further attacks of the kind, and in spite of a constitution originally of extraordinary strength, he never fully recovered his health.

In January, 1870, he had charge of the naval contingent that received the body of the philanthropist, George Peabody, when it was brought to this country by the British naval ship Monarch, and landed at Portland, Me. Brother officers who met him at Portland noted that he looked like one whose health was broken. To a young officer who nevertheless complimented him on having the appearance of good health, he said:

"Do you think so? I am very far from being a well man."

In fact Farragut's end was at hand. Remembering his great services, the Secretary of the Navy placed the steamer Tallapoosa under the Admiral's charge with permission to cruise in it with his family where he would. He thereupon went to the Portsmouth Navy Yard, then under the command of Rear Admiral Pennock, who had married a relative of Mrs. Farragut. The Admiral was in bed much of his time during the passage but when he heard the guns fired in his honor, as the ship entered Portsmouth harbor, he dressed himself in full uniform and went on deck. There, as he gazed at his flag flying from the mast-head, he said:

"It would be well if I died now—in harness."

A few days later, while wandering around the navy yard he went on board the old sailing sloop-of-war Dale that was lying dismantled at the wharf.

A brief look around her deck satisfied him, and then as he stepped ashore, he said to the old seaman who had charge of her:

"That is the last time I shall ever tread the deck of a man-of-war."

It was so. On August 14, 1870, at the house of the commandant of the navy yard, where " he was surrounded by his family and loving friends, including many of his old comrades in arms," and with the old flag above his head, he died. The body was laid away temporarily at Portsmouth, but in September the Navy Department brought it to New York. There "the municipal authorities took charge of the public funeral" that was held on September 30th. The public schools and offices, the custom house, the stock exchange and the leading mercantile houses were closed. The city edifices were draped, bells tolled, and minute guns were fired. A procession which included the President of the United States and members of his cabinet, many naval and military officers, veteran associations, 10,000 soldiers, the fire brigade and numerous civic societies, escorted the body, which was borne by sailors from the boat landing to the Harlem train at Forty-seventh Street. From there it was taken to Woodlawn Cemetery, the trustees of which had set apart for the purpose of the interment a beautiful plot of ground, where it now rests.

By a joint resolution approved June 22, 1874, Congress appropriated $20,000 for "a bronze statue of the late Admiral Farragut." This work of art was designed by Vinnie Ream and was erected in Farragut Square, Washington, where it was unveiled on April 25, 1881. The propeller of the Admiral's old flagship Hartford was used in casting the statue. A contemporary account says that when the memorial was unveiled, the procession contained so many naval officers and sailors as to astonish even those who had looked for great numbers of men of the service to attend the ceremonies.

The Farragut Monument Association, an aggregation of representative New York citizens, contracted with Augustus St. Gaudens for a statue of Farragut, which was erected in Madison Square, New York, and unveiled on May 21, 1881, in the presence of a great throng of people. This, the best known statue of him, was cast in Paris. "Of heroic size, it shows the Admiral in his navy uniform, his cap straight visored, and the trousers loose, his sword hanging from the belt. In his left hand he holds a marine glass. The right hangs naturally. The skirt of the coat seems to be agitated by the wind. The pose is easy and natural and the expression admirable in its combination of gravity and penetration. The instant that it was unveiled it achieved the success to which it is in every way entitled. Indeed, there are few, if any, statues in America to be compared with it in naturalness and power." Thus wrote a competent critic in the "Magazine of American History."

An inscription on the pedestal, written by Richard Grant White reads as follows:

"That the memory of a daring and sagacious commander and gentle great-souled man whose life from childhood was given to his country, but who served her supremely in the war for the Union, MDCCCLXI–MDCCCLXV, may be preserved and honored and that they who come after him and who will owe him so much may see him as he was seen by friend and foe, his countrymen have set up this monument, A. D., MDCCCLXXXI."

THE END

BIBLIOGRAPHY

ADAMS, HENRY. History of the United States, 1903.

ALLEN, J. Battles of the British Navy, 1852.

AMERICAN HISTORICAL REVIEW, 1904.

AMERICAN STATE PAPERS—Naval Affairs, 1834–1861.

ANNALS OF CONGRESS, 1801–1816.

ANNUAL REPORTS of the Secretary of the Navy.

BARNES, JAMES. Commodore Bainbridge, 1897.

—— Midshipman Farragut, 1902.

BENNETT, FRANK M. The Steam Navy of the United States, 1897.

BINNS, JOHN. Life and Recollections of, 1854.

BUSK, HANS. Navies of the World, 1859.

BUTLER, B. F. Butler's Book, 1892.

CABLE, GEORGE W. History and Present Condition of New Orleans, 1881.

CENTURY MAGAZINE.

CLAIBORNE, J. F. H. Mississippi, 1880.

CONGRESSIONAL GLOBE, 1860–1870.

CONNER, P. S. P. Home Squadron Under Commodore Conner, 1896.

—— The Castle of San Juan de Ulloa and the Topsy-Turvyists, 1897.

COOPER, F. Naval History of the United States, 1847.

DAHLGREN, M. V. Admiral John A. Dahlgren, 1882.

DAWSON, H. B. Battles of the United States by Sea and Land, 1858.

—— Historical Magazine, 1857, *et seq.*

DORSEY, SARAH A. Recollections of Henry W. Allen, 1866.

DOUGLASS, SIR HOWARD. Naval Gunnery, 1860.

FARRAGUT, LOYALL. Life and Letters of Admiral D. G. Farragut, 1891.

FOSTER, JOHN W. A Century of American Diplomacy, 1902.

GALAXY MAGAZINE.

HAMERSLY, L. R. Naval Encyclopædia, 1884.

—— The United Service Magazine.

HARPER'S MAGAZINE.

HARRIS, T. Life and Services of Commodore William Bainbridge, 1837.

HAYWOOD, MARSHALL DE LANCEY, Major George Farragut. (Pamphlet, no date.)

HEADLEY, J. T. Farragut and Our Naval Commanders, 1867.

—— Vice Admiral D. G. Farragut, 1865.

HOPPIN, J. M. Life of Admiral Foote, 1874.

HOSMER, J. K. The Color Guard, 1864.

HOUSE JOURNAL, 1801–1815.

JAMES, WILLIAM. Naval History of Great Britain, 1837.

KING, GRACE. New Orleans, 1902.

KIRKLAND, FRAZAR. Pictorial Book of Anecdotes and Incidents of the Rebellion, 1866.

KOUNTZ, JOHN S. Record of the Organizations Engaged in the Campaign, Siege, and Defense of Vicksburg, 1901.

MACLAY, E. S. History of the Navy, 1897.

MAHAN, A. T. Admiral Farragut, 1895.

———— The Gulf and Inland Waters, 1883.

———— Influence of Sea Power Upon History, 1896.

MONTGOMERY, J. E.   The Cruise of Admiral Farragut, 1869.

MOORE, FRANK.   Putnam's Record of the Rebellion, 1862–1866.

NILES, H.   Weekly Register, 1811, *et seq.*

OFFICIAL RECORDS of the Union and Confederate Armies, 1880, *et seq.*

OFFICIAL RECORDS of the Union and Confederate Armies, 1894, *et seq.*

OLIVE BRANCH, THE.   1816.

PARKER, F. A.   The Battle of Mobile Bay, 1878.

PARKER, JOHN C.   A Night with Farragut, in War Papers and Reminiscences, Commandery of Missouri, Loyal Legion, 1892.

PARKER, W. H.   Recollections of a Naval Officer, 1883.

PORTER, ADMIRAL D. D.   Incidents of the Civil War, 1891.

———— Naval History of the Civil War, 1886.

PORTER, D.   Porter's Journal, 1815.

RICHARDSON, JAMES D.   Messages and Papers of the Presidents, 1896.

RIGBY, W. T.   Historic Vicksburg, 1904.

ROOSEVELT, THEODORE.   The Naval War of 1812, 1897.

SANDS, REAR ADMIRAL B. F.   From Reefer to Rear Admiral, 1899.

SCHARF, J. T.   History of the Confederate Navy, 1894.

SCHLEY, REAR ADMIRAL, W. S.   Forty-five Years Under the Flag, 1904.

SCRIBNER'S MAGAZINE.

SOLEY, J. R.   The Blockade and the Cruisers, 1895.

———— Admiral Porter, 1903.

STARBUCK, ALEXANDER. History of the American Whale
    Fishery, 1878.

STEPHEN, JAMES.   War in Disguise, 1806.

WALKE, REAR ADMIRAL H.   Naval Scenes and Reminiscences
    of the Civil War, 1877.

WHARTON, FRANCIS.   International Law Digest, 1887.

WILSON, H. W.   Iron Clads in Action, 1896.

WINSOR, JUSTIN.   Narrative and Critical History of America,
    1889.

INDEX

Port Royal, U. S. S., at Mobile, 317, 319.

Portsmouth Navy Yard, Farragut dies at, 371.

Portsmouth, U. S. sloop, at mouth of Mississippi River, 180; in attack on Fort Jackson, 211.

Potomac River, mentioned, 259; 361.

Powell, Fort, defending Mobile, 305; attacked, 348; destroyed, 349; mentioned, 351.

Powhatan, U. S. S., at Pensacola, 156; blockades pass of Mississippi River, 169; sent to New York for repairs, 171.

Preble, Lieutenant Commander George H., work quoted, 38; in New Orleans expedition, 179.

Preedy, a British captain, effort of to discourage Farragut, 205, 206.

President, U. S. frigate, fight with British sloop of war Little Belt, 43, 44; mentioned, 52.

Price, General Sterling, mentioned, 314.

Privateers, Spanish-American, considered, 102 *et seq.*

QUEEN OF THE WEST, Union war steamer, 247; meets the Arkansas, 248, 249; fails in attack on Arkansas, 252; loss of, 280.

RACCOON, British sloop of war, mentioned, 63.

Raft, proposed for defense of New York harbor, 41, 186; to close Mississippi River at

Fort Jackson, 185 *et seq.*; strength of considered, 205; broken, 206 *et seq.*

Rafts, fire, below New Orleans, 187; work of in battle of Mississippi River, 213 *et seq.*; poorly handled, 225.

Randall, Captain Gideon, whaler, adventures of, 59 *et seq.*; mutiny of quelled by Farragut, 61, 62.

Randolph, John, tells Congress that it could not be kicked into fighting, 41; dislike for navy, 188.

Ransom, Lieutenant Commander George M., in New Orleans expedition, 179.

Read, Lieutenant C. W., on Confederate ram Manassas, 220; and ironclad Arkansas, 255.

Read, Midshipman J. H., with landing force at New Orleans, 236.

Ream, Vinnie, designs statue of Farragut, 372.

Red River country, mentioned, 254; importance of to Confederates, 280 *et seq.*; blockaded, 292; Banks' expedition to, 310.

Regla, on Havana Bay, pirate resort, 111.

Richmond, U. S. S., mentioned, 177; at mouth of Mississippi River, 179 *et seq.*; in attack on Confederate forts, 209; passing the forts, 215; at Vicksburg, 244 *et seq.*; before Port Hudson, 286, 289; battery of at Mobile Bay, 317; armored with sand, 318; mentioned, 321.

Richmond, Va., secession con-